Jews and Judaism in African History

Jews and Judaism in African History

RICHARD HULL

Markus Wiener Publishers
Princeton

Copyright © 2009 by Markus Wiener Publishers, Princeton, New Jersey

All rights reserved. No part of this book may be reproduced or transmitted in any form or by any means, whether electronic or mechanical—including photocopying or recording—or through any information storage or retrieval system, without permission of the copyright owners.

Cover illustration: Detail from *Jewish Wedding in Morocco*, 1837-1841, by Eugène Delacroix. Oil on canvas. Back cover illustrations: Falasha scrolls.

For information, write to Markus Wiener Publishers
231 Nassau Street, Princeton, NJ 08542
www.markuswiener.com

Library of Congress Cataloging-in-Publication Data
Hull, Richard.
　Jews and Judaism in African history / Richard Hull.
　　p. cm.
　Includes bibliographical references and index.
　ISBN 978-1-55876-495-8 (hardcover : alk. paper)
　ISBN 978-1-55876-496-5 (pbk. : alk. paper)
　1. Jews—Africa—History. 2. Judaism—Africa—History.
3. Africa—Ethnic relations. I. Title.
DS135.A25H85 2009
960'.04924—dc22
　　　　　　　　　　2008047643

Markus Wiener Publishers books are printed in the United States of America on acid-free paper and meet the guidelines for permanence and durability of the Committee on Production Guidelines for Book Longevity of the Council on Library Resources.

*To my wife, Jo, and to my sons,
Gordon and Timothy, for their patience,
enthusiasm, love, and encouragement*

Contents

Preface xi
Acknowledgments xix

CHAPTER ONE — Jews in Africa in Classical Antiquity 1
    The Early Semitic Thrust into Africa — 3
    The Great Exodus and the Foundations of Judaism — 7
    The Jewish Community at Elephantine — 14
    Jews in Egypt under the Ptolemies: The First Golden Age — 16
    The Early Jewish Diaspora to North Africa — 20
    Alexandrian Jews in the Roman Era — 22
    The Collapse of Alexandrian Judaism — 28
    The Challenge of Christianity — 31

**CHAPTER TWO — Jews and Muslims in North Africa
to the Seventeenth Century** 37
    The Arab Conquest — 39
    Jews under the African Fatimids:
        Dimensions of Mutuality and Toleration — 45
    Jews under the Mamluks — 50
    Revolutionary Times: Jews under the Almoravids
        and Almohads — 52
    Jews in the Mediterranean and Trans-Saharan Trades — 56
    Judeophobia Redux: The Central Sahara and the
        West African Sudan — 60
    Jews in Ottoman-Ruled Africa: A Symbiotic Relationship — 65
    The Sephardic Diaspora in the Maghreb — 68
    Morocco: Jewish Exiles in a Muslim Sultanate — 71

CHAPTER THREE — **Jews and Conversos in the Formative Years of the West and Central African Atlantic Slave Trade** .. **75**
    The New South Atlantic Economy — 77
    Sugar — 80
    Getting Started: The Early Years — 81
    The Iberian Factor: Anti-Semitism, Expulsion, and Diaspora — 86
    The São Tomé Factor — 89
    Expanding Frontiers of Violence and Chaos:
       The Angolan Wars — 94
    Transitions: Expansion to the Americas — 96
    The Plantation Economy and the Slave Trade
       Move Westward — 97
    An Intriguing New Nexis: Brazil, Kongo, Angola — 98
    The Amsterdam Factor — 102
    Jews, Conversos, and the West African Trade — 109
    The Curaçaoan Factor — 112

CHAPTER FOUR — **Jews and the Rise of South Africa** **117**
    The Early Entrepreneurs — 119
    The Lure of Diamonds and Gold — 124
    Jewish Randlords and Uitlanders — 128
    Jews, British, and Afrikaners — 131
    Jewish Political Leadership and the Union of South Africa — 133
    Jews and the Industrialization of the Country — 136
    The Roots of Modern Anti-Semitism:
       The Lithuanians and Latvians — 139
    The Rise of Zionism — 143
    Jews and South African Culture — 145
    The Early Quest for Social Justice — 146
    Zionism Redux: Flirting with the Israelis — 152
    Navigating in Treacherous Waters — 154
    Jews as Philanthropists and Business Innovators — 155
    Novelists, Writers, and Artists — 157
    Jews as Defenders of Civil Liberties — 158
    Jews and the Post-Soweto Era — 161
    Jews and the Post-Apartheid World: Exodus Redux? — 163

CONTENTS ix

CHAPTER FIVE — **Jews and Judaism in
Central and Eastern Africa** **167**
   New Immigration from Eastern Europe — 169
   Jews in Portuguese East Africa — 170
   The Lemba: The Earliest Jews of Southern Africa? — 173
   The Modern Jewish Impact on Zimbabwe and Zambia — 173
   Jews in East Africa: Kenya and Uganda — 181
   Jews and Judaism in Ethiopia — 185

CHAPTER SIX — **North African Jewry
since the Seventeenth Century** **207**
   Jewish and Muslim Coexistence in North Africa — 209
   Morocco: Jews and an Expanding Muslim State — 211
   Egypt — 224
   Jews of the Anglo-Egyptian Sudan — 233
   Algeria, Tunisia, and Libya — 235

References 251
Index 273

Illustrations

Unless otherwise specified, the following illustrations are details of images: **Page 1**: A Mosaic from the Great Synagogue of Alexandria; **Page 37**: Inside the Synagogue of Ben Ezra; **Page 75**: Elmina Castle on the Gold Coast (author's photo); **Page 117**: Lemba Village Counselor in South Africa (author's photo); **Page 167**: Falasha Villagers in Ethiopia; **Page 207**: Old Jewish Mellah, Fez, Morocco (author's photo).

Preface

This is a story about an aspect of African history that receives undeservedly little attention. It is a narrative about Jews and Judaism and the existence of both in Africa from antiquity to the present. Over the decades, we have been inundated with an avalanche of scholarly books on Christians and Muslims, but Jews are rarely mentioned and usually only in a footnote or passing commentary. This also holds true for most of our popular textbooks on African history and civilizations. True, Jews have been an often-marginalized minority out of the mainstream of history, yet they have played a colossal role in the history of the continent, one that is hugely disproportionate to their numbers. In many fascinating ways they have enriched Africa, culturally and economically, serving as innovators and middlemen, government servants and educators. Along the way, they have been victims as well as victimizers, mercenaries and proxies for others as well as adjuvants in long-distance trade and sustainable development. While some converted to other religions and were physically and culturally assimilated into indigenous societies, most retained their Jewish identity, albeit in various forms. Jews and Judaism have practically disappeared from Africa today, but their legacy will surely endure in many dimensions.

In this study we will treat "Jews" as people who either possess the faith or who are of Jewish heritage, whether or not they may actually adhere to the religion of Judaism. This would include people who might have been aware of their Jewish heritage but who may have converted, voluntarily or through coercion, to another religion or who chose secularity. In that category we have placed the so-called New Christians or *conversos*. In other words, we will focus on people and groups whose ancestors—the Hebrews and the Israelites—resided in the Middle East's "Promised Land," or Palestine territory. However, we will also take account of people whose lineage may not actually have originated there, such as the Jews of Ethiopia, even though their legends and epics link them to Jerusalem and to the Solomonic dynasty.

Many individuals and groups under examination had integrated to varying degrees into non-Jewish communities but may not have totally assimilated to the extent that they lost their Jewish identity. Recent DNA research suggests that a large number of today's Jews are distantly related to one another and may share a common gene pool traceable to ancient Palestine. Indeed, DNA data reveal a remarkable genetic unity among Jews throughout the world, suggesting relatively little intersection with other populations. While this may indeed be true, in Africa before the nineteenth century Jews were more likely to intermarry with indigenous peoples, even though Jewish genetic signatures appear in many regions of the continent. Indeed, as genetic research advances, we are discovering that Judaism in Africa was far more pervasive than hitherto recognized.

Jews of the world, and especially of Africa, share common traditions and ethical concepts which find their derivation from the same religious source. Jewish communities tended to set themselves apart or to invite being set apart. Most asserted they had a special connection with God and were His "Chosen People." Judaism compelled Jews to regard themselves as having a different past and future from non-Jews.

Judaism in Africa was an exclusive religion that with few exceptions did not seek converts or engage in violent crusades or jihads. As Norman Cantor puts it: "The covenant idea is intensely elitist. It singles out the people of Israel and raises them uniquely above all other people as a holy community" (Cantor

1995: 21). In Africa, they usually had their own calendar of festivals and rituals, certain dietary restrictions and fast days, and a different cultural rhythm. If a community were large enough, it became endogamous, narrowly marrying within the faith. Most members of the community would see themselves not as African Jews but as Jews living in Africa. Since antiquity, many congregations maintained a continuous dialogue with the Palestine communities in the Middle East. Throughout history, Jerusalem served as the anchor of Jewish identity. All of these factors contributed to a profound communal sensibility and durability.

Since the fourteenth century, the majority of Jews in Africa outside Ethiopia, the Rhodesias, and South Africa were Sephardic people of Iberian provenance, and their relationship with the land of Israel was intimate and enduring. As uncompromising monotheists, they were intensely resistant to the idea of accommodation and acculturation. Social separation offered a means to preserve the faith and to avoid genetic assimilation. It also assured a continuation of that special relationship with God. Some Jews worried that social integration would lead to a relaxation of religious observance. Many feared that traditional Judaism might be compromised by adopting the secular culture of the West or the polytheistic cultures of Africa. Some felt that only fidelity to the *halakhah*, or Jewish law, could ensure institutional consensus throughout the Jewish world. In time, some Jews would renounce their faith but seldom their values and cultural traditions.

This ideology of separation invited resentment, contempt, and often envy among the non-Jewish populations that surrounded them. Such separatism reinforced their alien status and often rendered them easy targets for negative stereotyping. In so much of the literature, from antiquity well into the twentieth century, Jews are objects of scorn and derision. They are stigmatized as possessing an "evil eye," of practicing witchcraft, of being treacherous and devious.

It is evident, then, that anti-Semitism and Judeophobia have haunted the African landscape since antiquity. By the late nineteenth century, Jews found themselves caught between the assimilatory imperatives of Western culture and Islamic culture and an abiding desire to retain a distinctive identity. The creation of the Jewish state of Israel in 1948 presented an intolerable dilemma for Jews living in the Muslim states of North Africa: they either had to support Israel or submerge their identity among fellow Muslim citizens in the emerging nation of their birth. Anguished equivocation led to painful decisions after the Suez crisis of 1956 and the Six-Day War of 1967. Nearly all Jews supported Israel in these crises, and in response to fears and the realities of Muslim reprisals the overwhelming majority left the continent of their ancestors in a mass new exodus to Israel or to Western Europe or North America. Also, many could not reconcile themselves to the inexorable wave of modern African and Arab nationalism or to the South African policy of apartheid. In 1948 there were more than one million Jews in Africa, with at least 754,000 in Arab-dominated countries. Today they number in the few thousands. In a few countries of sub-Saharan Africa, notably Ghana, Nigeria, and Uganda, new Jewish communities of recently converted Africans are emerging. But these communities are miniscule at this time, and they will not be discussed at length in this work.

Throughout African history, Jews have been seen as quintessential "outsiders," as strangers and aliens, as a marginalized minority holding a precarious position in a world that often persecuted and despised them while simultaneously welcoming them as innovators with seemingly esoteric knowledge and, often, exotic goods to sell. At times they were feared and envied, and in periods of crisis they often became scapegoats and were subject to pogroms and other more subtle forms of discrimination. When Jews were perceived as assets to wider society, rulers accorded them unique protections and privileges while imposing upon them special taxes and regulations. Although this was most pronounced in areas under Muslim control, the practice reached far back into pre-Islamic history and was implemented, successively, by the Egyptians, Greeks, Romans, and Christian Byzantine ruling elites. Even in the twentieth century, Jews faced discrimination under European colonial domination.

From antiquity, Jews painfully found that residing for generations in an African community was no defense against anti-Semitism. Though Jews occasionally enjoyed access to the centers of power, rarely were they able to exercise authority outside their own communities. If they had wealth or special knowledge useful to African leaders, they were extended special dispensations but few rights. Typically, they were not subject to customary judicial jurisdiction and thus enjoyed a degree of legal autonomy. But in the Muslim countries of North Africa, they were restricted from specific professions or occupations and compelled to wear certain garments and hairstyles that made them easily recognizable and more vulnerable to harassment and intimidation. Even when Jews were granted civil rights, restrictions were imposed on certain freedoms like residence and movement.

The Conundrum of Jewish Identity

Scholars and theologians will probably always debate the issue of Jewish identity. Who precisely is a Jew and what constitutes Jewishness are questions that have preoccupied Jews and their oppressors for centuries. Although there are no universally accepted definitions, most would agree that Jews are a distinct people. But are they a nation or an ethnic group? Decidedly, there are many components of Jewish identity, though religion and tradition are key. Some scholars argue that you don't have to be observant to be Jewish. Is a person who converts to another religion still considered to be a Jew? Renouncing the Jewish faith did not necessarily imply jettisoning the perennial values of Judaic traditions. According to the *halakhah*, a Jew by birth was one born to a Jewish mother, whether she was observant or secular, which seemed to imply that a Jew is defined by birth, not faith. The venerable Jewish polymath Maimonides concluded that Jewish lineage could never lapse, that a Jew is a Jew for all future generations.

Many scholars contend that the word *Jew* is a Greek derivation of a tribal name for the sons of Judah after their return from exile in Babylon. Robert Seltzer suggests that the English term *Jew* was derived from the Hebrew *Yehudi* (Seltzer 1980: 9). He postulates that the early Greeks and Romans identified Jews as a people whose traditions and religion originated in the Middle Eastern Kingdom of Judah. Yet he also argues that the word *Judaism* became widely used by Jews only in the last two centuries, and that the proper name for the Jewish people is *Israel*. The name *Israel* may indeed have originated as a territorial term and evolved into political and theological terms to describe people who worshipped Yahweh. This development may have occurred after the split of the united monarchy of Israel and Judah. Yahweh came to serve as the national god of both political entities. From that time, peoples who consider themselves of Jewish descent have a bond in the belief that they are Yahweh's unique people and thus share a common heritage and destiny. Nevertheless, in an African context it can be argued that religion is only one of the many elements of Judaism and that culture is another. Some scholars and theologians contend that a Jew may renounce the faith and remain subjectively and objectively a Jew by identity.

In the African diaspora, Jews flourished, spiritually and culturally, and managed to preserve a deep sense of their distinctive identity in a common heritage located in the Middle East. Thus, many saw themselves as a people apart, a nation in exile who regulated their lives by their own codes of law and institutions of governance. Yet after generations of interaction, Jews and indigenous populations often became physically almost indistinguishable. Much of that had to do with the dynamics of trade and commerce, for in many parts of Africa observant Jews and conversos functioned as intercultural links. Yet, such accommodationist inclinations could also work the other way, instilling in Jews an even stronger cosmopolitan sense of global solidarity. Indeed, throughout history, diasporically minded Jews with their geographically extensive family trading networks were exceptionally well prepared to take advantage of periods of globalization. Through these networks, they were among the first in the West to gain experience in finance, navigational technology, and unrivaled commercial intelligence. According to Paul Johnson, by the sixteenth century they were among the best-informed people in the world (Johnson 1987: 286-87). Even before the Great Age of European Discovery, that cosmopolitanism connected Jewish families across regions, oceans, and continents.

Perhaps it was their claims of non-African origin and their ambivalence toward local authority and allegiance that marked Jews as different, as the metaphorical outsider. Even when they integrated into indigenous African society, the Jewish self-perception as a unique people transcending narrow tribal or regional parochialisms endured.

Acknowledgments

This book would not have been written without the encouragement and insightful comments of graduate students in my seminar on Jews and Judaism in Africa since Antiquity. It is a course I have offered at New York University for more than a decade, and one that launched me on my journey across Africa and Europe and through several hundred published texts on the subject. I wrote this book as a course text for my seminars and colloquia because of an inability to find a comprehensive historical study of Jews and people of Jewish ancestry in African history. And after teaching undergraduate survey courses on African Civilizations for decades, I had become frustrated by the scant attention given in our popular textbooks and trade books to the role of Jews in the shaping of African civilizations.

Fortunately, over the past quarter century there has been an avalanche of specialized works on specific topics, countries, and periods. What I have attempted to do here is not to delve into archives and glean documents pertaining to Jews in Africa but to pour over the huge volume of secondary sources located in libraries on three continents in order to achieve a synthesis. Along the way I came to appreciate the enormous complexity of writing a general history of peoples of Jewish ancestry and heritage who inhabited a continent more than three times the size of the United States—a continent embracing scores of distinct civilizations and more than three thousand years of history—and then encompassing it all in a single brief volume. Obviously, for the sake of brevity and clarity much has been omitted, and not all periods and geographical areas have been treated equally. It is my hope, however, that this succinct book will challenge those who write broad surveys of African history—for students as well as for general readers—to give more attention to Jews in their narrative.

Much has been written of the contributions to Africa of Christians and Muslims, but perhaps because Jews have been such a small, often self-segregated minority, they have been overlooked and are usually consigned to footnotes at best. This is a pity, because they have played a disproportionately large role in the continent's rich history. This book focuses on the nature of the encounters between professing Jews and those who converted to Christianity and became so-called conversos. It also examines the relationships among Jews, Christians, Muslims, and Africans of other faiths and ethnicities.

Over the past five years, I have given several dozen public lectures before various religious communities here and in Africa in an effort to achieve balance, fairness, and sensitivity in regard to what is obviously a delicate and sometimes emotionally charged subject. I have received sage advice from rabbis and pastors, faculty colleagues and teachers, family and friends of all faiths. The result has been numerous drafts of this book and much editing. It is still far from a perfect work, and covering as it does some topics that will surely spark controversy, it will no doubt require further revision. In that sense, this is a work in progress and one that might inspire others to go beyond my own findings and interpretations.

I wish to give special thanks to the staff members and librarians at the Isaac and Jessie Kaplan Centre for Jewish Studies and Research at the University of Cape Town, and to their counterparts at the Brenthurst and Jacob Gitlin Libraries in Cape Town and Johannesburg. Also obliging were staffers at the University of the Witwatersrand's Kimberley Africana Library; at the Sam Cohen Library in Swakopmund, Namibia; and at the libraries of the University of Natal in Durban and Pietermaritzburg.

Especially helpful and gracious were the individuals in charge at the Oxford Centre for Hebrew and Jewish Studies at Yarnton Manor, who offered me accommodations and full access to their vast collections during my research.

Finally, I am indebted to those who read and offered valuable comments on various chapters of my manuscript or who spent time in conversation and guiding me to numerous sites in the field. They include Warren Dean, Seymour Gordon, Geoffrey Howard, Max Kortepeter, Reon Meij, Bruce Nichols, David Reimers, Candace Sandfort, Milton Shain, Les DeVilliers, David Voorhees, and Marcelle Weiner. I am, in addition, especially appreciative of the helpful and highly professional editorial assistance of Janet Stern, senior editor at Markus Wiener Publishers. And lastly, I wish to thank my university for providing me with two sabbatical leaves to enable me to undertake research in England, Morocco, and South Africa, and also for funds to purchase research materials.

CHAPTER ONE

Jews in Africa in Classical Antiquity

Major Clusters of Jewish Population from Antiquity to 400 CE

The Early Semitic Thrust into Africa

The story of Jews in Africa must naturally begin with the origins of the Jewish people. The grand narrative commences with the great Patriarch, Abraham, regarded by the Jews as the father of the nation of Israel and the man who molded this group of impoverished semi-nomadic Semitic speakers into a self-conscious religious community. With God's guidance Abraham and his nomadic clans some four thousand years ago migrated from their ancestral land of Ur in northern Mesopotamia in the Tigris-Euphrates River valley westward to the "Promised Land" of Canaan, embracing the whole of Palestine west of Jordan. There, God appeared to Abraham in a vision and made an everlasting covenant with him. Under its terms, He gave Canaan to Abraham and his clans and made them his specially chosen people in return for their pledge to worship Him, whom they would call "Yahweh," as their only god and to deny all other deities.

This epochal covenant sets forth a radical monotheism in a world that was essentially polytheistic. All other gods were to be considered "idols" or objects of human agency and cast out. Rites of divination, ancestor veneration, and magic were expressly forbidden. The book of Deuteronomy in Hebrew scriptures is designed to justify Abraham and his progeny as God's Chosen People above all others and all nations. To Jews, this covenant manifested a special bond between the people of Israel and their Lord. As God's Chosen Ones, Abraham's people believed they were superior in all respects to other religious and ethnic groups. Abraham and his followers apparently resisted integration into the indigenous populations even though some historians believe that they were actually related to the Canaanites.

The twelve tribes who claimed descent from Abraham settled for a while in Palestine between the Jordan River and the Mediterranean According to scripture, Abraham's grandson Jacob eventually led his people out of famine-plagued Canaan in the Fertile Crescent and southeastward into the African country of Egypt. It is written that shortly before this migration, Jacob's son Joseph had been captured, possibly by some of his jealous brothers, and sold into slavery in Egypt (Porten 1968: 1). He reputedly ended up in the royal court and became vizier to Pharaoh Amenemhat III (r. 1842-1797 BCE), arguably the greatest ruler of the "Middle Kingdom" period. As vizier, Joseph would have been one of the highest officials in the realm, second only to the pharaoh and strong enough to secure permission to settle the Israelite refugees in Egypt.

Africa's vast Nile Delta, already well known to peoples of the Middle and Near East, was seen as a point of both attraction and repulsion. In a region that for centuries had suffered under periodic drought and famine, the fertile Nile River valley and its delta was a place of refuge and economic opportunity. On the other hand, it was also regarded as a source of persecution and discrimination. Perhaps from the start many Jews perceived themselves as an exclusive community and remained outsiders in their host countries.

The Nile Delta and the lower valley of the Nile River contained rich deposits of alluvial soils of unrivaled fertility nourished by predictable annual flooding. Extremely well suited to intensive irrigated agriculture, it could sustain a dense population eager to engage in commerce. The Canaanite city-states had probably been trading with Egypt, via the isthmus of Suez, since about 3000 BCE. Egypt was by then importing timber from

Palestine (in modern Lebanon) as well as spices, incense, and precious stones from western Asia. Some trade routes extended to Mesopotamia far back in the pre-dynastic period. Thus, from the Old Kingdom in Egypt (ca. 2686-ca. 2181 BCE) or earlier, the peoples of Egypt and Palestine were living within a single zone of intercommunication (Miller and Hayes 1986: 385).

Ancestors of modern Semitic-speaking peoples, the Hebrews among them, may have been in this part of Africa as nomadic pastoralists and traders by 3100 BCE when the Nile country was united under the first pharaoh. Nevertheless, it was probably not until about 2080 BCE that the so-called Middle Kingdom of Egypt began to establish regular and systematic trade relations with peoples of the Fertile Crescent. Clearly, Syro-Palestinian culture in the eastern Nile Delta dates back to at least the eighteenth century BCE.

Foreigners were attracted to Egypt by the opportunities it offered in trade as well as agriculture and by its relative peace, stability, and high quality of living. Moreover, Egypt's magnificent cut-stone temples and tombs had become the envy of the ancient world. While Semitic-speaking peoples admired the Nilotic African civilization, they distrusted the Egyptians. According to Genesis, Abraham did not like Egyptians and feared they would exploit his own people.

The first foreign invasion of Egypt occurred in about 1674 BCE, when a mysterious band of Semitic-speaking warriors from western Asia swept across the Nile Delta with their swift chariots. The Egyptians called them Hyksos, which literally meant "alien people of the hill countries." Abraham's people may have preceded them by a few centuries, though some scholars hold that they followed the Hyksos by only a few years and may have been related to them. In any case, the Hyksos brought into Egypt Canaanite culture from the Levant. Indeed, they may have been Canaanites themselves. For nearly a century from the 1670s they controlled Canaan. By 1650 BCE they had also conquered the eastern portion of the Nile Delta, set up their own northern Egyptian dynasty, and used Avaris as their capital after massively fortifying it (Scheindlin 1998: 4).

Egypt's influence on these Semitic-speaking peoples of the Middle East was undoubtedly quite strong even though the Israelite immigrants constituted a discrete community, largely serviced by their own people and living apart from the indigenous Egyptians. During their sojourn in Egypt they developed unique rituals and dietary restrictions. Some scholars speculate that while in Egypt the Israelites may have been influenced by the ideas of the pharaoh Akhenaten (r. 1370-1362), who is said to have introduced a monotheism based on worship of the sun's disk (see Montserrat 2003: 220-24). Indeed, early in history the Israelites came to accept the notion of an omnipotent God who ruled supreme over all other supernatural beings and powers.

The Israelites' God was a single creator God, not merely a tribal ancestor. Some scholars question the historicity of the scriptures and postulate that the Israelites may have developed this awareness in Egypt and brought it back to the Middle East. Others believe their monotheism was acquired much earlier, during their residence in Mesopotamia. Not inconceivably, the early Israelites could have adopted the African notion that the supreme being could not be depicted in any form. For many Africans, graven images and other physical representations of God were considered idolatrous. But unlike the Israelites, indigenous Africans never lost the idea that there are pantheons of lesser deities who may be consulted to determine the will of the supreme being and who may be physically depicted in the form of statuary. Most Jews have always refused to acknowledge that the supreme being could be manipulated by divination or magic. Their monotheism, unlike that of other peoples, demanded monolatry, or worship of only one God from among many supernatural entities. Judaism recognized only prayer and religious conduct as the means of communicating with the divine.

The Great Exodus and the Foundations of Judaism

Trouble for the Israelites may have begun with the expulsion of the Hyksos in the 1570s. From the start, anti-Asian feelings ran high. Bezalel Porten notes that "given the general bias of Egyptians against Asiatics, a certain antipathy towards the Israelites would not be surprising" (Porten 1968: 44). While some Israelites became prosperous and rose to important positions in the Egyptian government, the majority probably toiled under the exactions of successive pharaohs who were continually coercing laborers to participate in the construction of public works. Pharaoh Ramesses II (r. 1304-1237), a prolific builder, may have resorted to massive enslavement to complete his projects (David 1998: 11). The Israelites resented this situation while struggling to survive a series of plagues and famines. Things finally came to a head and the fateful decision was made to return to the Middle East.

According to the scriptures' master narrative, this great exodus was led by Moses, an Israelite born in Egypt, raised in the royal court, and possibly married to an indigenous Egyptian or Nubian. It could have occurred during the Ramesside era (Hoffmeier 1997: 126). Then again, the book of Kings suggests that it took place 180 years before the founding of the Temple in Jerusalem: in other words, around the time of Pharaoh Dudimose in about 1447 BCE. Unfortunately, no written or archeological records exist to even lend credence to any exodus. The Egyptian records make no mention of it. Indeed, there are no references in Egyptian sources to Israelite settlers in the Nile Valley and Delta at the purported time of the Great Exodus.

If the Exodus did in fact occur, we have no idea how many people were involved. It could have consisted of a family or two or several clans. There is reason to believe that in any case many Israelites remained in Egypt. For Jews, this is immaterial. They adhere to the biblical story that Moses led such an exodus and that in the process he laid the crucial foundations of the Hebraic faith. Indeed, the first fifteen chapters of the book of Exodus describe in considerable detail the departure of the Hebrews—or Israelites—from the Egyptian "house of bondage." They recount that Moses was raised by the pharaoh's daughter and as an adult was chosen by God to lead his people out of the land of the oppressors. The Israelites' exodus took them across the arid Sinai Peninsula and ultimately into Canaan, the land originally promised to them by Yahweh in his covenant with Abraham and which by then had become a province of Palestine. Thus, the Israelites who had migrated from Egypt were linked to Canaan by the covenant narrative. The exodus was seen as God's will, and Moses as His instrument. It was He who led them out of captivity in Africa and back to the Promised Land. The idea of Jews as the Chosen People of Yahweh was reinforced when, en route home, Moses stopped at Mount Sinai where he received from God the Ten Commandments. Moses is therefore considered by most modern Jews as the founder of the Jewish religion and the supreme lawgiver. The Ten Commandments laid the essential foundations of the Hebrew legal code. In the Sinai desert, Moses rallied the Hebrew people around this supreme God, Yahweh, their savior and redeemer.

Moses never made it to Canaan. He died along the way and the exodus was probably completed by someone else. Once in Canaan, the migrants engaged in a series of successful wars against the indigenous population. They were now convinced that Yahweh had rewarded them by giving them victory over the Canaanites. Though possibly from the same cultural and genetic stock as the Canaanites, the Israelites had already rejected their possible common past as they developed their own identity.

The entire exodus experience gave Jews their collective identity as a special people endowed by Yahweh. This was when the word "Israel" first appears in Egyptian literature. Some historians argue that the experience may have infused the Israelites with an elitist mentality. Surely they were survivors against all odds, and they attributed their astounding success to their superior mental and physical capabilities, given to them by their God. To them, Yahweh was exclusive and intolerant of all other powers and their relationship with Him was special and enduring.

By 1200 BCE the Israelites had carved out a new Palestinian homeland for themselves. The Canaanites found themselves evicted from their lands and many migrated to other areas. The new inhabitants looked with scorn upon their fellow Semites, the Canaanites, and looked back with bitterness to the Egyptians of Africa because of their enslavement and to Abraham's stigmatization of them as unsavory people. After intermittent violent struggles with the irredentist Canaanites, the Hebrews took Palestine and Jerusalem and established a kingdom under David (possible reign: 1010-960 BCE). This heroic figure established Jerusalem as the political and religious center of the kingdom. Solomon (possible reign: 960-920 BCE), David's son and successor, constructed a large temple which became the center of Jewish religious observance.

Sometime before or after Solomon's death, the kingdom was bifurcated. Descendants of the Davidic line would rule Judah in the south, with its capital in Jerusalem. In the northern kingdom, called Israel, the faith was eventually modified to allow people to worship other deities in addition to Yahweh. By contrast, the people of Judah remained steadfast to Yahweh and came to be known as *Yehudi*. For centuries after the bifurcation, the area was wracked by political turmoil and instability and the two tiny kingdoms enlisted Egyptian support against the growing Assyrian menace. Ultimately, both kingdoms fell under foreign domination. By 732, the Semitic-speaking Assyrians developed a huge war machine and had carved out a vast empire which included Israel. Through diplomacy, Judah survived and preserved its religious traditions but became a vassal state of the Assyrian empire (Scheindlin 1998: 17-20).

By 670 BCE, the Assyrians had extended their own dominion southwards into Egypt and established a vassal dynasty by installing an indigenous pharaoh. During the reign of Josiah (640-609), Judah found itself in the middle of a great-power struggle among Assyria, Egypt, Babylonia, and the Indo-European state of Medes for control of the entire Middle East. After Assyria's defeat, Judah had to contend with Babylonian and Egyptian pressures. By 627, during Josiah's rule in Judah, the state was effectively an Egyptian satellite and Judaean troops were employed by the Egyptians to patrol strategic trade routes along the eastern Mediterranean coast (Miller and Hayes 1986: 384-85).

Judah eventually succumbed to the Babylonians. In 597 BCE their ruler, Nebuchadnezzar, defeated Judah, captured Jerusalem, and exiled its elites to Babylon. The hapless farmers were enslaved and sold into Egypt, while others, notably the defeated soldiers, poured into the Nile Delta as political refugees seeking asylum (Bleiberg 2002: 14). Thus, since at least the sixth century BCE Egypt has served as a major place of asylum for Judaean refugees. Even more traumatic than defeat and exile, in 586 BCE the Babylonians destroyed the sacred Temple in Jerusalem built by Solomon centuries earlier.

The Babylonian exile lasted from 586 to 538. Though the exiles adopted many elements of Babylonian culture, they held steadfastly to their own religious traditions. Some scholars postulate that it was during the exile that Jews acquired a unique theology and a national consciousness (Watzman 2001: 32). When Babylonia ultimately fell to the Persian conqueror Cyrus, the exiles were allowed to return to Jerusalem and rebuild their temple. Those who chose to return formed a province known as Yehudi, and its citizens came to be referred to as *Yehudim*, or Jews, and were identified with the tribe of Judah. Over the next two centuries, the religion of these peoples effectively became

Judaism. However, Edward Bleiberg implies that the ethnic use of the term "Jew" began during the First Persian Period in Egypt (525-404 BCE) (Bleiberg 2002: 19).

It was probably during the period of the Babylonian Exile and perhaps starting even a bit earlier, during the reign of Josiah, that the master narrative of early Jewish history was constructed. The Babylonian Diaspora may have stimulated Jewish belief in prophecy and messianism. The return of the exiles from Babylon mirrored the journey of Abraham from Mesopotamia to Canaan just as the exodus from servitude in Egypt mirrored the phenomenon of exile and return, a recurring theme of defeat, triumph, exile, restoration, destruction, and redemption (Cantor 1994: 28). The religion developed a vast literature, based on the accumulation of an extensive knowledge of sacred writings, myths, epics, and legends, drawn from many cultures, not least among them the Egyptians of Africa. The authors of the first five books of the Old Testament, the Pentateuch, perceived of themselves as preservers of the essential traditions of early Israel and Judah.

Unfortunately, many of the narratives must be taken on faith because they are unverifiable. Recent archeological work more often contradicts than confirms events and places described in the scriptures. Today, many secular Jews see the Hebrew scriptures, or Old Testament to the Christians, as invented history, designed to justify the special position of Jews in human history and to depict the ancient Israelites as an instrument of God's will. These biblical narratives, which included miraculous and supernatural events, were built on themes in orally transmitted folk traditions that had wide currency deep in antiquity (Cantor 1994: 16).

There is indeed today a growing debate over the historicity of the Old Testament. Some would argue that the Hebrew Bible is a narrative myth because so much of the evidence is unverifiable. Empirical research is lacking, and the need for archeological verification is recognized by many serious scholars and theologians. Maxwell Miller and John Hayes emphasize that "With one exception...there is no mention of Israel or the Israelites in extra-biblical sources before the ninth century BCE —that is, until well after the reigns of David and Solomon." They add, "The biblical Abraham, Isaac, Jacob, Joseph, Moses, and Joshua are not mentioned in any non-biblical records. Nor is there any reference to an Israelite sojourn in Egypt, the exodus, or the conquest of Palestine in any ancient source contemporary with the time when these events are said to have occurred." (Miller and Hayes 1986: 64) Even the biblical account of Israel's origins and history may not have been drafted until the reign of King Josiah (r. 640-609 BCE), according to archeologist Israel Finkelstein (see Watzman 1997: 33). During that time, Judah was subject to Egypt. Perhaps these dramatic biblical accounts were designed less for historical accuracy than to validate the Israelites as an instrument of God's will. The first five books of the Old Testament (the Pentateuch) may indeed be an effort to establish a mythical past for a beleaguered and traumatized Jewish people after the fall of the first temple.

James Weinstein asserts, "There is no archaeological evidence for an exodus such as is described in the bible in any period within the second millennium." He speculates that, "If there was an historical exodus, it probably consisted of a small number of Semites migrating out of Egypt in the late thirteenth or early twelfth century BCE, ultimately settling in southwestern Canaan, where their Egyptian heritage would allow them to melt into the local populace" (Weinstein 1997: 87-98). William A. Ward, writing in the same work, adds, "There is no direct Egyptian evidence to support the exodus story." He concludes that "we must see history in the Old Testament narrative not as it happened but as it was perceived to have happened, from the perspective of those to whom it happened" (Ward 1997: 111).

Regardless of these recent assertions, nearly all Jews from early times have seen themselves as descended from the ancient Israelite kingdom and linked to it by culture, religion, and, for some, ethnicity. The saga, embedded in the Hebrew Bible, became the enduring narrative for the survival of a people. Indeed, the Bible, a brilliant, inspirational, didactic, and stirring collection of stories, became the Hebrews' great national epic that shaped and sustained the Jews as a distinct people. From the time of their unhappy sojourn in Egypt the core thesis or ethos of the Jewish people has been one of persecution, exile, and return, and these themes recur through the duration of their centuries-long experience in Africa.

The conquest of Syro-Palestine and Babylonia by the Persian conqueror Cyrus in 539, and of Egypt by his son Cambyses in 525, led to the migration of many Judaeans to the Nile Valley (Porten 1968: 19). During this period of Persian domination, Egypt was a satrapy (province) of the Persian Empire, which also included Palestine and the Jewish communities in Judah, Mesopotamia, Iran, and western India. After the conquest, the Persians destroyed most of the Egyptian temples but spared the Jewish ones, an event that may have helped to lay the foundations of Egyptian anti-Semitism (Schafer 1997: 133). Large numbers of Jews were attracted to Egypt, and this great migration became the most enduring diasporic Jewish community in history, lasting well into the twentieth century. Persians brought many Jews into their armies. Jews were hired as mercenaries to fight the Ethiopians and Nubians, and they were settled in various frontier garrisons. Jewish military captives were eventually freed and spread out over Egypt. Cambyses's successor, Darius I (r. 522-486), built roads and established a royal mail system—services that probably only contributed to the diaspora (Thompson and Ferguson 1969: 110).

The Persians considered the Jews as essential allies in their rule over Egypt. Peter Schafer says that Jews tended to side with the Persian rulers on issues affecting indigenous Egyptians

(Schafer 1997: 123). Others hold that Jews were friends of Persia because of its role in their national rebirth. Jews therefore helped to defend Persian interests in Egypt against local anti-Persian rebellions. This may have been a miscalculation. In 404 BCE Egyptians staged a revolt against Persia and blamed the Jews for its failure. Egyptians henceforth hated the Jews because they were seen as their "rulers' servants." Persian rule continued and the region remained under its suzerainty until the Macedonian Alexander the Great took it in 332 BCE. Interestingly, Egypt would remain under the rule of a foreign power for more than six centuries until its independence from the British in 1922 CE.

The Jewish Community at Elephantine

Elephantine was a place on the Nile where war elephants may have been acquired from the Nubians (Kaplan 2000: 58-59; Porten 1968: 4-22). It evolved into a military colony cum garrison town which included women and children. It served as a fortress, protecting the southern border, as well as a gateway to Nubia. Nubia was derived from the Egyptian word *nub*, meaning gold. By the fifth century many Jewish soldiers were stationed at the fortress town of Elephantine Island. Indeed, Jews were settled in garrisons on both sides of the Nile, and for centuries, Jews and Greeks had been hired by Egyptian authorities as mercenaries to fight Nubians and Ethiopians. It is said that the pharaohs used both groups in their campaigns against Nubia and Ethiopia (Kush) between 594 and 89 BCE. Some contend that Jewish mercenaries led the epochal battle against the African city of Napata and destroyed it.

Elephantine was only the largest of the garrison communities with Jewish populations. From there, many commercial expeditions were sent south into Nubia. At Elephantine, Nubian traders sold ebony, panther skins, ivory, and monkeys (David

1988: 267). From time to time, Nubia was a colony of Egypt and sent tribute in gold, ostrich feathers, leopard skins, cattle, slaves, and precious stones. Papyri with Aramaic writing found on Elephantine Island near Aswan suggests that by the early fifth century BCE Jewish communities were as far south as the first cataract (Porten 1968: 34). Aramaic was the daily language of the Jews of Egypt, and by 300 BCE it was widely spoken even in Jerusalem.

The Elephantine settlement marked the start of the extension of Jewish influence into Africa's interior. A Jewish mercenary community flourished in this remote Persian-ruled Nubian frontier town and was prosperous enough to boast a temple as large as Solomon's in Jerusalem (Kessler 1982: 42). The Elephantine Jews did not yet have the Talmud and other rabbinical interpretations of the laws set forth in the Hebrew Bible, and Jewish sacrificial worship was practiced at the temple during the Babylonian captivity. Joseph Modrzejewski maintains that "from the time of the exile until the reconstruction of the Temple in Jerusalem after the return of the Jews from Babylon, between 587 and 515 BCE, the sanctuary at Elephantine was the only place in the world where Jewish sacrificial worship was practiced" (Modrzejewski 1995: 36).

Sometime between 410 and the 390s BCE, the temple at Elephantine had been obliterated and the Jewish community had disappeared, possibly a victim of Egyptian nationalism. Egyptians saw the Jews and the Persians as their oppressors. The conflict between Jews and indigenous Egyptians had been simmering for decades and was both political and religious in nature (Schafer 1997: 133). Jews were seen as proponents of the hated alien rule because they refused to support the liberation of the Egyptians. The Elephantine incident may have been the first anti-Jewish reaction in history. It was arguably the first recorded anti-Semitic attack (see Schafer 1997: 135).

Egypt's influence on the Hebrews was strong because of their long sojourn in the Nile River valley. Nevertheless, they constituted a discrete community, largely serviced by their own people and living apart from the Egyptians and other indigenous populations. Still, there was some intermarriage with Egyptians and assimilation in both directions. Some locals joined the Jewish community at Elephantine, and some Jews assumed important administrative positions and garnered significant wealth from commerce. Numerous scholars suggest that the Jews at Elephantine were also syncretistic in their worship, drawing freely on indigenous rituals.

Jews in Egypt under the Ptolemies: The First Golden Age

The conquests of Alexander the Great marked the end of antiquity and the commencement of the classical era. Intensive Jewish settlement in Africa began after Alexander's conquests in the fourth century. Egypt became one of the major centers of the Jewish diaspora in the Hellenistic and Roman world. There were substantial Jewish and Greek communities in Egypt when Alexander the Great, a Greek Macedonian, expelled the Persians and annexed the kingdom in 332 BCE. During Alexander's invasion, Jewish soldiers helped to defeat the Egyptians, and in doing so they won the favor of the new regime. Jews minimized acculturation by living in cohesive, well-organized communities. Similarly, Greeks and Egyptians had been co-existing for centuries before the takeover, though among them there was considerable intermarriage. In any case, Alexander's conquests ensured that the Jews in Egypt would be Hellenized, and that the major language spoken by the Jews would ultimately be Hellenistic Greek. Indeed, it can be argued that by the end of the Babylonian Exile centuries earlier, Hebrew ceased to be the sole Jewish language.

Alexander and his successors were unprecedentedly tolerant of Jews, according them a special status and allowing them to settle freely. Ptolemy I Soter, one of Alexander's Macedonian generals, was placed in charge of Egypt, and when the Greek Empire broke up after Alexander's untimely death in 323, he became ruler of an independent kingdom (Barclay 1996: 20-21). Soter established the Greek Ptolemaic dynasty, which would rule over Egypt until 30 BCE when Rome annexed Egypt to its own empire. There was a huge influx of Jews into Egypt during the reign of Ptolemy I Soter (305-283 BCE), who is reported to have brought back 100,000 prisoners of war after his conquest of Palestine in the early 300s (Thompson and Ferguson 1969: 112). Many became slaves of his soldiers. Many also came in as mercenaries in Ptolemy's armies. Soter gave these soldiers generous amounts of land and encouraged civilian Jews to settle in the new metropolis of Alexandria. It was during his rule that Alexandria's Jewish population emerged as a significant force in the development of the city (Modrzejewski 1995: 87). Before long, Alexandria achieved recognition as a great center of Jewish culture.

Following Alexander's conquests in the fourth century BCE, a Macedonian variant of Greek culture and politics began to pervade the Middle East and the eastern Mediterranean. For the next eight centuries or so, the Mediterranean zone was strongly influenced by Greek- and Latin-speaking peoples and their institutions. Both Palestine and Egypt thus became part of this vast new empire. Within a short time, Alexandria had displaced Athens as the commercial and cultural center of the Mediterranean world. Indeed, after Alexander's conquest, the intellectual center of the Hellenic world shifted from Athens to Alexandria. Alexandria became the meeting place of East and West...a multicultural and international city of classical antiquity. In the third century BCE it became the largest city of the ancient world, and its 180,000 Jews constituted a third of the city's population. Scholars speculate that there may have been more Jews in Egypt at the time than in Palestine (Seltzer 1980: 174). There were two self-governing Jewish quarters in Alexandria, but Jews were allowed to live in other parts of the city as well. Jews were also present in the Egyptian countryside: in towns, villages, and on farms along the entire Nile River. They may have contributed to the great library with its works of astronomy, medicine, math, physics, and geography. The library alone contained at least 700,000 scrolls, and the library complex also housed a museum, observatory, zoo, and botanical garden.

Relations between the early Ptolemies and the Jews were good. Ptolemy II Philadelphus freed all Jewish slaves, and links between Palestine and Jews in Egypt remained close (Gruen 2002: 64-65). Egyptian Jews looked to Jerusalem as their spiritual center, and Jews kept close cultural ties with Judea. The Temple to Yahweh remained the central focal point for the diasporic Jewish communities in Egypt. Jews took frequent pilgrimages to the temple, and most of them paid an annual tithe to its stewards.

L.A. Thompson and J. Ferguson argue that throughout the Ptolemaic period in Egypt there was little evidence of anti-Semitism. They suggest that relations between the Greek communities and the Jews remained relatively peaceful and friendly (Thompson and Ferguson 1969: 116). Modrzejewski takes issue with that view. He argues that anti-Semitism predated Christianity, that numerous motifs portrayed Jews as alien intruders, and that there was widespread hostility towards Jews in much of the Ptolemaic period. He sees it as the result of the Egyptian Jews' desire to be both citizens and different (Modrzejewski 1995: 71). Jews were accused of religious particularism, and Greek authorities reproached them for their conscious and willful separatism. The Greek authorities allowed them a large measure of religious freedom but did not grant them, as a whole, the full citizenship enjoyed by resident Greeks and Macedonians. Nor did they extend those rights to the indigenous Egyptians.

Only a few prominent Jewish families or individuals ever attained citizenship.

Jews became progressively Hellenized, even though they tended to live and work apart from the rest of Egypt's populations and still considered Palestine their homeland. From Alexander the Great's conquests in the fourth century BCE Greek culture and language became pervasive throughout the Middle East and the eastern Mediterranean. Already by the third century BCE most Egyptian Jews had abandoned Hebrew and Aramaic and communicated mainly in Greek, the predominant language of Egyptian government, trade, business, and social life (Marlowe 1971: 83; Barclay 1996: 31).

The Jewish literati became concerned that Hebrew had become practically unknown to Egyptian Jewry. It is said that in response Ptolemy II (d. 246 BCE) commissioned seventy-two Jewish scholars to translate the first five books of the Torah, or Pentateuch, into Greek (Keller 1966: 35). Shaye Cohen holds that the purpose of the translation was "not to make Judaism accessible to non-Jews but to make it accessible to Jews" (Cohen 1999: 24). Consequently, the early Hebrew Bible was translated into a language that every Alexandrian Jew could comprehend. This was an unprecedented accomplishment because the Torah had never been translated into another language, and this first translation was into a language that was not even Semitic.

In this context, it is worth remembering that in antiquity the populations of the eastern Mediterranean were predominantly speakers of Semitic languages. "Semitic," a term borrowed from the name of one of Noah's sons (Shem), refers to a language family which includes Hebrew, Aramaic, Arabic, and others. This new, Greek-language version of the Torah came to be called the Septuagint (Latin for "seventy"). The translation represented a considerable intellectual breakthrough for the Jews, and over the next three centuries Egyptian Jews would produce an impressive literature in Greek. More will be said of this later.

The Early Jewish Diaspora to North Africa

The Jewish population of Cyrenaica may be as old as that in ancient Egypt. Berber traditions reveal that the Phoenicians spoke a Semitic dialect, called Punic, and were originally from Canaan. Fascinating legends maintain they had been expelled from Palestine by Joshua possibly in the ninth century BCE, sailed westward along the Mediterranean coast, and built Carthage, near the site of modern Tunisia (Barclay 1996: 232-33). In any event, Jewish merchants and traders followed the expansion of Phoenician trading colonies all along North Africa's Mediterranean shores.

Towards the start of the fifth century, Carthage became the first maritime and commercial power in the western Mediterranean, its fleets strong enough to keep Greeks off the African coast west of Cyrenaica. Carthage reached its zenith in about 400 BCE, having attracted a population of possibly 400,000. Carthaginian Jews helped blaze chariot trade routes deep into the interior and ultimately across the Sahara desert via the Fezzan. West of Egypt, Mediterranean Jews established themselves in all the major coastal towns, especially in Cyrene and Berenice in present-day Libya. The latter was considered a virtual Jewish city-state by 200 BCE (Keller 1966: 35). They also spread to the high plains of what is today central Algeria and Morocco. In Numidia and Mauretania they intermarried with the Berbers, who themselves may have originated centuries earlier in southwestern Asia. Recent DNA data supports the theory that some 30,000 years ago the ancestors of today's Berbers emigrated from the Levant.

Clearly, trans-Saharan links date to the late Punic era. The Garamantes of Fezzan traded with Punic towns along the coast of Tripolitania. In time, Tripolitania, not Egypt, became the most important termini of the great trans-Saharan trade routes. Incrementally, Jews occupied desert oases as metalworkers, jewelers, and financiers. Judaized Berbers, as middlemen, traded with the Garamantes, especially during the subsequent Roman era, exchanging olive oil, glassware, and wine for slaves and ivory (Oliver 1991: 79).

Ultimately, the entire North African coast fell under Roman influence. Phoenician-Berber cities adopted Roman culture, and Latin became the language of business and government in the coastal towns. The magnificent coastal communities that emerged during the process of Romanization depended on their hinterlands for trade. Roman presence in North Africa reaches back at least to 264 BCE with the opening of the Punic wars with Carthage. By 200 BCE Rome would become the center of the Mediterranean world. It conquered Greece not long after 150 BCE and defeated Carthage in 146 BCE after a protracted diplomatic and military struggle. Much of what is today Tunisia was annexed and organized into a province called "Africa," a corruption of the Lebu-Berber word *Ifriqiya*, a term used for centuries to identify this region of North Africa. Roman rule extended westward along the coastal plain. Aqueducts brought water from the interior Atlas Mountains and fed into a vast coastal irrigation system. In time, Africa province became the breadbasket, or granary, of the Roman Empire.

During the Roman period, possibly in the first century CE (designation for Common Era or Christian Era), camels were introduced into the Sahara. At first used largely in cavalries, in time they became a conveyor of goods and revolutionized the trans-Saharan trade in the Roman era. As pack animals camels proved ideal for desert conditions, with a capacity for storing huge quantities of water in their body cavities and able to move for up to forty days swiftly and sure-footedly in sandy soils without solid food. They came to be regarded as the "ships of the desert." By the second century CE camel use in the central Saharan trade had become widespread, though even more so after about 360 CE with the introduction of single-hump Dromedary camels imported from Arabia (Ogunremi 1982: 96-108). Nomadic Judaized Berbers acquired them and penetrated southwards towards the Niger and Senegal River valleys.

By the first half of the second century CE Roman/Berber expeditions had ventured as far as Lake Chad in West Africa. It was in this period that the earliest trading centers south of the Sahara began to emerge in response to steadily strengthening commercial demand from the vibrant coastal cities of North Africa. Trade was often through Judaized Berber intermediaries who were in frequent contact with sub-Saharan Africans who dealt in gold, ivory, and slaves.

While Emperor Julius Caesar added western Tunisia, eastern Algeria, and the Tripolitanian coastal strip to his expanding empire, his successor Caligula in about 40 CE annexed what is today western Algeria and northern Morocco. In the process, many Berber dynasties were liquidated and their lands confiscated. As we shall discover, eventually all of Africa north of the Sahara would fall under Roman hegemony. In the Middle East, the Jewish kingdoms of Judea also capitulated to the Romans. By the close of the first century CE all of the eastern Mediterranean coast and Egypt had been incorporated into a huge administrative, cultural, and economic empire centered in the city of Rome on the Italian peninsula. The Fertile Crescent, lying in the Middle East between the Mediterranean and the Arabian Desert, continued to serve as a bridge between Asia and Africa and as a point of maritime contact with Western Europe. And Alexandria, in Egypt, with its huge markets, was the great international commercial city of the Roman Empire, linking East and West.

Alexandrian Jews in the Roman Era

Jews in Egypt found themselves in a precarious position as the Ptolemaic period gave way to direct Roman rule. At the time,

Egypt was home to as many as a million Jews, or approximately ten percent of Egypt's total population (Modrzejewski 1999: 74). It is said that more than 100,000 Jews lived in Alexandria alone, comprising nearly forty percent of the city's population. It was the largest Jewish community in the ancient world between the third century BCE and the close of the first century CE.

Jews worked in nearly every profession, and some had become extremely rich and powerful in several trades, including shipping. Even Jewish artisans and small shopkeepers prospered. By the Roman conquest, Jews had become an important economic force in Alexandria and were thus tolerated and treated as autonomous, self-governing people. Caesar granted them religious freedom by recognizing Judaism as a legal religion with full protections under Roman law.

The local Egyptian and Greek populations in Alexandria, however, had always been notoriously anti-Roman. Because the Roman authorities desperately needed allies, they were prepared to make concessions to the Jews in return for their collaboration. There had been Jewish soldiers and officers in the Ptolemaic army before the Romans arrived in Egypt; however, most were stationed not in Alexandria but in military posts around the country. Indeed, the Jews of Egypt had supported Caesar's campaign there as far back as 48 BCE, when a Jewish detachment of the Ptolemaic army at Pelusium allowed into Egypt relief forces for Caesar's army. Hence, Alexandrian Jews at first welcomed the advent of direct Roman rule. In doing so, they alienated important sections of the Alexandrian population, including the local Greeks, who were persecuted by the Roman authorities. Greeks could not have their own citizens' council, or *boule*, while the Jews were allowed to retain their own *politeuma*, a semi-autonomous political institution that had its own courts (Gruen 2002: 78-79).

However, Jewish hopes of privilege under Roman rule were soon dashed. Indeed, the rights of the Jews in Egypt fluctuated with each new Roman emperor and prefect. When Egypt became a province of the Roman Empire in 30 BCE, following the defeat of Mark Antony and the death of Cleopatra VII, provincial society was reorganized in a manner that excluded Jews and subjected them to discriminatory taxation. The Romans did not recognize them as Hellenes and classified them instead with the indigenous Egyptians (Collins 2000: 12). Except for an accommodation under the emperor Tiberius, who allowed Jews to retain their clubs, which were an extension of their synagogues, Jews now became second-class citizens in every respect. Flaccus, the Roman prefect in Egypt, abolished Jewish citizenship and thus made all Jews "foreigners" or resident aliens with few legal rights. They were forced to live in a special section of Alexandria, the first ghetto in world history (Gruen 2002: 55-56). Jews had to leave their downtown shops and homes for the urban periphery. While the Romans did grant the Jews some privileges that other so-called foreigners did not enjoy, many Jews felt aggrieved and called upon Herod Agrippa, a Jewish king in Palestine, to mediate, but his arrival in Alexandria only added fuel to the anti-Semitic mobs (Pollard and Reid 2006: 199).

Anti-Roman feelings often assumed the form of anti-Judaism. As noted above, relations between Jews and indigenous Greeks and Egyptians had been strained and confrontational for centuries, but they turned violent in the Roman period. Some scholars have concluded that the Jews had always been hated by the urban masses who envied their economic success.

Anti-Judaism played into Roman hands under the emperor Gaius Caligula. Caligula, who came to power in 37 CE, viewed Jewish exclusiveness as politically subversive. The Roman prefect in Alexandria had demanded that statues of the emperor be erected in all places, including the synagogues. When the Jews refused to allow statues of the emperor in their synagogues and rejected all Roman gods, they were accused of being unpatriotic

(Schafer 1997: 136). The Jewish faith tolerated no icons or images of God and recognized only prayer and proper religious conduct as the means of communicating with the divine. The mere thought of a statue of the emperor in a house of worship was anathema.

The Romans, on the other hand, hated monotheism and found enormous satisfaction in their worship of a pantheon of deities. They saw Judaism as a rival to imperial culture. Indeed, Judaism was seen as a threat to the very unity of the Roman Empire (Aberbach 2000: 9). Thus, by the end of 37 CE, the Jews were decreed to be "foreigners," and Greek mobs were allowed to attack the Jewish communities (Mokhtar 1990: 133). Some of the most influential writers of the early Roman Empire attacked Judaism. The highly influential Roman historian Tacitus (55-118 CE) scorned many Jewish customs and saw Judaism as a grave threat to the traditional deities and religious institutions (Slingerland 1997: 129).

Roman ambitions of forging a unified imperial culture were hampered by the separate lifestyle of the Jews. Most Jews did not see themselves as Egyptians, or for that matter as Egyptian Jews, but as a separate people living in Ptolemaic and, later, Roman Egypt. They saw themselves as possessing a unique past and a special destiny of their own. Their own set of core values rarely squared with those of the Romans, Greeks, or Egyptians among them. Jews in Africa were always torn between the assimilation of Western culture and the desire to retain their own identity and distinctive set of values. Moreover, Jews in Egypt never lost their cultural and religious links to their national homeland in Palestine. Diaspora Jews nearly everywhere in the ancient world remained outsiders in their host societies. It was not uncommon for indigenous populations to resent them for their seeming clannishness. By the opening decades of the Christian Era, there was very little marriage between Jews and indigenous Egyptians and Hellenes.

With the coming of the Romans, Greek-Jewish relations deteriorated, and one of the earliest anti-Jewish pogroms in history occurred in Alexandria in 38 CE. By this time, Roman authorities had begun to side with the local Greeks in their ethnic rivalry with the Jews. Greek mobs pushed Jews into a small area of the delta and pillaged their homes and businesses. The Roman authorities suppressed the pogrom, but it represented a watershed for Roman-Jewish relations. Some see the pogrom as an outgrowth of essentially political struggles for power between Jews, Greeks, and local Egyptians. In any case, in its aftermath a special tax was imposed on all Jews aged three to sixty-two. Many Alexandrian Jewish intellectuals exiled themselves to Jerusalem and never returned (Haas 1997: 102). Under the emperor Claudius in about 42 CE, limited franchise rights were restored, but in return Jews had to pledge to cease proselytizing among the Egyptians (Gruen 2002: 60-61).

Westward, in the coastal cities of North Africa, the Roman authorities, between the reigns of Augustus and Caligula, extended the franchise to large numbers of indigenous people. And in many of the cities this enfranchisement led to greater social integration and acculturation between the Roman and Italian settlers and the indigenes. This policy of colonization and aggressive Latinization alarmed many Jews, who saw it as a threat to Judaism. On the other hand, Romans became progressively impatient with Jewish intransigence.

Despite Roman rule, Alexandria in the first century CE was culturally a Greek and Jewish city. Jewish influence and numbers were steadily growing, and Jews surely played a major role in the city's cultural renaissance. Jews were successfully drawing people into their faith, and Romans feared expansionist Judaism. Philo, the great Alexandrian Jewish scholar and one of the greatest thinkers of diaspora Judaism, sought to reconcile and blend Jewish and Greek Platonism (Cohen 1995: xii). He tried to combine the wisdom of the Old Testament with Platonic-Egyptian thought to achieve a synthesis of biblical doctrine and Platonic philosophy. Philo fused Judaism and Hellenism, taking post-biblical Jewish thought as a base and weaving Stoicism and Platonism into it. He interpreted Judaism through Greek philosophy. By undertaking comparative studies of Greek philosophy and Hebrew theology, Philo and his followers were transforming Judaism into an international religion and Jews into a multi-racial people (Pollard and Reid 2006: 198). Not all Alexandrian Jews supported this endeavor, and they continued to side with rabbinical Judaism. The Greeks, on the other hand, resented Philo's work and accused Jewish scholars of trying to assert the superiority of Hebrew culture over Greek.

Ironically, Philo, who died in 50 CE, later came to be seen as a father of the early Christian Church. It is important to remember that Christianity came to Alexandria through its Jewish community (Runia 2002: 210-11). Indeed, the first Christians of Egypt were Alexandrian Jews. Christianity had come to Egypt from Jerusalem in about 41 CE at the beginning of Emperor Claudius' reign. Cantor maintains that the Church "had become intrinsically more Greek in its doctrine, absorbing fully Alexandrian Platonism, which had been largely developed by Philo the Jew" (Cantor 1994: 157).

By the second century Christianity was becoming virulently anti-Jewish. Many Jews looked down upon the growth of Christianity with "cold indifference, furious contempt, and active condemnation." And Christians responded with malice and vindictiveness. Nevertheless, the early Christians came to regard the Septuagint as the authoritative text of the Old Testament. Haas suggests that the Septuagint became the key agency for transmitting many Jewish elements into Christianity (Haas 1997: 97).

The existence of Jews in Africa became even more precarious after the disastrous Jewish war of national liberation against Rome, which raged from the Middle East across North Africa from 66 to 70 CE and resulted in the Roman destruction of the second temple in Jerusalem (Barclay 1996: 75-77). With the destruction of the temple in 70 CE, Jews no longer had a center to unify them. The ideology of the temple had had a powerful unifying effect on diasporic Jews, and with its loss morale plummeted.

The Roman emperor Titus is said to have enslaved more than thirty thousand Jews and exiled them to North Africa. A number of them are believed to have settled on the island of Jerba, a Jewish community possibly founded as early as 580 BCE after the destruction of the first temple in Jerusalem (Udovitch and Valensi 1984: 17). After the war against Rome, all Jews in the Roman Empire were subjected to a special tax (Barclay 1996: 77). Unlike other minorities in the ancient world, Jews were taxed for their religion. The trauma of the Jewish war and its aftermath forced Jews and Judaism in Egypt to become more introspective.

The Collapse of Alexandrian Judaism

For centuries Jews and Judaism had flourished in Africa west of Egypt. By the second century CE, Jews were prospering economically in nearly every large seaport town along the North African coast. Carthage was rebuilt by the Romans and it became an early center for both Christianity and Judaism. By 296, thanks to Jewish initiative, Roman Carthage was minting gold coins, possibly with ore from the goldfields of the Upper Senegal River Valley of West Africa (Iliffe 1995: 50). On the high plains of what are today Algeria and Tunisia the Romans introduced olives and barley. The Latins, with the help of the local Jews, transformed the coastal littoral into the granary of Rome, furnishing the empire's cities with abundant cereals.

In North Africa as well as in Egypt, many Jews had become tough business competitors in their dealings with local entrepreneurs. And this aroused envy. Jews were increasingly viewed as cunning, avaricious, secretive, exclusivist, and rejecters of Christianity. Their strong communal structures only alienated them more from the general populace. The Jews of antiquity viewed themselves as citizens of one nation and one religion, seemingly not cognizant of their separation from each other by their diverse languages, practices, ideologies, and political loyalties. The Jews of Africa had become a people who dwelled apart.

In 73 CE a fanatical Jew from Palestine incited the poor of Cyrene to revolt. The Cyrenaican Jews rallied behind this messianic ruler, named Lucuas, who raised expectations of a divine intervention on behalf of all Jews. The revolt was quickly and brutally suppressed. Yet for unknown reasons the Jews again rebelled against Roman rule in Cyrenaica in 115 CE (Barclay 1996: 78-81). What began as a conflict with their Greek neighbors spread rapidly to Egypt and Cyprus. The Roman army was forced to intervene, and the conflict consequently escalated into a war against Rome itself. It was Jews against Roman Legions, the local Greeks, and the Egyptians. The Jewish rebels wreaked considerable damage in Cyrene, destroying roads, public buildings, and even numerous Roman temples. The revolt spread to Alexandria and eastward as far as Mesopotamia. It was finally suppressed by Trajan's armies in 117, but not before the great synagogue in Alexandria was destroyed (Haas 1997: 99).

The revolt of 115-117 CE led to the near elimination of Hellenized Jewry from Egypt and North Africa. It was seen as a great victory for the Egyptian Greeks. The Jews lost their lands in both areas through confiscations. The Jewish population of Alexandria and Cyrenaica plunged dramatically. Whole communities vanished. Several hundred thousand Jews were killed or enslaved. Their major synagogues were destroyed, their centers of Jewish studies were closed, and Judeo-Hellenistic literature was practically erased. In the decades following this trauma, most Jewish literature tended to be of an apocalyptic nature (Marlowe 1971: 84).

While remnants of Judeo-Alexandrian literature were preserved—notably the Septuagint and the works of Philo—Judaism per se was rejected by the Roman authorities. In fear and dismay many prominent rabbis and their families moved to Palestine. Those who remained were involuntarily relocated to new settlements beyond the city walls. The great library at Alexandria—so cherished by Jewish scholars—had already been destroyed in 47 BCE in a fire during violence between Roman and Egyptian militaries.

Jewish-Roman relations deteriorated further under Emperor Hadrian. He forbade the practice of genital mutilation (circumcision)—a decision that may have sparked the Bar Kochba Revolt of 132-135 CE in Palestine. As a consequence of the revolt, Jerusalem was reconstituted as a non-Jewish city, and the name of the country was changed from Judea (land of the Jews) to Palestine (land of the Philistines). After this war, the Romans forbade proselytization in return for the right of Jews to practice their faith (Aberbach 2000: 69). In North Africa, many Jews fled to the mountains in what is today Mauretania and Morocco and began to convert the local Berbers. The Judaization of many Berber communities may have largely been the consequence of the dispersal of Cyrenaican Jews who, after the repression ordered by the Roman emperor Trajan, fled into the Sahara and to Mauretania. Some got as far as Tuat (Tawat), where they introduced the *foggara*, an ingenious system of oasis irrigation.

Thus, Jews were expelled from the coastal towns and cities of North Africa and fled into the high plains of central Algeria, Morocco, and Mauretania. In those areas, Berbers of Numidia and Mauretania were producing valuable exports of corn and olive oil. Saharan Berbers started breeding camels and pushed southwards into the desert oases south of the Atlas Mountains. Jews may even have involved themselves in the gold trade emanating from West Africa by 280 CE. Later, Jews would move back to the coastal areas, notably to what is today Tunisia.

After the early first century the Jewish population of Alexandria practically disappeared. But the Greek version of the Hebrew Bible (Septuagint) survived, as did the works of Philo. Ironically, they became an integral part of Christian tradition. Those who lived farther up the Nile fared better, though most of them remained small tenant farmers and tax-paying peasants.

The Challenge of Christianity

Christianity began to emerge as a mass religion, and by 150 CE Alexandria had become a major center of eastern Christianity. The Judean church leadership in Alexandria had been purged and was followed by a Judeophobia pervasive in the city's culture. Still, Christianity in Africa was no longer a Jewish phenomenon but a distinct religion no longer exclusively made up of Jews. A Jew-hating ethos was thus injected into the church episcopate, and it would persist through the ages in North Africa and beyond.

Gradually and quietly Jews began to make a comeback in Alexandria. Their population began to grow and they started to prosper again in the late Roman period, especially in the late fourth and fifth centuries. Haas notes that Jews made up a significant portion of the city's intellectual elite and occupied "virtually every social status and economic position within the city, including teachers, philosophers, and mathematicians" (Haas 1997: 113). By late antiquity they may also have dominated the medical profession. Some became large landowners or merchants of goods such as alum and wine. A number were even slaveholders. By the early third century Jews were allowed to hold municipal office. They were further empowered when the Roman emperor Caracalla granted Roman citizenship to everyone in the empire in 212 CE. The central synagogue in Alexandria was completely rebuilt by the third century and re-emerged as an important center of political as well as religious activity.

Nevertheless, the Roman authorities saw Christianity as a growing threat and sought to play the Jews against the Christians as well as the Greek population. By about 200 CE, Christianity had begun to pose a threat to Judaism as well. The Hebrew scriptures were adopted by the Christians as the "Old Testament," and the emperor Diocletian (284-305) claimed he was the "elect of God" and ruled through God's will. Jews found themselves the target of growing persecution again. At the same time, however, Christian leaders were deeply divided over doctrine and were faced with deep schisms and numerous heretical movements.

Canons 49 and 50 of the Ecclesiastical Council of Elvira in 306 were severely exclusionary of Jews. Some scholars claim they aimed to insulate Christians from Jews and to arrest the diffusion of Judaism among the Gentile populations. After this, we see an increasingly hostile ecclesiastical attitude towards the Jews. A growing number of negative stereotypes relative to the Jewish faith appeared in the major works of Roman literature. Benjamin Isaac maintains that "The Romans adopted some...of the traditional anti-Jewish ideas, put their own slant on them, and developed more" (Isaac 2004: 80).

Jewish life began to deteriorate in the fourth century when the Roman Empire officially converted to Christianity under the emperor Constantine (r. 306-37). Constantine converted to Christianity in 312 and within a year had passed an edict according Christians complete freedom of worship. Christianity was thus recognized as a legitimate religion. Nevertheless, a law of 329 carried the death penalty on Jews who persecuted Jewish converts to Christianity (Isaac 2004: 461).

The emperor Theodosius went even farther than Constantine. In 384 he issued an edict formally declaring Christianity the official religion of the Roman Empire. He ordered the closure of all temples and other religions buildings dedicated to the old deities (Battenson 1943: 31). He allowed the church to install its own courts, which shortly developed their own body of law, called "canon law." Constantinople, the New Rome, was constructed on the site of Byzantium, an early Greek city on the Bosporus. Now a wholesale conversion to Christianity was underway. By 350 CE Christianity became a state religion in Ethiopia with the forging of an Aksumite-Constantinople axis. By the sixth century the whole of Nubia had become Christian, from Aswan to the Blue Nile.

By the 390s, Roman policy had become pro-Christian, and the faith spread like wildfire in Alexandria and all along the North African coast. Saint Augustine, one of the foremost Christian theologians of all time, was an African born in Algeria in 354. As Bishop of Hippo he wanted to isolate Jews to prevent their contaminating the fragile Christian communities. His thoughts about Jews were legalized in the Theodosian Code. By the last decades of the fourth century Jewish scholars were distancing themselves from Hellenism, and the Alexandrian and Egyptian Jewish communities were becoming more fully Hebraized.

After 375 CE, Roman rule in the West crumbled, and by the opening of the fifth century, the Christian Church had become enormously influential. Arguably, it now represented the major culture in Alexandria. Jewish and Christian conflict erupted in Alexandria in 414 CE—instigated by the fanatical patriarch Cyril—and within a year the government had expelled a large portion of the Jewish population (Pollard and Reid 2006: 274). Jews were also struggling to survive in the coastal cities of North Africa. By 500 CE their numbers had fallen by more than half since the onset of Christianity.

Jewish-Christian conflict had always manifested strong economic overtones, as Jews had become fierce competitors in maritime occupations. Also, Jews dominated the cloth exports.

Jewish-made luxury consumer goods were marketed throughout the Mediterranean by merchants centered in Alexandria. Jews were moreover very close to the Palestinian patriarch in the Middle East who made regular trips to Egypt to collect tithes for the Temple in Jerusalem.

New threats to Jews and their faith came from across the Mediterranean. By the opening of the fifth century a Vandal kingdom had been established in North Africa by Germanic tribal chieftains. In 429-39 CE the Vandal king Genserich overran Spain and swept into North Africa via Gibraltar. Originally from the Baltic area of northern Europe, the Teutonic Vandals conquered much of the coast, laying waste to many of its once-vibrant port cities. As they gained control over the eastern coastal plains, Berbers strengthened their hold over the interior. Many Jewish traders and farmers retreated to the hinterlands and joined the Berbers—some of whom we have learned were already Jewish converts. Remarkably, all of Morocco and Algeria were untouched, while Cyrenaica remained within the Egyptian orbit. The Vandals gained control of the maritime trade in the western basin of the Mediterranean, focusing on Tunisian coastal areas. These and subsequent Germanic invasions introduced an entirely new ethnic element into the North African demographic. Equally momentous, they brought an ignominious end to more than four centuries of Roman domination.

Indeed, in 476, with the death of Roman emperor Romulus Augustus, the empire in the West ceased to exist. The eastern half of the old Roman Empire survived and began to flourish under the emperor Justinian (r. 527-565), who ruled from Constantinople. The resurgent Byzantine Empire then launched campaigns to regain its western provinces, including North Africa. Beginning in 533, the Byzantines initiated seaborne attacks, and with Berber assistance they conquered the Vandals and expelled them from the continent, their Arian form of Christianity eventually replaced by Orthodox Catholicism.

Byzantine rule over North Africa was even more destructive than that of the Vandals. Punitive taxes were levied and non-Christian religions were brutally suppressed. During the Byzantine period the position of Jewries in North Africa deteriorated. An edict was issued by Justinian in 535 or 553 that excluded Jews from public office, forbade the practice of the faith, and resulted in the transformation of numerous synagogues into churches. Many Jews fled to the Berber communities in the mountains and into the Sahara. In 626 CE, Christian Byzantine militaries ejected the Persian army of occupation from Egypt, and within a decade Byzantine emperor Heraclius decreed a forced conversion of Jews (Gerber 1992: 13).

The process of Jewish decline was paralleled by an array of fresh writings emanating from Jewish theological centers in the Middle East and culminating in the sixth century with the massive Babylonian Talmud (ca. 500 CE), a rich compilation of oral traditions. Carl Ehrlich calls the Babylonian Talmud "the most influential work in Judaism over the last millenium and a half" (Ehrlich 2003: 23). Norman Cantor maintains that this work "promoted Jewish consciousness while reflecting an ambience of social anxiety and intellectual withdrawal" (Cantor 1994: 81-82).

Indeed, for intellectuals this was a dark age of introspection and re-assessment of Jews' relationships with seemingly hostile dominant cultures that swirled around them and threatened their survival as a people and a faith. Holy texts were reexamined to reflect perceived new realities. In the Babylonian Talmud, for example, the Genesis narrative concerning Noah is recast in a way that claims that the descendants of Ham are cursed by being black. Ham is depicted as being black and sinful and his progeny as degenerates. Edith Sanders argues that these oral traditions grew out of a need for Jews to rationalize their subjugation of Canaan in ancient times. In any case, in the Babylonian Talmud Ham was blackened and transformed into an ancestor of black peoples. Henceforth, the Hamites became identified with

Africans, who were to be regarded as sinful and inferior (Sanders 1969: 521). This vicious myth took root, was adopted by Christians and Muslims, and became a justification for enslaving Africans. Such a denigrating characterization must have made it even more difficult for Jews in Africa to relate to their dark-complexioned gentile neighbors.

Byzantine rule in Africa was short-lived. In 641, adherents of a new faith, Islam, swept into Egypt and seized Alexandria and most of the countryside. Arab armies extended their conquest westward into Libya. The rise of Muslim naval supremacy in the eastern Mediterranean opened the way to further Muslim conquests in North Africa, and by 705 Byzantine Africa had been conquered. Henceforth, the entire coastal region of North Africa west of Egypt was referred to by the Muslims as al-Maghreb, meaning "the West."

The indigenous Berber chieftaincies in the interior mounted a fierce resistance but lacked the unity to succeed. By 711 CE the Muslim armies had reached the Atlantic coast of Morocco and were poised to cross into Spain. This Muslim Arab invasion and occupation was a crucial watershed that signaled the effective end of the Classical era in Africa and the beginning of a new epoch full of great danger to Jews and Judaism in much of Africa north of the Sahara. While Judaism may have been the first non-African religion to penetrate the continent—with Christianity following—it was Islam that became the most aggressive and dramatic in its expansion and arguably the most successful. The next chapter will explore the Jewish response to this new threat.

CHAPTER TWO

Jews and Muslims in North Africa to the Seventeenth Century

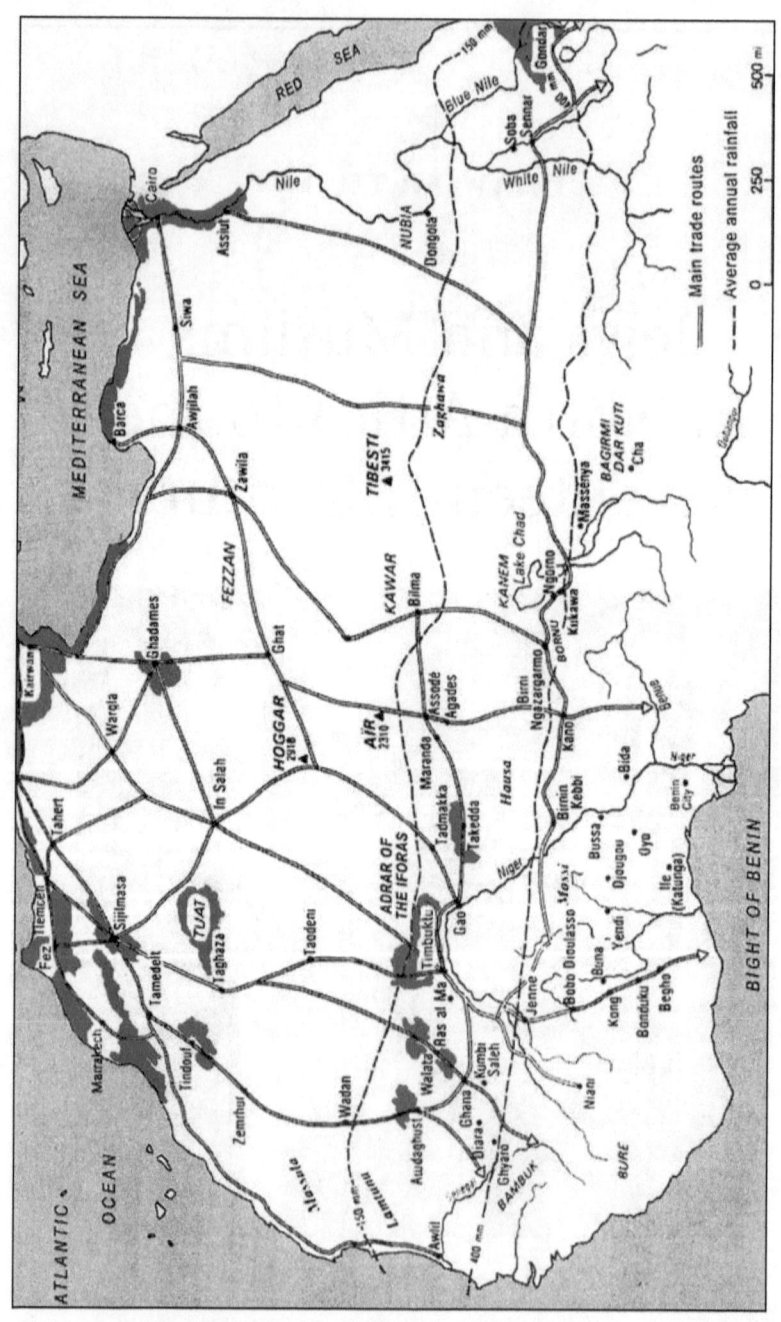

Major Clusters of Jewish Population ca. 1550

The Arab Conquest

The Arab conquest of North Africa commenced with the invasion of Egypt in 639 CE, and within about five centuries Islam would become the predominant religion of the region. The expansion of Arab power and the Muslim religion followed the death of its founder, the Prophet Muhammad, in 632 CE. Muhammad drew heavily on the traditions of Islam's two predecessors, Judaism and Christianity. By the time of Muhammad's death nearly all the Bedouin tribes of the Arabian Peninsula had been welded into a remarkably cohesive and ethnically homogeneous religious community.

In North Africa, Islamization drew its initial impulse from conquest, or Holy War (*jihad*). In late 639 CE, thousands of well-armed Muslim Arab men poured into Egypt and within three years they had evicted the Byzantines, who were unpopular among the indigenous populations. These youthful jihadists were intent on destroying the very foundations of Christian and Judaic institutions as well as traditional African religious systems. They would seek to replace them with those based on Islamic tenets. Intolerant of other deities, they would accept no other God but Allah. Local populations would have to adapt—which most did—or be eliminated. Initially Jews and Coptic Christians, ignorant of Islam, saw the Arabs as liberators from persecution by the Byzantine Orthodox Church. That perception changed quickly. Within three years Christianity ceased to be the official religion of Egypt, replaced by yet another religion rooted in the Middle East.

As the Arabs from Syria and Arabia swept into the region of Cyrenaica and Tripoli west of Egypt they encountered determined opposition from both the Berbers and the Byzantine Empire. Evicting the Byzantines from the coastal cities to the west became difficult because of their formidable navy. The Arabs also had to contend with the durable Berber Numidian kingdoms which held the southern plains. The Muslim invaders thus moved south of the coastal littoral, and in about 670 they founded Kairwan in the Tunisian hinterland, just two days' journey from the Mediterranean and away from danger of Byzantine attack. Kairwan was initially established as an Arab base of operations against the surrounding Berber populations, but it eventually blossomed into one of Africa's greatest centers of Muslim culture and learning.

In the early years, the Arab Muslims were remarkably united while the Berbers lacked unity and coordination of command. Nevertheless, by 700 the Arabs had built up their own navy and had taken the strategic city of Carthage, effectively ending Byzantine rule over North Africa. They also defeated the powerful but loosely knit federation of Berber Zenata tribes. Their armies, which became increasingly Berberized, reached the Atlantic Moroccan coast by 711, sweeping all of northwest Africa under their nominal control. Henceforth, the Arabs referred to the entire coastal region of North Africa west of Egypt as *al-Maghreb*, meaning "the West."

From the Maghreb they crossed the Strait of Gibraltar into Spain and defeated the Visigoths. They pushed onwards beyond the Pyrenees, and at the Battle of Tours in 733 the Frankish forces under Charles Martel defeated them and halted further expansion. All the conquests in southern Europe, including Spain, were placed under Arab governors based in Africa at Kairwan. John Willis contends that the Muslim armies that swept into the Iberian Peninsula and southern France were as much Judaized Berbers as they were Muslim Arabs (Willis 1971:

155). On the other hand, many local Jews in Spain readily assisted in the invasion, having tired of Visigothic oppression.

By 733 Muslims had completed the conquest of a vast region of the world, extending from the Pyrenees in Western Europe eastward across North Africa and through the fertile crescent of the Middle East to Persia. With breathtaking speed, the vast Mediterranean Sea had been transformed into a Muslim lake. The theocracy constituted one enormous common market. Centuries would elapse before so much of the world would again be brought into a single economic and political union. This remarkable globalization offered the Jews, whose contacts already stretched over wide geographical areas, a wonderful opportunity to expand the scope of their enterprises. But this opportunity came with a price.

In Egypt—the jewel of Africa—the Arab invaders gave the subject populations of Jews and Christians the stark choice of either converting to Islam or accepting the status of "protected tributaries" (*dhimmi*) in return for surrendering land and incurring a poll tax on all males over the age of fourteen. As dhimmis they were eventually forced to wear special garments and colors to distinguish them from the Muslim populace (Hunwick 2006: 5-9). Dhimmis were also forbidden to ride horses or to bear arms. This is significant because from that time onward Jews and Christians were exempted from military service in Muslim-ruled countries (Schroeter 2002: 3-11). On the other hand, without weapons they were deprived of staging armed opposition or coups against Islamic regimes no matter how oppressive they might be. As a trade-off, Muslim rulers and masters were expected to guarantee their physical and fiscal security and to allow them the freedom to practice their own religion (Deshen and Zenner 1996: 87).

Another important concession was their freedom to travel and reside anywhere throughout Muslim domains. Hence, Jews especially would move easily and safely around the Muslim and

Christian worlds for the sake of business as well as for contracting marriages for their offspring. Thus, as merchant families they remained a mobile and cosmopolitan community, operating an extremely diversified trade in staples and luxuries and serving as interpreters and diplomats (Schroeter 2002: 3).

Forced conversions were rare. Muslims saw Jews and Christians as *al-kitab*, or "People of the Book." They recognized that they all came from a common Judeo-religious heritage in the Middle East (Diaz-Mas 2003: 52). However, while Jews may have been free to practice their faith, they were forbidden to proselytize or to erect new synagogues without the consent of Muslim authorities. Some scholars argue that Muslim hostility to *kaffirs* or unbelievers was not motivated by any deep-seated theological hatred but from a concern that their seemingly deviant religious beliefs would contaminate Islam and weaken the faith. However, make no mistake: from the beginning, Jews especially were transformed into a subordinate population constrained to pay humble deference to their Muslim superiors.

At first, the Arabs in Egypt depended on Jews and Coptic Christians to administer much of the vast state apparatus. However, by the eighth century the Arab population had grown to the point where the Jews and Christians were no longer essential, and they were gradually excluded from public office. Ultimately, many affluent Jews converted to Islam to avoid taxation levied on non-Muslims, and they came to be called *Mawali*, or assimilated Muslims. Milton Shain asserts that "under Islam the Jews were never an 'outsider' to the same extent as in Christian Europe" (Shain 1998: 45). In the marketplace, at least, they interacted with peoples of all faiths.

Globally and locally, Islamic unity was challenged from within the faith. Shortly after the Prophet's death, fundamental divisions within Islam began to emerge. In the Middle East, the Arab-ruled Umayyad Caliphate in 750 lost out to the Abbasids, who would rule until 1000 CE. The Abbasids moved their capital from Damascus eastward to Baghdad in Iraq and began to rely increasingly on non-Arab nationalities to assist in governance (Lewis 1976: 12-14).

The Abbasid revolution transformed the caliphate from an Arab entity into a Muslim empire. Mecca remained the Holy City of Islam, much as Jerusalem continued to be the focal point of Judaism. Mark Cohen argues that "The ties to Palestine, dating back to Roman times, survived the Abbasid centralization of imperial authority in Iraq in the middle of the eighth century" (Cohen 1980: 4). Gradually, the ruling elite throughout the caliphate became multi-ethnic. Indeed, the Abbasid rulers maintained their vast empire by recruiting mercenaries, especially Turkish slaves called *Mamluks*, whom they forcibly converted to Islam.

Ultimately, North African Muslim rulers began to assert their independence from the Middle East–based Abbasid caliphs, and by about 800 CE the Maghreb was effectively independent of Abbasid rule. In less than a century, real power in Egypt rested with Turkish military governors and their ethnically diverse mercenaries.

In the Maghreb, Arab feelings of racial and religious superiority were resented by indigenous Berbers, many of whom had converted to Islam and yearned to be treated as equals. Inevitably, schisms appeared in the faith. In the Kharijite rebellion of ca. 739, Berber Muslims fought the armies of the Umayyads and were forced to flee southwards into remote desert oases. In 757, they built their new capital, Sijilmasa, and began to revive and expand trade with the Sudanic areas of West Africa (Abun-Nasr 1987: 49). Indeed, it was the Kharijites who historians believe were responsible for reviving the ancient routes to the Niger River valley via Lake Chad and the central Sudan. The region between the headwaters of the Niger and Senegal rivers was proving to be enormously rich in alluvial gold, and writers of the time were describing it as the "land of gold."

Sijilmasa quickly prospered and became a cosmopolitan city of the Sahara. Sanhaja Berbers, Jews, blacks, Andalusians, and Arabs from various parts of the Maghreb and Spain were attracted to the magnificent emporium. Before long, it became an important entrepot for trade southward to Walata and the emerging black African empire of Ghana (Levtzion 1973: 34-38). This was a time of dramatic state building, and in 789 a refugee descendant of the Prophet Muhammad established a kingdom based not too far away, in Fez (Blady 2002: 288). In the eighth and ninth centuries, still more Berber states arose to challenge the authority of the eastern rulers in Baghdad.

How did Jews fit into this fascinating story? David Corcos maintains that Malekite traditions discouraged Muslims from dealing in precious metals. He specifies that the marketing of gold in powder form, in ingots, or in wrought form was simply not in conformity with the Muslims' Malekite beliefs (Corcos 1976: 40; see also Diaz-Mas 2003: 53). Thus, they were willing to let Jews trade and work in gold, which became the Western Sudan's most lucrative export. Consequently, because much of the fabrication and minting of gold was done by Jews, it was they who became a powerful presence in the expansion of the western Sudanic trans-Saharan gold trade.

From approximately 800 to 976 CE, Sijilmasa flourished as home to famous rabbis and as an active center of Judaic studies. Jews lived in small peri-urban communities surrounding the city, where they worked as gold- and silversmiths and played significant roles in the movement of gold along the caravan routes extending west of the vast Sahara desert. Similarly, Kairwan—in today's modern Tunisia—reached its peak under Ibrahim II (r. 875-902) as an important point on the caravan route between Egypt and Spain. Kairwan's markets were filled with products of its huge textile industry as well as with citrus fruits from the coast which were exchanged for wheat from the northern plains. Jews were tolerated by the Muslim authorities, for they brought wealth and culture to this amazingly sophisticated and dynamic urban center. Moreover, from the eighth to the eleventh century, the academy at Kairwan was a famous center of Jewish scholarship and produced information that was useful to Jew and Muslim alike. In Kairwan's numerous *yeshivot*, Jews wrote important medical treatises which were later translated into Latin and circulated in Europe (Seltzer 1980: 345).

As the ninth century closed, most of the Muslim west—the Maghreb included—was no longer controlled by the Baghdad-based Abbasid Caliphate. And it would not be long after the fall of the Abbasids in the tenth century that Egypt became the center of the Muslim world. Inexorably, the center of gravity in North Africa was moving eastward.

Jews under the African Fatimids: Dimensions of Mutuality and Toleration

Early in the tenth century a new dynasty emerged in the central Maghreb, the Fatimids. The Fatimids were Berber Ismaili Shiites who denied the legitimacy and supremacy of the orthodox Abbasid Caliphate in Baghdad and claimed descent from the Prophet through his daughter Fatima. The Fatimids rose to power in Kairwan in 910, with much of their wealth obtained from the fabulous international gold markets of Sijilmasa.

Fatimid empowerment was quite rapid. Their fleets sacked the Italian city of Genoa in 934 and gained control over Mediterranean trade. In less than two decades they would conquer most of northern Tunisia and Algeria. In 969, with the aid of slave mercenaries and Berber auxiliaries, they peacefully took Egypt from the Turkish military officials who had tenuously ruled on behalf of the Baghdad-based Abbasids (Hrbek 1992: 37).

The capture of this vital link between the markets of the East and West completed the indigenous Berber reconquest of North

Africa and released the region from the hegemony of Baghdad. With remarkable speed and brilliant military execution, Maghrebian Berbers had succeeded in establishing an African empire which extended from Morocco to Egypt. I. Hrbek asserts that the entire Maghreb had been Islamized by the tenth century, and that "only in some regions and towns were there still some small Christian and Jewish communities" (Hrbek 1992: 37). While Christian intellectuals had almost all turned to writing in Arabic, Jews resisted and tenaciously clung to their unique culture and religious traditions. Nevertheless, commercial correspondence was usually conducted in Judeo-Arabic—an Arabic dialect written in Hebrew letters.

In 973 the Fatimid caliph and his family, seeking stronger commercial ties with the East, abruptly moved their base from the Maghreb to Egypt, leaving behind a Berber family, the Zirids, as their deputy in the Maghreb. In time, the Zirids became independent of the Fatimids and established their own state. Shortly before this occurred, the Fatimids had established their new Egyptian capital, called Cairo, and amassed a huge fleet in the Mediterranean, which eventually controlled much of the eastern seaborne trade. Commerce became free, intensely competitive, and private (Gubbay 1999: 67).

The Fatimids' importance in Islamic and Jewish history is in their role in reorienting Mediterranean and Indian Ocean trade. Under their leadership, Egypt became the most important entrepot for trade between the Indian Ocean and the vast Mediterranean. Much credit for the integration of disparate Mediterranean markets goes to the so-called Jewish "Maghrebian traders," who in the eleventh century pioneered the institutionalization of business contract enforcement, a procedure based on interpersonal trust and mutually accepted sanctions for violating that trust. These "Maghrebian traders" were so named because a century earlier their ancestors had migrated from Baghdad to Fatimid-ruled Tunisia on the Maghrebian coast and then were brought to Egypt when the Fatimids relocated to Cairo (Greif 2006: 60-61). The practice of contract enforcement contributed enormously to the expansion of trade in the Mediterranean Basin and beyond.

Undeniably, Jewish merchants of Egypt of all stripes grew rich from this long-distance trade and also as suppliers of African gold to the royal mint. Abu Zikri Kohen from Sijilmasa was a key broker in the trade between Cairo and India. There were many others like him who traveled extensively to Middle and Near Eastern markets, learning foreign languages, accumulating strategic knowledge of different cultures, and building substantial fortunes. Quietly though surely the Jews had become the globalists of the medieval world.

The domains of the Fatimids reached beyond the Nile, and for the first time since the Ptolemies, Egypt ruled an empire in Asia Minor. Indeed, Fatimid rule extended eastward to Damascus from 978 to 1076. The Caliphate held sway over nearly all of North Africa and Egypt, as well as Syria, Palestine, and Arabia (Gubbay 1999: 65)

The Fatimid rulers became patrons of the arts in all the major cities, especially in their own capital of Cairo. They took advantage of the fiscal and administrative skills of Jewish merchants, and under them Jews as well as Christians became important tax collectors. Ali Killis, a Jew, was the first vizier of the Fatimid empire.

The Fatimids also began to mint gold coins, and by 975 there were Jewish-operated mints in Fez, Marrakesh, Sijilmasa, and elsewhere. Nehemiah Levtzion observes that "the economic and political expansion of the Fatimid Caliphate was much aided by the gold of the Sudan" (Levtzion 1973: 127-31). In the tenth century, the demand for gold from the Sudan soared when, on behalf of their Fatimid overlords, Jews began to mint large quantities of dinars. It should be emphasized that gold constituted the basis of the Muslim monetary system in the Middle

East and the Mediterranean World. Indeed, the coveted Fatimid dinars contained substantial quantities of West African Sudanese gold.

Not surprisingly, West African Sudanic empires such as Ghana arose in response to the growth in this trans-Saharan trade. Jews set up operations in the major towns of the western Sudan, but, unlike Muslims, they made no effort to convert the local populace or their rulers to the Judaic faith. They remained very much in the background while their more aggressive Muslim counterparts pressured African rulers to renounce their traditional religious beliefs and become Muslims. Some traditional leaders—notably the ruler of Ghana in the eleventh century—resisted and were overthrown.

Jewish life flourished under the Fatimids, and as we've already discovered, by the eleven century the city of Kairwan in modern Tunisia had become a major center of Jewish learning and economic activity. Jewish scholars traveling between Europe and the Middle East rested, studied, and taught in Kairwan. Robert Seltzer tells us that "academies were established by important talmudists and prosperous Jewish merchant families supported Jewish scientists and philosophers" (Seltzer 1980: 345). Egyptian and Maghrebian Jewry flourished, and Jews from the old Abbasid territories began to migrate to Africa.

Mark Cohen notes that in the Fatimid period the yeshivas of Palestine and Iraq became increasingly dependent upon Maghrebian and Egyptian Jews for financial support (Cohen 1980: 5). This was an exciting moment when the Muslim Middle East looked to Africa for fiscal support and theological inspiration.

Distant Fez had also become an important Jewish intellectual center. Isaac Alfasi (1013-1103), one of the most influential talmudists in the world at that time, lived there. And according to Seltzer, his digest of talmudic law became a classic of early postgeonic rabbinical law (Seltzer 1980: 346). From the eleventh century, extensive communication existed among Jewish co-religionists in the African, European, and Eastern Muslim world. Fez, for example, enjoyed especially close ties to Jewish scholars in Spain.

The great Spanish rabbi Samuel Ha-Levi, chief minister at the court of Granada, did much to promote Jewish learning throughout the world. He gave much of his personal fortune, made in international commerce, to intellectuals wishing to study the Torah and become rabbis. By the time of his death in 1055, Ha-Levi had supported large numbers of Jewish students in North African communities (Marcus 1972: 298). Gerber reveals that in the eleventh century, Jews of Tunis were exporting both merchandise and manuscripts to Spain, Egypt, Syria, and India (Gerber 1980: 33).

Muslim-ruled Fez would eventually become a major publishing center for Jewish theological works, Hebrew being the lingua franca. Indeed, though many scholars wrote in Arabic, Hebrew script was invariably used. Unfortunately, life for Jews in the Maghreb was never secure, and in a pogrom in Fez in 1033, thousands of men were murdered and their women sold into slavery. Despite this huge humanitarian tragedy, Jews did not totally abandon their community. The traumatized survivors stayed on and rebuilt against all odds. Fez endured well into the twentieth century as an important center for Jewish learning.

The Fatimids sacrificed local support in moving eastward, and their concentration on Egypt led the Berbers in the west to renounce their allegiance in 1048 and to form their own independent states. Interestingly, the Fatimids responded not with military force but by allowing huge numbers of nomadic Arab bedouin tribes of the Middle East, mainly the Bani Hilal, to pass through Egypt and settle westward in Ifriqiya. It was perhaps the largest Arab diaspora in history and one which, if gauged by its impact, has not been repeated. Unfortunately, these Hilal Arab immigrants proved to be quite destructive in the Maghreb. They overran Cyrenaica, Tripolitania, the Fezzan, and much of Ifriqiya before settling mainly in Morocco. Along the way they sacked numerous cities, notably Kairwan in 1057 (Gerber 1980: 13).

With this huge new population of immigrants interspersed throughout the countryside, many more indigenes were converted to Islam. Indeed, the Bani Hilal diaspora resulted in an acceleration of the process of Arabization and Islamization among the indigenous populations. Fearing assimilation, many Jews fled to Muslim-ruled Spain, or *Sephared* ("the East"), as the Jews called it. On the other hand, H.Z. Hirschberg says that some Jews after the mid-eleventh century began to move southward in the face of growing turmoil in southern Morocco. These refugees settled in the market communities of black-ruled western Sudan (Hirschberg 1963: 321). Tantalizingly, recent DNA research suggests that many Africans from Mauretania through Senegal may be descendants of these groups of Middle East provenance.

Jews under the Mamluks

Meanwhile, the Fatimids in Egypt became fatally dependent on their slave army of captives from the Near East, Asia, and Nubia. Fatimid weakness spelled vulnerability in the coastal seaports of the southern Mediterranean. Italian merchants and pirates, mainly from Pisa and Genoa, raided the almost-defenseless ports in their struggle for control of the western Mediterranean. Conflict with the Christians always had a religious dimension, and the First Crusade of 1095 marked a new and more dangerous era in Christian-Muslim rivalry for the profitable trade. Christian fundamentalist rulers in the West had begun to impose their beliefs on the Islamic Middle East, which reacted with historically unprecedented violence. The Western imposition only fueled dormant Islamic militancy and brought economic destabilization to the entire region.

In 1171 the Shiite Fatimids were overthrown by their Syrian-born Kurdish vizier, the great Saladin. Saladin restored the Sunni branch of Islam, and Egypt has remained Sunni to this day. Perhaps even more important, he overran Syria and ruled it from Egypt, thus re-linking Africa with the Middle East. In 1187 he defeated the Christian Crusaders and recaptured Jerusalem for Islam.

After Saladin real power shifted to a self-perpetuating caste of Mamluk military forces who ruled through their own appointed leaders. *Mamluk* is a term meaning "owned." Indeed, these fearsome cavalrymen originated as slaves purchased in their youth from the shores of the Black Sea near the south Russian steppes, sold to the Egyptian rulers, and forcibly converted to Islam. Gradually, their ranks were swelled by Christian Circassians, Armenians, Slavs, and African Nubians. The Mamluks were ultimately freed and achieved fame and power for their equestrian skills and for their handling of weapons, notably the bow and lance. They effectively controlled Egypt from 1250 until the Ottoman Turkish conquest in 1516-17 (Oliver 1977: 163).

The Mamluks became Egypt's greatest builders since the Ptolemies of antiquity, and Jews became active collaborators in the construction industry. Trade with the Italian city-states also flourished, thanks in large part to the intercession of Jews on both sides of the Mediterranean. Egypt itself gained even greater prominence as the key commercial bridge between Asia and Europe.

But in 1380 another group of Mamluks ascended to power, and they are remembered today for their rapacity and debilitating internal quarrels. They became purveyors of weapons, military materiel, and even mercenaries to numerous West African Sudanic states, which in turn led to the expansion of Islam at the expense of the traditional non-Muslim populations. By the early sixteenth century, the Hausa emirates of today's Nigeria and neighboring Kanem benefited from their arms trade with the Egyptian Mamluks. Many Jews in Egypt, faced with economic decline, emigrated to the Italian city-states, notably Venice. By this time, Venice had no serious challenger from any rival naval power. Nevertheless, while the Venetian merchant families welcomed the Jews, especially those in the textile trades, they confined them to a small quarter of the city, called the *ghetto,* a word which later became a generic term for the segregation of Jews worldwide.

Revolutionary Times: Jews under the Almoravids and Almohads

In the western Maghreb a new militantly fundamentalist group emerged among nomadic Sanhaja Berbers of southern Morocco and the western Sahara. Known as the Almoravids, they were fervent Sunni adherents of the Malikite school of law. They were also deeply interested in trans-Saharan commerce. Not surprisingly, their power would come to rest on control over a major caravan route from southern Morocco to the western Sudan. The movement, founded by a West African Muslim trained in Kairwan, actually began in the Senegal River valley and quickly split into two branches (Trimingham 1970: 23-31).

One group of jihadists went southward and captured Awdaghast and Silijmasa. In about 1055, the Almoravids seized the northern and southern termini of the strategic trans-Saharan routes between Ghana and Morocco. They also captured a key port town on the Niger leading to Gao. In 1070 they created a new capital at Marrakesh in order to command the vast plains. By 1083 they had overwhelmed the entire Maghreb west of Algiers, and within three years the northern branch had crossed the Mediterranean and entered Andalusia in Spain in order to organize its resistance to Christian expansion. The Almoravids were able to finance their operations by securing much of the West Africa gold trade and by developing agriculture along Morocco's Atlantic plains. In the jihad's aftermath, the trans-Saharan gold trade grew prodigiously. Gold dinars minted in Almoravid territories would find robust markets in Catholic-ruled Western Europe (Bovill 1958: 16-31).

Islamic culture in southern Spain now began to expand into North Africa. The union of Spain with the Maghreb opened the way to the movement of Jews and others. Though Jews had lived in relative peace in Morocco for many centuries, their condition improved when the Almoravids came to power in 1062. With the connection to Muslim Spain, many Saharan-based Jewish intellectuals, including Alfasi in 1088, immigrated there.

Before the Almoravids, Jewish life in Spain had been insecure. A group of Muslim fanatics had sacked Cordova in 1013, destroying its world-renowned library. And less than a half-century later, thousands of Jews would be massacred in Granada. In the early years of Almoravid rule, Jews, Christians, and Muslims enjoyed easygoing interaction. In this relatively peaceful atmosphere, Andalusian culture began to permeate North Africa as people moved back and forth across the Mediterranean. Prosperity followed in the eleventh century from growing exports of African gold and the adoption of gold coinage throughout the Muslim world.

Inevitably, the Almoravid state—weakened by costly battles against the Christian menace—taxed its populations heavily and quickly lost popular support. Tensions and oppression followed. Looking for scapegoats, in 1146 they launched a purge against all non-Muslims and shut down most of their churches and synagogues. Even Muslims of opposing sects were brutalized.

In response, Islamized Berber farmers in the Atlas Mountains formed a new movement—the Almohad—and launched a popular rebellion. The Almohads easily and quickly overwhelmed the Almoravids in Spain and then turned to Morocco and eastward, seizing Marrakesh in 1147 and Ifriqiya in 1160, putting an end to Bani Hilal Arab expansion and uniting the Maghreb for the first time under a single Berber authority. By 1170, much of the Iberian Peninsula and the entire Maghreb as far as Tripoli had fallen under their control.

With a modicum of peace restored, commerce flourished again throughout North Africa and the Mediterranean. The gold trade especially reached a new peak with Almohad rule over Spain and the Maghreb. Gold (along with silver) constituted the basis of the Muslim monetary system, and beginning with the Almoravid and Almohad incursions into Europe, the trans-Saharan gold trade helped to fuel southern European cultural and economic growth. Indeed, after 1252, gold began to replace silver as Europe's main currency. West African gold became essential for the monetization of the medieval Mediterranean economy and for the maintenance of the balance of payments. Many historians of Europe fail to recognize that from the eleventh to the seventeenth century the Sudanic region of West Africa served as a leading gold supplier to this international economy. More specifically, West African gold was vital to the Andalusian mints of Spain. The Almohads alone were able to boast of twenty-one mints there and in North Africa. Their dinars were in great demand in Muslim and non-Muslim markets throughout the Mediterranean. Urban life prospered and merchants from the Italian city-states began to trade in the Muslim currencies.

But life for non-Muslims in Almohad Spain was difficult. John Iliffe says that "Almohad rule was rigorously Islamic; Christianity was virtually eradicated from the Maghreb, and Jews found Almohads exceptionally intolerant" (Iliffe 1995: 47). In Spain, Judaism and Christianity were outlawed, marking one of the few instances in Islamic history that a government had led a campaign against its dhimmis. Elizabeth Isichei is careful not to exaggerate this situation and argues that Christianity was already in rapid decline, partly because it lacked a monastic tradition, unlike the Copts in Egypt (Isichei 1995: 179).

Some Jews fled to the few Christian outposts in Spain where they were welcome. In Morocco, the Almohads forced Jews to embrace Islam or face eviction. This may have been the beginning of a significant Sephardic emigration to Egypt. The great Sephardic Jewish philosopher Moses Maimonides left Cordova, Spain, and eventually settled in Cairo in 1165 (Deshen 1989: 37). Maimonides was enormously influential in the Muslim world as a jurist, philosopher, and physician. He was a prolific writer, and his *Guide to the Perplexed*—written in elegant Arabic—attempted to reconcile Jewish doctrines with Aristotelian logic. He also authored a widely read code of Jewish law that made him Jewry's pre-eminent legal authority. During his long sojourn in Africa, Maimonides recast Judaism by offering a philosophical interpretation of the scriptures far removed from the conventional readings (Nuland 2005: 211-24).

Eventually, the Almohad Caliphate overextended itself and was riven by internal dissension. Muslims turned on each other in cycles of unending violence. Christians took advantage of the turmoil, and their stunning victory in the Battle of Las Navas de Tolosa in 1212 marked the beginning of the end for Almohad rule in Africa and on the Iberian Peninsula. In the same year, a Zenata tribe in northern Morocco captured Marrakesh, moved the capital to Fez, and governed a somewhat diminished Morocco for two centuries as the Marinid dynasty. In 1269, the Marinids defeated the last Almohad caliph and established an independent state based in Fez (Ki-Zerbo and Niane 1997: 37-38).

By 1248, all of the Iberian Peninsula except Granada lay in Christian hands; Granada remained under the control of the Nasrid dynasty for nearly another century and a half. The new situation on the Iberian Peninsula provided unique opportunities for the Jews, who already enjoyed years of commercial and cultural contact with the peoples of North Africa. They mastered their languages as well as their business culture. Predictably, Jews became essential clients of the new Christian rulers and merchants and assumed a vital role in connecting the Christian and Muslim Mediterranean worlds in trade as well as in diplomacy.

Jews in the Mediterranean and Trans-Saharan Trades

The Christian kingdom of Aragon in Spain played an especially important role in the African trades. From the 1160s, successive monarchs of the House of Barcelona extended their power throughout the Mediterranean. Interestingly, while Muslims tended to be seen as competitors, Mediterranean Jews often became their behind-the-scenes allies and agents. Jewish immigration to the Mediterranean island of Majorca coincided with its conquest by King James I of Aragon in 1229. The Spanish Catalans were determined to use the Mediterranean islands as a springboard to North Africa and beyond.

Jews already figured importantly in the Catalan trade, and James encouraged Jewish merchants and professionals with their intimate knowledge of the Maghreb and its southern hinterlands to live in his kingdom. Thus, many prominent Moroccan Jews moved to Barcelona and Valencia, and historians believe the Moroccan-Jewish émigrés in Barcelona introduced their Christian associates to North African Muslim trading opportunities (Abun-Nasr 1987: 138-39).

Jews were already quite familiar with the trans-Saharan networks. Seltzer notes that "prosperous North African Jewish merchant families participated in the Saharan gold trade and maintained close economic ties with the kingdom of Aragon in Spain" (Seltzer 1980: 348). Indeed, by the thirteenth century, Jews of the oases towns of Tuat (Tawat) and Sijilmasa monopolized the trans-Saharan trade. It has already been noted that

Sijilmasa was the seat of an important Jewish community and was an embarkation point for the rich markets of the western Sudan. It attracted huge caravans from the western and central Maghreb and from lands to the south of the Sahara. Complementing this, the Saharan city of Tlemcen served as a key link between the trans-Saharan trade and Europe.

Roland Oliver maintains that Barcelona Jews became active in organizing the long-distance trade with Tlemcen, which was the only emporium in central Maghreb with a strong connection to Africa's resource-rich interior. It was strategically located along the caravan route between the Atlas Mountains and Sijilmasa (Oliver 1977: 366). In time, Tlemcen became a kind of protectorate of Aragon. Remarkably, tiny Aragon spread its net wide: forging strong commercial ties with Marinid Moroccans based in Fez and Marrakesh, as well as eastward to the Zayyanids based in Tlemcen and the Hafsid state in Tunis (Ki-Zerbo and Niane 1997: 41-42). Yet in so many respects it was the Jews who actually provided the essential bridges to these important Muslim entities. If you will, they were the essential facilitators.

Aragon by the mid-thirteenth century had begun to gain control over the major camel caravan routes between North Africa and southwestern Europe. By then, they had established direct and extremely fruitful contact with the Zayyanid rulers in Tlemcen. Relations between the Catalonians, who were part of Aragon by then, and the Zayyanid state became especially close (Benbassa and Rodrigue 2000: lii). Between 1284 and 1286 King Pedro of Aragon employed Jews as middlemen in commerce with the Maghreb (Lobban and Mandy 1997: 211). The link with Tlemcen was formalized in 1286 with the conclusion of a Jewish-brokered commercial treaty between Aragon and the Zayyandis. Jamil Abun-Nasr suggests that by then "colonies of Jews were engaged in commerce both in the central Maghreb and further along the caravan routes to the western Sudan" (Abun-Nasr 1987: 40).

The Italian city-states like Florence and Venice would also see the advantages of trade with Africa. Since the twelfth century Muslim rulers had allowed Italian merchants to establish operations in the major coastal towns of North Africa, from Tripoli to Ceuta. The western coastal ports, particularly Oran, were popular with merchants from Pisa and Genoa. But anti-Semitism was also strong in the Italian city-states, and in the thirteenth century Jewish cartographers from Genoa, Venice, and Pisa moved to the comparatively freewheeling Balearic island of Majorca, where they drew up charts, called *portolani*, of the coastlines of North Africa.

In 1339, Angelino Dulcert of Majorca was the first to put the gold-rich West African kingdom of Mali on a map. Thirty-six years later, a Majorcan atlas attributed to Abraham Cresques, of Jewish birth, was drawn for Charles V of France. In striking detail it depicts the western Sudanic cities of Timbuktu, Niani, and Gao and clearly indicates the caravan route from Sijilmasa to Timbuktu via Tawat (Tuat). A year later Cresques was commissioned by Prince Juan of Aragon to devise a world map, or *Mappa Mundi,* which also placed the West African empire of Mali on it and portrayed its ruler, or *mansa*, in all his majesty (Rotberg 1965: 42).

Thus, the Jews of Morocco and Majorca provided considerable information on the trans-Saharan trades. Hirschberg says, "There can be no doubt that these Jewish and New Christian cartographers received from Jewish traders the particulars required for the making of the maps of the Sudan and the routes leading to it." Corcos emphasizes that the "Jews of...Sijilmasa and Toowat (Tuat) monopolized trans-saharan trade." With perhaps moderate exaggeration, he argues that they controlled exclusively all business with Black African lands on the far side of the immense desert, adding, "for the simple reason that with 'Malekism' having finally become dominant, the Muslims left the Sahara entirely to the Jews" (Corcos 1976: 73). They were unmistakably a force to contend with in North Africa's coastal markets as well. For sure, by the fourteenth century certain mercantile families had become economically powerful and the small European Christian merchants could hardly compete.

We also know that relations between Morocco and Mali were good in the 1330s and '40s during the Marinid period. Mansa Musa's splendid pilgrimage to Mecca via Cairo in 1324, with its fabulous quantities of gold, put the West African gold exporter on world maps. As bright as this may have seemed, the future looked uncertain. As Marinid authority disintegrated and Mali itself was hit by dynastic rivalries, contacts diminished and trade stagnated.

The story of African-Mediterranean commerce is incomplete without an examination of what are today modern Tunisia and Libya. Ifriqiya, Tripolitania, and eastern Algeria had become by 1236 an independent state ruled by Hafsid kings at Tunis. In those heady days, the Ifriqiyan economy benefited enormously from its middleman position in African-European commerce. And a series of solid trade treaties with Venice, Pisa, Genoa, Florence, and Aragon sustained it (Oliver 1977: 177). These European city-states became major clearinghouses for West African gold and were therefore key players in international trade (Epstein 1996: 26).

Thus, the Hafsids eagerly concluded treaties with Christian merchant communities, and in response European agents began to settle in the Hafsid-controlled ports. Many Spanish Muslims and Jews also immigrated to Hafsid cities, where they eventually constituted a powerful Andalusian presence. Not surprisingly, Hafsid-ruled Tunis developed into a dynamic and immensely prosperous commercial city-state (Ki-Zerbo and Niane 1997: 34-37).

Judeophobia Redux:
The Central Sahara and the West African Sudan

Throughout history Judeophobia and anti-Semitism have loomed just under the surface in Jewish relationships with Muslims and Christians. In the early days of Muslim rule on the Iberian Peninsula—before the Almohadic fundamentalist jihads—Jewish-Muslim relations were fairly cordial and commercially productive. In that era of prosperity, many people felt confident and were in no mood to expend energy on resurrecting old grievances and nursing new prejudices. Cities like Cordoba boasted libraries, public buildings of architectural monumentality, and bustling markets. Opportunity abounded for nearly all, and no one was threatened. Then came the traumas of the jihads emanating from Africa and the uncertainties and tensions they engendered. Somehow Jews were able to survive them. But with the economically destabilizing reconquest, or *reconquista*, of the peninsula by Christians, tensions in some regions began to resurface.

Judeophobia and anti-Semitism reached a crescendo in 1391 with a vicious pogrom in Seville that rapidly spread across Andalusia. Some 50,000 Jews may have perished. To survive, some chose baptism and became *conversos,* or so-called New Christians. (More will be said about conversos in our next chapter.) Large numbers of remaining practicing Jews, along with many conversos, were forced into exile. This abrupt departure marked the first major Sephardic dispersal from the Iberian Peninsula. Many refugees immigrated to North Africa and confronted the indigenous Jewish communities (Benbassa and Rodrigue 2000: liv). They arrived with much-needed skills, and by the fifteenth century they had become prosperous and numerous along the Mediterranean littoral and in the inland market towns.

Tuat was an important destination, having already gained

attention as a center dominated by Jewish brokers and goldsmiths and as a key entrepot for caravans from Morocco and Tunis before their continuation southwards across the desert. Thousands of these Sephardic exiles trekked onward to Morocco. There, they played important roles in the political and economic life of the sultanate and strongly influenced the culture and architecture of Morocco's cities. Fez, for example, took on the appearance of a Spanish city by the early fifteenth century, and management of the municipality's finances soon fell under the supervision of these Sephardic exiles (Deshen 1989: 36-37). At mid-century Fez's royal mint was already under Jewish management. And Jewish gold- and silversmiths set up business there and in almost every large oasis settlement. Moreover, in the second decade of the sixteenth century, Fez found itself as a world center for Hebrew book production, a business operated by Sephardic Castillian exiles who were engaged as scribes of Hebrew manuscripts (Benbassa and Rodrigue 2000: lii; see also Gampel 1997: 256).

This sudden infusion of Sephardic Jews received a mixed reception. David Corcos notes that "until the first decade of the XIV century, the Berber character of the Moroccan Jews prevented any sympathy with Jews of Andalusia or Grenada on account of the Arab culture with which they were deeply imbued" (Corcos 1976: 36). Jewish immigrants seem to have fared far better in Ifriqiya under its enlightened Muslim ruler, Abu Faris (1394-1434).

By the early fifteenth century, however, the wealth of many Jews had become a point of envy and anger among Muslims, particularly conservative sheikhs in the rural areas. This may have been the cause of renewed persecution. Portents of trouble ahead appeared in 1437 when some Jews were hacked to death in Fez. The sultan intervened before it got out of control and resettled almost the entire community in an inhospitable quarter in the city's desolate salt marsh. The quarter was called *mel-*

lah (Arabic for "salt"), and the Fez mellah became a prototype for the classical Moroccan Jewish ghetto of the sixteenth and seventeenth centuries (Stillman and Zucker 1993: 67-71).

This drastic move placed great hardship on the Jews because it removed them from the economic center of the city. It was also a humiliation, for it became a constant reminder of their second-class citizenship. Milton Shain, in a wider study on anti-Semitism, asserts that "it was precisely when Jews presented themselves as economic competitors that the anti-Jewish stereotype took on a distinctive malevolence, allowing for exclusion and ghettoization" (Shain 1998: 40). The Fez action seems to prove his point. But if Jews were so hated by the populace, why did the sultan intervene to halt their annihilation? Shain and others in the years ahead could rationalize that ghettoization was a means of protecting Jews from angry mobs, as the mellahs were walled and gated, and Jews would re-enter them at day's end before the gates were closed.

There were good reasons to protect Jews. Islamic authorities in many parts of the world had come to regard them as a vital source of revenue for state coffers through the array of special taxes levied on all non-Muslims. Moreover—as will be evident later in this chapter—Muslim monarchs and regents and their Jewish subjects had established mutually profitable business partnerships and alliances. Thus, it was usually in their interest to protect their Jewish denizens from attacks upon their person and property. Certainly in North Africa the Islamic trading states would have suffered economically without Jewish commercial connections and business acumen.

Anti-Semitism and Judeophobia simmered in the late fifteenth century in many caravan centers of the Sahara. There were also rumblings in the *madrasas* or Qur'anic schools in the larger towns. It all came to the surface when an anti-Jewish riot broke out in Tlemcen in 1467, although the riot was suppressed. In 1492 things came to head in Tuat when al-Maghili, a brilliant fundamentalist shaikh from Tlemcen, incited a devastating massacre that convulsed the entire city (Trimingham 1970: 98).

The year had gotten off to a bad start for Muslims when, on the Iberian Peninsula, the last Nasrid king of Muslim Granada was overthrown and went into exile in Africa. The Muslim world was shocked, and in less than a decade this last independent Muslim state would fall completely to Christians, and henceforth all of Spain would live under the shadow of Catholic rule. Fourteen ninety-two was also a traumatic year for Sephardic Jews. King Ferdinand of Spain and his wife, Queen Isabella, gave their Jewish subjects less than a year to convert to Christianity or be evicted from the country altogether. Four years later Jews suffered the same fate in Portugal. As we shall see in our next chapter, these actions triggered the largest Jewish diaspora in history. Thousands emigrated to the Maghreb, where in the minds of fervent Muslims they posed as an even greater commercial and religious threat than the earlier Jewish émigrés (Blady 2000: 294-95).

The Muslim fundamentalist sheikh and lawyer al-Maghili was particularly alarmed by the growing economic and political power of Jewish merchant families in Maghrebian and Sudanic cities (Hunwick 1985: 30). He railed against Jewish-Muslim trade partnerships, which by then had apparently become quite common, especially in Tuat (Gerber 1980: 117). This city was an ideal target for an anti-Jewish pogrom, serving as it did as the gateway to the *bilad-as-sudan*—the land of the blacks—where caravans converged. Indeed, it had become an important commercial crossroads where traders from Tunisia and Egypt exchanged goods for Sudanic gold and slaves (Hunwick 1985: 164). And it was a city where Jews had prospered and become influential in its cosmopolitan life. Jewish success and the growing disparities in quality of life prompted anger and envy. Maghan Keita notes that Jewish wealth through the trans-Saharan trade "became so ostentatious that it served as a rationale for reprisals against them...which finally resulted in restrictions against Jewish-Islamic partnerships and the banishment of Jewish merchants from several quarters of the West African Sudan" (Keita 1989: 153).

Al-Maghili called upon fellow Muslims to "rise up, kill and enslave the infidels—pigs, who care not for the name of Muhammad. Rise up and kill the Jews" (Hunwick 2006: 13).

Al-Maghili's pogrom in Tuat in 1492 led to the destruction of the city's synagogues and the confiscation of Jewish assets. It also caused a significant disruption in trade. The city's Muslim authorities were angered by the incident and promptly expelled al-Maghili, but not before most of the Jewish population had fled. Many of these hapless refugees ended up in Sudanic cities of the West African sahel, particularly in Timbuktu and Gao, where they established new commercial enterprises. Al-Maghili, a hero to Islamic militants, pursued them. He persuaded the Askiya of Songhay, Muhammad Touré, to arrest Tuatis living in Gao and to ban Jews from entering the empire altogether. Significantly, Songhay was territorially one of the world's largest Muslim theocracies, holding hundreds of important markets and portions of most of the major international trade routes.

For another decade the charismatic and articulate al-Maghili composed a number of political tracts, including the enormously influential *Obligations of Princes,* which advised Muslim rulers on how they might guard against opposition elements undermining their powers and mystique. The treatise bears an uncanny resemblance to Machiavelli's *The Prince,* which followed by only a few years. Al-Maghili also served as a consultant to numerous West African Islamic rulers, including the Emir of Kano in Nigeria's Hausaland.

Initially, al-Maghili succeeded in persuading the authorities to boycott Jewish trade, to restrict or eliminate their artisanal activities, particularly goldsmithing, and in the case of Timbuktu to expel them altogether. For decades thereafter, his political tracts were widely read in the Sudanic states, and he is today known as Africa's black Machiavelli. Nevertheless, he was not popular with the Timbuktu Muslim literati, who complained that his anti-Jewish behavior in Tuat had interfered with the trans-Saharan trade. In the end, they persuaded Songhay's Askiya to rescind his Judeophobic policies.

Jews endured these anti-Semitic outbursts. Indeed, when the astute North African merchant Leo Africanus visited Tlemcen in the early sixteenth century, he noted "there is a large quarter that contains some five hundred houses of Jews, nearly all rich" (Hunwick 1985: 66). At the time (ca. 1510) Jews constituted about 3 percent of the city's population (Hunwick 1985: 164).

Nevertheless, these pogroms reveal much about the fragility and unpredictability of Muslim tolerance for those of the Judaic faith. In West Africa, Jews came to the painful realization that the only way to survive in this Muslim "sea" was to convert to Islam. Eventually nearly all of them did, and by the end of the seventeenth century Judaism had practically disappeared from the region.

Today, communities in Senegal, Mali, Ghana, and Nigeria are rediscovering their genetic heritage through DNA and by uncovering ancient texts found in the homes of Muslim families.

Jews in Ottoman-Ruled Africa: A Symbiotic Relationship

Events in Egypt took a decidedly different turn. We have seen that in 1250, the Ayyubid dynasty was overthrown by its own Mamluk troops, who were descended from slaves purchased from horsemen of the Eurasian steppe. Generations of Mamluk generals would henceforth directly rule Egypt until 1517.

A great turning point in North African history was reached with the arrival of the Ottoman Turks in the early sixteenth century. The Ottomans advanced from Asia Minor and militarily occupied Byzantium, the heartland of eastern Christianity. The ascendancy of the Ottoman Turks as a global power dates to their conquest of the Byzantine capital at Constantinople in 1453, which put an end to the Eastern Roman Empire. The name was changed to Istanbul, and it became the capital of a vast Muslim world empire. By the close of the sixteenth century, the Ottoman Empire extended across southeastern Europe, northern Africa, and western Asia. Syria and Palestine were also brought into its realm.

The conquest of Egypt by the Ottomans in 1517 opened a new chapter in the history of Jewish communities in northern Africa. With the Ottoman seizure Egypt lost its sovereignty again and became a province within an essentially western Asian empire. Egypt's ruler was henceforth a viceroy (called *pasha*) nominally under a Turkish sultan who resided in Istanbul. Under the early Ottomans, the Mamluk establishment continued to perform its old functions, though now under the supervision of an Ottoman viceroy and a janissary garrison.

From Egypt, the Turks pushed westward into the Maghreb. They took Algiers in 1529 and added Tripoli in 1551. They gained mastery over the coast of Algeria and Tunisia, establishing Turkish-dominated states. Their armies moved southward to the frontiers of Morocco, where they were stopped. For a time, the Ottomans controlled the entire Mediterranean from Algiers to Albania.

Obviously, Arabic-speaking Jews (Musta'rab) in North Africa fell under the sway of this new imperial power. (Seltzer, 456) The Ottoman Empire was Muslim in religion and Turkish in official language. Still, by 1570 the Ottomans had extended themselves enormously and were therefore forced to rule their tributary states indirectly, through indigenous leaders or through their slave troops, called Janissaries, who formed frontier garrisons. Under the reigns of Suleyman the Magnificent (1520-66) and

Selim II (1566-74), Egypt boomed. Pilgrimage caravans from West Africa en route to Mecca passed through the bustling city of Cairo. Trans-Sahara trade now grew in the east as well, from Darfur and Sennar.

At the time of the Ottoman conquest of Cairo, most Jews lived in a walled, gated, filthy, and grossly overcrowded Jewish Quarter. The economy was only a shadow of what it had been before the European powers found an alternative route to Asia, via sub-Equatorial Africa. But life for most Jews in Egypt had changed almost imperceptibly. They tended to be poor and without power or influence.

Both the Ottoman and Mamluk empires were Turkish Sunni states, and therefore the legal position of dhimmis (non-Muslims) remained largely intact. Nevertheless, Jewish life improved measurably under Ottoman rule. Cairo, especially, was an open society, and Jews were not only tolerated but welcomed as people with much-needed skills. While most Jews continued to reside in the ancient quarters, the elite lived widely and freely among the general populace. In Cairo women were quite independent and could own inherited property (Kraemer 1992: 263). As was customary, dhimmis compliantly paid the *jizya* (poll tax) and in return enjoyed freedom of worship. Though they were allowed to maintain their own courts, the merchants often resorted to the Muslim courts and *shari'a* law in their business concerns. Jews became so proficient in international trade that the government appointed them as *iltizams* (Sonbol 2000: 62). These powerful customs officials enjoyed the privilege of collecting duties on exports and imports. And it was in large measure through that agency that some Egyptian Jews became rich and influential in the mercantile sector of the economy.

Turkish policy was aimed at maritime control, with little concern for hegemony over peoples of the hinterland until the last quarter of the sixteenth century. Consequently, interior authority was fragmented in the early Ottoman era. But almost everywhere the Jewish elite—though few in number—were useful to the Turks for their technical and financial skills, which were scarce in Ottoman society yet essential for sustaining the cumbersome administrative structures of the empire.

By the end of the sixteenth century, Jews had also become powerful in the financial administration of Egypt—arguably as strong as they were in the Fatimid period. In 1577 a Jew became director of the Cairo mint, and another was appointed Inspector of the Currency at the Customs House in Alexandria (Shaw 1991: 34). In financial and commercial matters Jews were seen as indispensable. Before long they became tax collectors, a position that enabled them to accumulate considerable wealth and political power. As we shall discover, this was a process of Jewish advancement that would recur throughout African history. Through the sixteenth century, Jews in Egypt made steady gains in the economy, and the Ottoman authorities in Cairo benefited greatly from this new wave of Sephardic exiles who were welcomed to the Ottoman Empire by a Muslim regime in search of talent regardless of religious orientation.

The Sephardic Diaspora in the Maghreb

In those days, common hostility to the Iberian Christians prevented any direct conflict between the Ottoman and Moroccan states. In the late fifteenth and early sixteenth centuries, Portuguese and Spanish Christians captured a number of seaports along the North African coast, including Tangier, Algiers, and Tunis. Portugal seized strategically vital coastal towns, beginning with Ceuta opposite Gibraltar in 1415. Moreover, with the conquest of Grenada in 1492, the Spanish terminated nearly eight centuries of Muslim rule in southern Spain. Though seaborne trade continued to flourish, Christians and Muslims continually raided each other's Mediterranean commerce and the coastal ports. When Ferdinand and Isabella, rulers of Aragon and Castile respectively, married and united Spain, the Christians became an even more formidable threat: not only to Muslims but to Jews as well.

It has already been noted that the Christian kingdoms of Aragon, Castile, and Portugal had held substantial Jewish and Muslim populations for centuries. Generally all three faiths manifested a high degree of tolerance towards each other despite periodic anti-Semitic pogroms. Indeed, Spain had been remarkable among European lands as a place where the three religions could coexist, albeit in a state of tension. For generations, Jews had acted as intermediaries between the Christians and Muslims, especially in business matters. The Sephardim were involved in a wide range of occupations as both professionals and artisans. Some served important Christian families as financial advisers. Jews in Castile and Aragon especially were employed by royalty to manage their estates and their financial investments. Others held important positions in state administrative bureaucracies. We also need to be reminded here that Jews on the Iberian Peninsula had been prominent in international commerce for centuries and tended to be multilingual. In sum, by the opening of the fifteenth century, a small minority of Jews played a role in medieval Spain far out of proportion to their numbers.

But perhaps the most valued field of service to Christians was in the area of finance. The Catholic Church forbade Christians to lend at interest to other Christians, and Judaism prevented the same of their own coreligionists. On the other hand, Jews and Christians were at liberty to lend to each other. As we have seen, anti-Semitism had become apparent in the late fourteenth century and reached its height in the pogroms of 1391. After the pogroms of that year, a number of campaigns were launched to forcibly convert the Jews to Christianity. The mass conversions at the end of the fourteenth century produced an entirely new social and economic group, the conversos, or New Christians. By the 1480s, Spain had a large population of peoples of mixed Judeo-Christian ancestry. Nevertheless, the mass conversions did not eliminate the ethnic prejudices of the Old Christians, and a kind of "ideology of pure blood" emerged that stigmatized Christians of Jewish heritage. Not surprisingly, such people usually made efforts to conceal their genealogies from public scrutiny.

By the late fourteenth century, Jewish religious leaders had become alarmed by the decline of interest in traditional (talmudic) Judaism. By contrast, the Catholic authorities perceived conversos as a kind of "fifth column" of crypto-Jews seeking to undermine the purity of the Christian faith and thus rendering it potentially vulnerable in the face of Islam. It must be recalled that for centuries the Iberian Peninsula had been under Muslim rule, and Muslims and their institutions were still deeply imbedded in Iberian culture. Thus, Christians remained insecure in the face of the perceived Islamic threat. These feelings gave new fuel to the embers of an anti-Semitism that had always been just beneath the surface.

As we have already seen, things came to a sudden and unexpected climax in 1492 when Ferdinand ordered all Jews to convert to Catholicism or leave the country within months. This touched off a massive exodus, mainly to neighboring Portugal. However, four years later a similar order was made by the Portuguese authorities, and Jews fled to the more tolerant Ottoman Empire and to the Sultanate of Morocco, where they had enjoyed age-old trade links.

Morocco: Jewish Exiles in a Muslim Sultanate

In the Maghreb, Morocco was arguably the greatest beneficiary of the epochal Sephardic diaspora of the 1490s. As in the Ottoman Empire, the arrival of these exiles led to significant changes in Moroccan politics and economy. Jews were already serving in Tangier as mercantile intermediaries in transactions between Christians and Muslims. Historically, Tangier had been the port of entry for Europeans seeking business in the sultanate. In fact, it was Tangier—a safe distance from the capital—that was the seat of diplomatic representation.

After the Jewish expulsions from Spain, Portugal, and in 1499 from recently conquered Granada and Andalusia, the Moroccan authorities allowed the exiles to settle in the inland cities, especially Fez, and granted them a high degree of judicial and legislative autonomy in their own communities. Jews were already an important minority in Morocco, numbering about 30,000. By 1512, their numbers had swelled by another 10,000 or more.

As the sixteenth century wore on, Jews and some conversos assumed roles in government as interpreters, spies, physicians, court advisers, official trade negotiators, and managers, if not owners, of profitable mercantile enterprises.

From at least the mid-fifteenth century, Morocco had been almost xenophobic in the face of its troubles with Portugal and Spain and the humiliating fall of Granada. Christendom was virtually at its door. And to make matters worse, the Ottoman Turks were a rising and equally aggressive power.

By 1509, Spanish Christians had begun to occupy coastal communities in what are today Algeria, Tunisia, and Libya. Tlemcen was sacked in 1542, and it was reported that fifteen hundred Jews were killed or taken prisoner (Hunwick 1985: 66). Muslims, too, were victims of the Spanish and Turkish depredations.

Morocco also found itself surrounded on the north and east by potentially hostile regimes. It recognized the need to diversify its trade as well as to develop a modern military force. With the help of the new Jewish exiles and Muslim refugees from Andalusia and Granada, the sultanate commenced a major effort to build a formidable defense while at the same time expand the country's global trading networks. Initially, Jews negotiated imports of English cloth while arranging for the export of copper, pelts, ostrich feathers, saltpeter, and sugar. The timing was perfect, as English and Dutch demand for sugar could not yet be met from New World plantations (Abun-Nasr 1987: 219).

Morocco was inexorably drawn into the international struggle for control of the western Mediterranean. Spain's victory over the Ottoman Navy at the Battle of Lepanto in 1571 ended Turkish monopoly over trade in the eastern Mediterranean. The Spanish fleet had thus stopped the westward seaborne advance of Islam. It was the largest naval encounter in world history since the Battle of Actium in antiquity, and its success only emboldened the Iberians. They now sought to extend their dominion over the western Mediterranean as well, and Morocco came into their sights.

Morocco was already preparing for the inevitable invasion, again thanks in part to its Jewish compatriots. The Iberian Sephardic exiles had brought with them exceptional knowledge of munitions. For centuries in Spain they held occupations in metallurgy and gradually became Europe's foremost experts in weapons manufacture. When the Christians expelled them from Spain, they took this knowledge with them. Further, Weston Cook observes that "Spanish Jews played a role in the transmission of gunpowder manufacture in Morocco" (Cook 1994: 285).

Even before Lepanto, Jews and conversos had become the key purveyors of armaments to the Royal Moroccan Army and were architects of their foundries and armories. They were instrumental in the establishment of Morocco's formidable firearms industry in the 1530s, the first in Africa and the last until well into the twentieth century (Chase 2003: 109).

Initially, arms- and weapons-manufacturing machinery had been acquired from England and paid for largely in sugar and saltpeter, the latter used by the English to produce their own gunpowder. But in time, Morocco became self-sustaining, its factories turning out state-of-the-art harquebuses, canons, crossbows, lances, and swords. Moreover, the sultan's armies were modernized and trained by highly skilled Hispano and Marisco Andalusian mercenaries seeking revenge for the Christian takeover of their homelands.

The final moment came in 1578 in the decisive Battle of Al-Kasar-al-Kabir, also known as the Battle of the Three Kings because it directly engaged the monarchs of Spain, Morocco, and Portugal. It was a stunning defeat for the European powers, the first by an African state since Roman antiquity. The Portuguese army had been decimated. The kings of Morocco and Portugal were killed. The Portuguese king had no heirs, so in 1580 the entire Iberian Peninsula was united under King Philip II of Spain. Just eight years later, Spain's navy, the world's largest at the time, was devastated in a terrible storm off the British Isles as it prepared to engage the English in war.

In Africa, Ahmad al-Mansur ascended to the Moroccan throne and, flushed with victory and anxious to replenish his treasury, turned his attention to the rich gold fields of the Songhay empire to the south. A huge army was assembled, staffed mainly by imported Christian and Muslim mercenaries and a small numbers of Jews. After months crossing the Sahara, they engaged the Songhay forces on the plains of Tondibi in 1591 and, though vastly outnumbered, handily defeated them. Songhay's renowned archers were simply no match against Morocco's musketeers (Hiskett 1984: 39). The Askiya fled and the Moroccans, headquartered in Timbuktu became a hated occupying force. Many of the city's leading literati, including dozens of Jewish scholars, were exiled to Morocco, where they continued their Qur'anic and Torah studies.

Tondibi marked the beginning of the end for the largest and most politically and culturally advanced theocracy in sub-Saharan Africa. After years of guerrilla warfare, the Songhay remnants liberated themselves. In 1612, the beleaguered and demoralized Moroccan occupiers departed, having never gained control of the gold resources, but leaving behind in ruins what was the greatest of the empires of pre-colonial Africa.

Clearly, in the Mediterranean world the fifteenth and sixteenth centuries had been marked by momentous demographic changes and great power realignments. And peoples of Jewish ancestry played key roles vastly disproportionate to their numbers. In this same period, changes of equal magnitude would occur in Atlantic Africa. It is to that region we will now venture.

CHAPTER THREE

Jews and Conversos in the Formative Years of the West and Central African Atlantic Slave Trade

Major Clusters of Jewish Population ca. 1600

The New South Atlantic Economy

The trade in humans from Africa to the Atlantic sugar islands and ultimately to the Western Hemisphere commenced in a systematic way in the mid-fifteenth century and flourished for more than four centuries. Probably from thirteen to fifteen million Africans were involuntarily transported across the Atlantic. Many millions more died in the violence that slave raiding and transportation entailed. The participants in the Atlantic slave trade included Portuguese, Italians, Spaniards, French, English, Germans, Dutch, Danes, Swedes, and literally hundreds of African ethnic groups. Christians, Muslims, and Jews all participated in the construction of the Atlantic slave system, a highly complex operation requiring multifaceted organization and extensive synergy of effort. No single nation or religious or ethnic group must bear full responsibility for the trade. Each one played pivotal roles at different junctures in history. As David Brion Davis put it, this was "the world's first system of multinational production for a mass market" (Davis 1994: 14). Humans, reduced to mere commodities, were compelled to produce a wide array of labor-intensive goods, ranging from coffee, tobacco, cotton, and rice to precious minerals like gold, silver, and diamonds. But few commodities required more slaves than cane sugar; thus historians tend to make a direct connection between slavery and sugar.

People of Jewish ancestry played a large role in the development of the South Atlantic economy and the integration of West and Equatorial Africa into the Atlantic commercial system. In the sixteenth and seventeenth centuries, they forged many trans-oceanic connections on all sides of the Atlantic littoral. They were a community of people with shared familial relationships, common historical background, and similar cultural practices that bridged the Atlantic. Their transatlantic trading and social networks were critical in shaping Atlantic commerce and culture in the sixteenth, seventeenth, and eighteenth centuries. Some Jews and *conversos* (Jewish converts to Christianity; also called "New Christians") settled, intermarried with local Africans, and founded important merchant families in port towns along the coast of West and Central Africa and on offshore Atlantic islands.

In terms of absolute numbers, Jews and people of Jewish ancestry were a tiny minority in the Atlantic system compared with Christians. Yet their international importance in the creation and operation of the Atlantic economy sharply contrasted with their modest share in the actual production of cash crops. Nevertheless, they played key roles at critical junctures, especially from its inception to the late 17th century.

Jewish and converso entrepreneurs were major players in the rise of the international mercantilist (state-controlled) form of capitalism in early modern Europe. Less well known is the contribution of a number of Jews and conversos to the launching of the Atlantic slave trade and the early establishment of the New World sugar plantation system. Indeed, certain Jews and conversos, along with many Christians, were critical to the process of refining and marketing commodities—notably sugar—and worked as contractors in acquiring slaves in Africa and in financing their trans-Atlantic shipment along with many of the commodities they produced. In Angola and Brazil, Jews bought large numbers of slaves and sold them to New World Catholic planters on credit or in exchange for sugar. They also loaned plantation owners capital to build sugar mills and acquire expensive cane-crushing machinery. In Africa, in collaboration with indigenous traders (*pombeiros*), they outfitted and financed slave-seeking caravans into the interior or dealt directly with bush traders and armed marauders at the source. In Ralph Austen's words, it was the Jews' "ability to transfer assets and information among themselves across the entire economic network" that made them so successful (Austen 1998: 68). It was a relationship often based on a combination of trust and kinship.

Together with Italian Genoese and Venetians, Jews were key in establishing the earliest sugar plantations in the Atlantic islands off Africa. Subsequently, they took a leading role in transferring the technology and management of sugar production to the New World, initially to Brazil which, with their crucial assistance, in the late sixteenth to mid-seventeenth centuries became the world's premier sugar exporter. Ultimately, they were instrumental in the sugar revolution of the West Indies in the late seventeenth and eighteenth centuries. They helped to establish the first sugar plantations in Africa and in the New World. By 1695, after Dutch authorities had granted Jewish merchants permission to plant sugar in Dutch Surinam, Jews there owned more than forty sugar plantations employing over nine thousand African slaves.

Meanwhile, Spain and Portugal and their possessions in Africa and South America were officially "free" of all Jews after about 1499. However, many of those who converted to Christianity and became New Christians, or conversos, continued to uphold Jewish traditions. At least up until the 1680s, it was common for many in the diaspora to return to their faith and become so-called crypto-Jews. This was possible because, in Africa and South America, converts were distantly removed from traditional rabbinical control and could redefine their relationship to Judaism in their own manner. Although according to Jewish law a convert ceased being Jewish—as did his or her children—the Spanish refusal to accept converted Jews as Christians because of their "blood" perpetuated for generations a stigma against being

Jewish. Hence, the erasure of Jewishness was not total in any sense.

New Christians, or conversos, tended to be Christians only in public, while remaining more or less loyal to Judaism in their private lives. They also continued to share a common language with Jews, either Judeo-Spanish—also known as Ladino—or Portuguese. Many were thus forced to lead an existence suspended between Christianity and Judaism. Still, as individuals and as extended families, they developed strong bonds among themselves, and the scale and intensity of these interlocking relationships were such that their communities may be considered participants in what can be described as an "Atlantic community." Many of them would hold a collective image of themselves as descendants from the biblical tribe of Judah, and that memory gave them a sense of confidence and, at times, solidarity in the face of persecution and in their dealings with African Muslims and non-Muslims alike.

Sugar

Slavery and sugar went hand in hand, and Jewish involvement in the commodity reaches far back into history. From the eleventh century Jews in the Mediterranean basin had been active in the making and marketing of sugar from raw cane in the Mediterranean basin and, along with the Muslims, were prominent in the international trade in sugar (Verlinden 1995: 240). Indeed, sugar refining was an important Jewish and Muslim occupation in Egypt and in the Levant until well into the fourteenth century. The Italian republics were introduced to sugarcane production when they occupied territory in Palestine after the First Crusade. At first, the Levant furnished much of Christian Europe with cane sugar. Gradually, slave-worked cane sugar cultivation spread westward, carried by Jews and Muslims to Sicily in the central Mediterranean. Eventually, the expanding commercial networks of Aragon and Catalonia in the thirteenth and fourteenth centuries brought Jews and Muslims of the Iberian Peninsula into even closer relations with the Levantine commerce in sugar and slaves (Blackburn 1997: 52)

Already by the fourteenth century large numbers of slaves from Italian colonies in the Black Sea and Balkans were being exported throughout the Mediterranean world. Slaves—white and black—were sold in the great slave market in Constantinople, and some found their way as far west as Lisbon (Forbes 1988: 27). Catena Cayetana notes that in 1404 a few Genoese Jews obtained a permit from King John I of Portugal to plant sugar in the Algarve in Spain (Cayetana 1989: 64). The Genoese, Christians as well as Jews, acted as trade liaisons between the Mediterranean and the Atlantic, and it was their capital and techniques that helped to launch production in the Atlantic islands.

The Iberians found themselves unable to compete with Italians and Muslims in the rich Mediterranean commerce in sugar and spices from the Levant and in trans-Saharan gold from West Africa. Already by the fourteenth century they had begun to look to the Atlantic in hopes of forging maritime routes to Indian Ocean spice markets and sub-Saharan African gold. Not surprisingly, individual Italians would play a major role in Iberian discovery and colonization.

Getting Started: The Early Years

Utilizing Genoese merchant families as fleet commanders, Portuguese probes into the Atlantic began in earnest in the fourteenth century during the reign of Afonso IV (1325-1357). Lanzarotto Malocello discovered the Canary Islands between 1325 and 1339 (Verlinden 1995: 92). These early and somewhat tentative probes culminated in 1415 with the capture of Ceuta, across from Gibraltar, as well as portions of the northern Mauritanian coast. The conquests only intensified Portugal's urge to find a sea route to Asia, as well as to exploit the gold resources of the African interior.

Exploration greatly accelerated under the Portuguese Prince Henry, dubbed "TheNavigator" (1394-1460), who assembled a collection of mainly Jewish experts in the field of cartography and navigation. Judah Crescas, a Majorcan Jew, was appointed director of Henry's nautical laboratory in Sagres at the southwestern tip of Portugal (Blackburn 1997: 100). He helped to map out the early expeditions utilizing information gained from North African Muslim sources. Among other consultants was Abraham Zacuto, a famous Renaissance Talmudic scholar and astronomer, and author of the pathbreaking work *Almanach*. His tables of celestial positioning enabled Henry's ships to determine latitude at sea without reckoning from the sun (Sachar 1994: 332). Without Zacuto's input, it would have been difficult if not impossible for the Portuguese to have embarked on their Great Age of Discovery in the mid-fifteenth century. Now, with international expertise, Henry's sea captains were able to master oceanic navigation. They pushed southward down the coast of Morocco. Cape Bojador was reached in 1434; the region of Arguin by 1443 (Knight 1988: 3).

The Atlantic slave trade had its origins on the tiny Atlantic islands off the African mainland. It was there—the Azores, the Canary Islands, the Cape Verde Islands, and São Tomé—that the roots of the New World plantation economy are to be found. Slaving probably first began along the Upper Guinea coast, serving the Cape Verde Islands, Madeira, and Portugal. New Christians, seeking refuge from the persecution of the unfolding Inquisition at home, took an early interest in the trade (Brooks 1993: 122).

The Atlantic slave trade may have actually begun in 1441

when a Portuguese raiding party captured ten Berbers and Muslims on the West African coast off Mauritania and sold them in Lisbon. In that same year, a New Christian, Antao Concalves, secured the first captives on African territory and transported them to Lisbon (Blackburn 1997: 102). The Canary Islands were also destined to become importers of slaves after the indigenous population died off from disease and near-genocidal exploitation.

It is important to remember here that the Atlantic slave trade was begun with African slaves being transported to Western Europe, not to the undiscovered Americas. Thus, the Old World Atlantic slave trade was a precursor to the New World Atlantic slave trade. Prince Henry, recognizing the potential of the slave trade, declared it a state monopoly, and in 1444 the first license was issued to import slaves. The Old World phase of the Atlantic slave trade was launched. Between 1446 and 1462, a series of trade agreements were made with African coastal rulers covering both slaves and gold.

In 1449 Henry commissioned a trading port on the island of Arguin just off the coast of Mauritania. It became the first slave port established along the West African coast and—between 1450 and 1464—the main Portuguese slave market. Henry secured Papal bulls, or edicts, to legitimize his activities. In about 1452, Pope Nicholas V permitted the Portuguese to enslave "enemies of Christ" and infidels, giving moral sanction to the trade. Added religious justification came with the Pope's Romanus Pontifex (1454), which allowed the sale of captives if arrangements could not be made to convert them to Christianity. It also proclaimed that in the name of Christianity, "pagans" could be expelled from their own lands and subjugated in perpetual servitude (Schorsch 2004: 161). A year later, another bull awarded the Crown a commercial monopoly of Atlantic Africa south of Cape Bojador, and with that mandate the Portuguese began to extend the slave trade southwards along the West African coast (Saunders 1982: 5).

Henry died in 1460, but his bold initiatives were sustained. In 1466, the Cape Verde Islands were settled as a base for trade with the Upper Guinea coast, and periodic slave raids on the mainland ensued. Slaving in this region was not new. Ibn Khaldun of Tunis in 1370 mentioned in his writings the importance to Morocco of slaves its traders imported from the Canaries (Unger 1995: 54). Tony Hodges notes that between 1469 and 1474 the entire trade of Guinea was leased by the Crown to a New Christian, Fernao Gomes, a Lisbon merchant, in return for his pledge to explore approximately 320 miles of coast annually (Hodges 1988: 71). In about 1470 his ships had sighted the equatorial island of São Tomé. Within five years the equator had been crossed, and by 1483 Diogo Cão had reached the mouth of the Congo River and visited the coast of northern Angola.

In 1479, the kingdoms of Castile and Aragon had been joined to form a unified Spanish kingdom. A partition agreement that year gave Castile the Canary Islands and awarded Portugal a monopoly of the West African trade. The new Spanish monarchs, Ferdinand and Isabella, called on Genoese capital to plant sugar and establish sugar mills in the Canaries.

Subsequently, the Tordesillas agreement of 1494 partitioned the world along a longitudinal line running west of Cape Verde. Thus, much of the south Atlantic fell within the Portuguese sphere.

After establishing Elmina castle on the Gold Coast of modern Ghana in 1482, the Portuguese Crown focused on the gold trade itself and relegated slave trading to private merchants. Portuguese caravels began to barter slaves there for gold from the interior. The Elmina castle complex became the Portuguese entrepôt in the gold trade and a bastion against future European interlopers.

Years before these events, sugarcane had been introduced to Madeira Island. It grew abundantly and quickly replaced wheat and wine as the major export. Slave-produced sugar on Madeira would become an undertaking not of Lisbon investors but of Sephardic Jewish merchants, notably Samuel Abravanel, and Genoese financiers and merchants (Braudel 1973: 815). By the 1470s, Portuguese ships were taking Madeira sugar to Lisbon and Flanders for distribution. The Atlantic sugar trade had thus begun.

By the 1490s, Madeira had become a prosperous sugar colony and the largest single producer of sugar in the western world (Schwartz 1985: 316). At first the indigenous population had been pressed into labor, but they were few in number and not culturally oriented to mass organized labor. Consequently, in increasing numbers, slaves were obtained from along the Upper Guinea coast and shipped to the islands and to Lisbon. The first great sugar island of the modern world was entirely dependent on African slave labor.

Overnight, Lisbon and Seville emerged as Europe's most important slave markets, and many wealthy residents, including some Jews, acquired slaves as domestic workers. By 1500, nearly ten percent of the population of both cities consisted of African slaves (Blackburn 1997: 52). Madeira's sugar exports were largely controlled by non-Iberian Europeans, including Jews. Christopher Columbus—allegedly a converso—who lived for more than a decade in Madeira, took sugar plants from the Canaries with him to the West Indies. But the crop did not gain wide acceptance in the early period of colonization, probably for lack of labor. Nevertheless, within a decade, Lisbon had emerged as the great European market for sugar, a commodity that soon became a staple of the western diet. Indeed, what had been a luxury food for European nobility eventually became a staple for the masses, especially after the introduction of tea and coffee and the need to sweeten them.

The Tordesillas agreement of 1494 partitioned the world along a longitudinal line running west of Cape Verde. Thus, much of the south Atlantic fell within the Portuguese sphere. Even before, in 1479, the kingdoms of Castile and Aragon were joined to form a unified Spanish kingdom. A partition agreement that year gave Castile the Canary Islands and awarded Portugal a monopoly of the West African trade. The new Spanish monarchs, Ferdinand and Isabella, called on Genoese capital to plant sugar and establish sugar mills in the Canaries.

The Iberian Factor: Anti-Semitism, Expulsion, and Diaspora

Jews had been on the Iberian Peninsula, an area known to them as Sefarad, since at least the sixth century BCE. From the era of Islamic rule until the fourteenth century, they lived throughout the peninsula in separate autonomous communities. We must recall that, before the twelfth century, learned Sephardic Jews served as key ministers of finance and ambassadors for Muslim rulers. They were valued for, among other assets, their banking and commercial skills and were sought after for their capital. Unlike the Qur'an and New Testament, the Jewish texts imposed no religious prohibitions on loaning money at interest.

Beginning in the thirteenth century, a number of Jews in Catholic Spain had begun to gain economic and political influence as tax collectors, court physicians, and intermediaries between Christians and Muslims. (Livermore 1976: 126) They prospered even more as New Christians. Nevertheless, by the fourteenth century, prejudice had grown against the Jewish minority, directed in part against their leading role as financiers and tax collectors under the employ of kings, nobles, and the Catholic Church.

Historically, some Jews had held government contracts to collect taxes, customs, and tolls under Christian and Muslim dynasties. But tax farming was quite oppressive and weighed heavily on the general population. As the key moneylenders, Jews invited both respect and anger, both of which were then generalized to the Jewish population as a whole. As we have seen, the first major pogrom against them occurred in 1391 in the major cities of Spain. Thousands of Jews were forced to emigrate or to convert to Christianity and become New Christians. Many of those who left found new homes in North Africa and in the Ottoman Empire and brought with them vital artisanal and professional skills. Those who stayed behind and converted escaped many restrictions and soon moved into important positions in Christian society. Others integrated through marriage into Christian families, but this practice only contributed to greater antagonism between them and the so-called uncontaminated or "Old Christians."

From the start, these newcomers to the faith were suspected of being insincere Christians. By the early fifteenth century, they were accused of secretly practicing Judaism and were therefore heretics who must be punished by a religious court of the Inquisition. As false converts and heretics, they were labeled with the pejorative appellation *Marrano* (pig) or crypto-Jews. Catholics also discriminated against these New Christians for lacking *limpieza de sangre*, or purity of blood. This obsession with blood purity may have reflected the trend of intermarriage between Jews and Christians that had been occurring for well over a century. Thus, Jews were discriminated against on the basis of both religious heritage and ethnicity.

Violent religious intolerance spread across the Spanish countryside with terrifying speed. Finally, in 1478 a Papal bull re-established an Inquisition into heresy in Castile and Aragon (Perera 1995: 163). This intimidating and terrorizing Inquisition continued intermittently for 350 years (Tambs 1996: 39). According to Henry Kamen, its purpose was to eliminate Semitic culture from official Catholicism (Kamen 1983: 40). But the medievalist Norman Cantor maintains that it was also motivated by a desire to centralize royal power against the rising nobility, many of whom by then were New Christians or at least part ethnically Jewish (Cantor 1992: 12). Jews who remained impenitent were commonly burned alive at public executions. Victor Perera says that "One of the most painful ironies of the Inquisition is that among the harshest persecutors of Jews and relapsed conversos were Jewish converts who had risen to high rank in the Church" (Perera 1995: 169).

We have already noted that the anti-Semitic tide reached a crescendo in March 1492 when King Ferdinand and Queen Isabella issued the Edict of Expulsion, giving Jews four months to accept Christian baptism or emigrate (Tambs 1996: 46-47). It is interesting that Ferdinand himself reputedly had a Jewish grandmother. Cantor contends that Spanish Catholics by the late fifteenth century had come to believe that Christ would return only when Jews and Muslims had been converted to the faith and the Church would be triumphant in the world (Cantor 1992: 14).

This Edict of Expulsion touched off a massive exodus—far exceeding that of the late fourteenth century—with Jews fleeing to Italy, North Africa, the Ottoman Empire, and nearby Portugal. Kamen says that in a matter of months about 150,000 Jews left Castile and 30,000 left Aragon. They were joined by approximately 700,000 conversos (Tambs 1996: 49). Some Christians who owed large sums of money to Jewish bankers used the expulsion as an excuse to rid themselves of their debt. Jewish properties were seized, and the émigrés were forbidden to take with them gold, silver, and other assets. Interestingly, the state-sanctioned expulsion of Jews gave Christian debtors an unprecedented legal opportunity to avoid paying obligations. David Brion Davis informs us that "the continuing persecution and exclusion, especially of the New Christians or Marranos, did lead to a desperate search for new commercial opportunities in the New World" (Davis 1994: 14). And as we shall discover, it also led them to search for ventures on the islands and along the coast of Atlantic Africa.

Jews fared no better in Portugal. Indeed, toleration of the Spanish Jewish (Sephardic) refugees by the Portuguese Crown was short-lived. In December 1496, the new Portuguese king, Manuel, issued his own expulsion edict against the hapless Spanish refugees and Portuguese Jews. He may have done so to please his future wife, a daughter of the Spanish monarchs Ferdinand and Isabella, in hopes of eventually unifying the Iberian Peninsula under a single crown (Tavares 1997: 99). Also, some Christian merchants may have feared the potential competition with Jews for the lucrative sugar trade. Significantly, Jews who agreed to accept Christian baptism were allowed to remain and joined the community of New Christians. But for centuries thereafter, the Marranos were caught between Judaism and Christianity and moved back and forth between the two faiths and two cultures. Many became alienated from both and were secularized in the process. Others integrated themselves into Catholic Iberian culture.

The São Tomé Factor

For many decades hence, the Portuguese overseas possessions would serve Iberian Jews and conversos as a refuge from anti-Semitic discrimination, including the infamous Inquisitions. Initially, the expulsion resulted in a significant number of Jews emigrating, voluntarily or otherwise, to the tiny Atlantic island of São Tomé, some 120 miles off the coast of the kingdom of Kongo. Though uninhabited when the Portuguese "discovered" it in about 1470, it lay strategically near the Equator and at the confluence of wind systems that could drive both northbound and southbound Atlantic maritime commerce. European mariners soon realized that this pattern of winds and currents rendered the Atlantic, that great "ocean sea," a highway to both the Americas and the Far East.

Portugal's Crown sponsored the settlement of São Tomé, and in 1485 a royal grant allowed its residents to trade from the Niger Delta southwards. The São Tomé merchants (*tomeans*) soon pioneered a regional system that connected African markets around the Gulf of Guinea, from Angola to the Gold Coast, through the trade in cattle, salt, and cloth and through trafficking in humans (Curtin 1990: 43-44). Already in the 1480s the Portuguese had begun to acquire captives in the "slave rivers" of the Bight of Benin. For a century thereafter, São Tomé served as the key base for trade in the Bights of Benin and Biafra, the centers of slave traffic in the Gulf of Guinea.

First occupied in 1485, its rich volcanic soils and humid tropical weather made São Tomé ideal for sugarcane cultivation, which, incidentally, was probably introduced there from Madeira in 1493. Yet two obstacles stood in the way of its development into a valuable cash crop: an absence of people knowledgeable in the art of sugar growing and no indigenous population to plant, cut, and grind the crop. Skilled Iberian converso exiles and slaves from the Congolese and Angolan hinterlands quickly solved the problem and transformed the island into one the world's principal sources of cane sugar.

Ultimately, it was São Tomé—not Madeira or the Cape Verde Islands— that became the direct antecedent of the New World plantation system (Curtin 1990: 21-22). Almost from the beginning the island's colonization was associated with sugar cultivation. Here, the techniques of the Mediterranean sugar complex were combined with an ideal soil and plentiful involuntary labor procured initially from the two mainland kingdoms of Benin and Kongo.

Actually, the tragic story of São Tomé's emergence as a flourishing plantation economy begins with Jewish orphans. In 1493, when Portugal was flooded with Sephardic refugees from Castile in Spain, the children of Jews who refused to convert were forcibly baptized, and nearly two thousand were ultimately shipped off to São Tomé to be raised as Christians and trained to become producers of sugarcane and operators of sugar mills. Approximately six hundred survived and became an important element in the tomean planter community (Hodges and Newitt 1988: 18). Robert Garfield says that the orphans—who were forcibly baptized—were eventually married off to Africans by design, and that by 1510 a mixed population of *mestiços* had emerged (Garfield 1990: 646). Some of their descendants became rich and powerful on the island and laid the foundations not only of the trans-Atlantic slave trade but of the modern plantation system of agriculture that further evolved in the New World.

The slave trade between the mainland and the island of São Tomé and its tiny neighbor, Príncipe, was underway by 1494; within five years, more than nine hundred slaves had been landed from the continent. There were by then a number of *fazendas* (plantations) on the island, some of them owned by Kongolese nobles who were based on the mainland. Labor shortages were initially a problem, and Kongolese female slaves were brought to São Tomé partly as "breeding stock" for white male settlers as well as for their male slaves. Almost from the start, then, it is difficult to speak of a "purely" Jewish community, even though elements of Judaic religious and cultural identity endured in many forms. By the mid-sixteenth century, the *fazendeiros* (plantation owners) on São Tomé were mainly of mixed race (Garfield 1990: 647).

Initially, São Tomé drew mostly from the Gulf of Guinea for its slaves. The first recorded European slave ship from Elmina on the Gold Coast of West Africa was in 1499 (Vogt 1973: 456). A year later, the Crown allowed the tomeans to trade freely with all the Portuguese territories, and between 1500 and 1509 their orbit expanded northward to the Upper Guinea coast (Ebl 1997: 62).

A brisk trade in humans soon developed between São Tomé, Elmina, and the kingdoms of Benin and Kongo. But in coastal terms this was not an entirely new trade pattern. John Thornton notes that "the growth of Kongo's trade had to draw on a well-developed system of slavery, slave marketing, and slave delivery that preexisted any European contact" (Thornton 1992: 97). In any case, tomeans assumed dominant positions in the slave trade between the Bight of Biafra and the equatorial Congolese coast. Already, tomeans had begun to organize slave caravans into the interior, boldly challenging the Kongolese monarch's monopolies and ignoring his pleas to Portugal to cease this interference. King Mbemba Nzinga had hoped to open a wide bilateral trade with Portugal by converting to Christianity and accepting baptism as Dom Afonso I. Assuming this new persona, Afonso would rule from 1506 to 1543. But from the start, he and the tomeans competed bitterly for control over the slave trade.

As early as 1514 he complained to King Manuel that the slave trade was out of control and was threatening to reduce the kingdom's manpower and destroy its once robust and diversified economy. Despite a lengthy correspondence between the two monarchs, Manuel did not act and Afonso established a commission to ensure that no free subjects were captured and shipped as slaves to São Tomé (Davidson 1964: 191). The Oba (king) of Benin shared Afonso's concern and in 1514 sent a mission of his own to Lisbon to complain of tomean interference. Having no success, the Oba attempted to ban the sale of male slaves from his kingdom. Nevertheless, both African monarchs failed to stem the trade as European demand for slave labor became too great and as African rulers bought European goods and had to pay for them in human bodies, the only commodity the white intruders truly desired (Ryder 1969: 52-75). In a world without financial institutions, and thus with little capital or specie in commercial transactions, slaves were often produced by African rulers seeking to retire trade debts to European merchants.

It must be noted here that trading in humans was already common in many African societies. In these pre-capitalist, mainly barter economies, wealth was obtained and exhibited by controlling the labor of others. Without the notion of private ownership of land, people themselves constituted capital and could readily be used as items of exchange. Even before the arrival of the Europeans, rulers of West Central Africa—including Benin—were shipping slaves along the Atlantic coast to the Akan peoples of West Africa to work in their gold mines. The Akan religious prohibitions on working beneath the earth's surface forced them to seek laborers elsewhere (Wilks 1993: 31-37).

The scale of that Atlantic coastal trade was miniscule compared to what would soon follow. But expansion could not occur without an infusion of Europeans, with their skills and access to overseas capital, markets, and trade goods. Moreover, larger ships were needed to make the trade in humans truly viable. European monarchs endeavored to promote colonization—even to coerce it—when dealing with conversos. Massacres of New Christians in Lisbon in 1506 drove even more peoples of Jewish ancestry to Africa, giving further impetus to the slave trade: prohibited from dealing in gold and spices, many Jews sooner or later gravitated to human trafficking. Malyn Newitt holds that until 1535, São Tomé received many of the former Jews exiled under the anti-Semitic persecutions of Portuguese king Dom Manuel (Newitt 1988: 9). Jews and New Christians who had committed offenses as minor as petty theft had to face either prison or exile to Africa. Such peoples, variously called *degredados* (degraded ones) or *lancados* (castoffs), found themselves in Africa without capital but not always without skills in commerce. Slave trading thus provided them with an opportunity to start life anew and to recover their losses.

By 1516, more than 4,500 slaves were being imported annually from the mainland, making West Central Africa the largest source for the Atlantic slave trade. Many were re-exported from São Tomé and the neighboring island of Príncipe to the Gold Coast—where Portuguese Crown agents bartered them for gold mined in African-controlled territories—or to European marketers in Lisbon, Seville, and Valencia. Some scholars maintain that the 140,000 or more slaves imported into Europe from Africa between 1450 and 1505 served as an important new labor force in the wake of the deadly Bubonic plagues that had decimated nearly a third of Europe's population only a generation or so earlier.

Probably by the second decade of the sixteenth century, Kongo had become commercially dependent on the lucrative trade with São Tomé. São Toméan traders aggressively bartered ivory, brass, and raffia fabrics for mainland slaves. Additionally, the Portuguese used palm cloth manufactured in the African Kingdom of Loango, on the coast north of the Congo River, as a currency to buy slaves. Local demand for cotton cloth grew explosively and Portugal did not produce enough of its own to export. Consequently, slaves were taken from the Upper Guinea coast of West Africa to plant cotton and indigo on Cape Verde. There, African weavers and dyers manufactured textiles that were then exchanged for slaves along the entire coast of West and Equatorial Africa. In this way, the Portuguese gained entry to the Atlantic slave trade with a minimum of capital investment (Thornton 1992: 60).

Expanding Frontiers of Violence and Chaos: The Angolan Wars

A number of tomeans—New Christians as well as Old Christians—played key roles in the transformation of Central Africa into a vast labor reservoir. The Atlantic trade, already tensing relations within African societies, had a politically and socially destabilizing impact. Kongo raiders, armed with European weapons, invaded the populous south, taking prisoners but failing to expel tomean traders, many of whom were also seeking captives for the slave trade.

In the ensuing civil war between Kongo and its rebellious provinces, Afonso's desperate and futile efforts to restrict São Tomé trading activities only led the aggressive tomeans to shift their activities to the hapless kingdom's outer provinces, especially southward to the Ndongo kingdom that the Portuguese would call Angola, after the title of its ruler, the Ngola. Despite a reassertion in 1526 of Afonso's pleas, Lisbon left the Kongo and its problems to the treacherous tomean oligarchy. São Tomé-based ships bought slaves on the mainland in a vast arch from the Niger Delta southward beyond the Congo estuary. Most of these Africans were youthful farmers in the prime of life who had lost their freedom as prisoners of war or who were victims of slave raids on their villages.

Plainly, the trade was fueled by political turmoil in the interior African states—turmoil instigated by European and mixed-race traders and government officials on the Loango and Angolan coasts. In 1556, Ngola (Angola) defeated Kongo in the Battle of Caxito and established itself as an independent entity. Four years later, Portugal stopped supporting the Kongolese royal trade monopoly in Central Africa and let the tomeans trade directly with the Angolan coast (Vansina 1966: 61). Angola was then declared a Portuguese colony in 1571, and, in the decades that followed, its military governors on their own hired interior warlords and bandits to capture—through raids and kidnapping—young men and women who had been dispossessed by the incessant civil wars.

Transitions: Expansion to the Americas

Early on, São Tomé's success in its entrepreneurial activities made it evident that sugar and slaves held enormous promise as keys to imperial wealth and power. James Rawley indicates that São Tomé became a prototype for New World sugar plantations, and that the plantation system, or *engenho*, which incubated on the island, was transferred to the Americas (Rawley 1981: 26).

Already by 1544, São Tomé was producing nearly 2,250 metric tons of sugar a year, and within six years it would serve as Europe's principal source of sugar and as an important source of wealth for Portugal. It was also the center of slave traffic in the Gulf of Guinea and Angola. As the world's largest sugar producer, it boasted between five and six thousand slaves (Galloway 2003: 60). By then, São Tomé's New Christians, or conversos, were dominant on the island and were resented by others who socially discriminated against them as people of Jewish ancestry. Questions of purity of the blood, which had hounded those of Jewish ancestry in Spain, were being raised by the island's so-called Old Christians. An especially prominent target was Filipe de Nis, a Portuguese New Christian who had formerly been a Jew named Solomon Marcos. An important slave trader on São Tomé and in West Africa from the 1550s to the 1570s, he had married one of his slaves and later returned to Europe and reverted to Judaism (Israel 1992: 372).

São Tomé's golden age was short-lived. Sugar production peaked between 1575 and 1580 and declined precipitously thereafter. Labor unrest and intrigues among the planter elites were taking a toll, and the island's tiny size restricted further expansion of cultivation. More will be said of São Tomé's problems later. Here it is important to recognize that, at this point, the vast lands of the Americas were opening up to colonial exploitation and a new giant—Brazil—would soon emerge on the stage.

The Portuguese had traditionally furnished the Spanish-American colonies with slaves, as Spain had no African territories of its own. The Atlantic slave trade to the Americas had begun in earnest in 1518 when Carlos V of Spain granted the first royal license, or *asiento* (a monopoly contract), to carry African slaves directly to Spanish-American colonies (Postma 1990: 3). Slaves could now be shipped to the Spanish West Indies directly from

Africa free of customs duties paid in Spain. The so-called Middle Passage between Portuguese São Tomé and the Spanish West Indies was formally opened in 1532. Still, nearly two decades would elapse before slaves were landed in Brazil directly from African soil.

The Plantation Economy and the Slave Trade Move Westward

Portugal claimed Brazil in 1500 but largely ignored it because of interests in Asia. The first landing party of the Portuguese flotilla included a Polish Jew who served as the expedition's interpreter. Much to his disappointment, no one could speak the languages he knew and little useful information was subsequently collected. Nevertheless, in 1502, a New Christian, Fernao de Noronha, received a contract to trade in Brazil for slaves—presumably Amerindians—and exotic timber (Forbes 1988: 35). Sugarcane was allegedly brought by 1516 to the country from Madeira by conversos, and the first exports, a half decade later, were from an area just north of Pernambuco. Despite an exceptionally good environment for sugar cultivation, the project initially was less than successful. Though some African slaves had apparently begun to be employed in the sugar industry around 1526, planters relied almost entirely on local Indians (Cardoso 1983: 168). In about 1542, New Christians from Madeira—though reputedly based in Lisbon, Oporto, and São Tomé—began constructing sugar mills in Pernambuco itself. It was not long before more were built in Bahia and, by the early 1600s, in the Rio de Janeiro area. Consequently, sugar exports from Brazil rose dramatically, and the colony became exceptionally valuable to metropolitan Portugal's booming economy. In 1549, Thomas de Souza, reputedly of Jewish ancestry, became the colony's first governor-general and presided over the expansion of the sugar plantation economy (Johnson 1987: 249).

Conversos in Brazil were excluded from slave importing because it was a monopoly of the West India Company. Instead, many operated as brokers "buying from the company large consignments of slaves and selling them on the installment plan to the planters" (Marcus 1970: 75). But some went beyond this. In 1550, Diego Dias Fernandes (of Jewish ancestry) owned one of the first five *engenhos* (plantation plus mill) in the colony (Cohen and Peck: 217). And in the late sixteenth century, Erasmo Schetz—a German Jew whose business was based in Antwerp—was majority partner in the largest *engenho* in southern Brazil. But Schetz became an absentee owner, turning management over to (presumably Christian) German and Flemish overseers dispatched from Antwerp.

By the mid-sixteenth century, Jews and conversos had secured a large share of the African, transoceanic, and New World overseas commercial operations of Portugal. They helped to finance the long-distance voyages and the merchandising of the products of Africa and its offshore Atlantic islands.

An Intriguing New Nexis: Brazil, Kongo, Angola

The slave trade from Kongo to northern Brazil was officially established in 1559 when an Alvara, or royal decree, allowed each sugar mill owner to import up to 120 slaves from the African kingdom (Cardoso 1983: 172). By the 1570s, Portugal's northeastern Brazilian captaincies of Pernambuco and Bahia had emerged as prosperous plantation economies.

Still, these labor-intensive economies could not develop without a steady supply of labor. J.H. Galloway says that from the start of the Brazilian sugar industry, especially from the 1520s to 1570s, most slaves were American Indians (Galloway 2003: 72).

He adds that the first African slaves in Brazil were technicians in the mills and boiling houses and may have gained that knowledge from São Tomé or Madeira. Nevertheless, by the 1610s, Brazil had become dependent on African slaves for the drudgery of harvesting. As sugar gained in value, so did Africans.

Indeed, from the mid-sixteenth century, African slaves rapidly displaced Amerindians as cane workers in Brazil. The Portuguese had discovered that Indian slaves were less productive than Africans, and that many were dying from smallpox and other European-borne diseases. The exploding European demand for sugar seemed to coincide with the catastrophic decline of America's Indian populations. Moreover, pressure against enslaving indigenes was emanating from the highly influential Catholic missionaries, who based their argument on religious and humanitarian grounds. The moral assertions of Bartolomé de las Casas, a Spanish priest of Jewish ancestry, were especially convincing. Las Casas had visited the New World and was appalled by the treatment of the "native populations," even fearing their ultimate extinction. In the 1520s, he was instrumental in organizing a movement in Spain and Spanish America in their defense. After intensive lobbying, the king was won over, and this led in 1542 to the "New Laws," which banned Indian slavery altogether in Spanish colonies. Eventually Brazil, another Catholic colony, followed suit. Henceforth, planters of Latin America would have to look to Africa for nearly all their slave labor. Jonathan Schorsch believes it was de las Casas who persuaded Carlos V to permit the shipment of slaves directly from Africa rather than via the circuitous route through Lisbon's slave markets (Schorsch 2004: 35).

Pragmatically, African slaves had to be imported in large numbers to maintain or increase levels of sugar production. African and European slavers were ready for the challenge. The tomeans had already assumed an early dominant position in the lucrative

Angolan trade and were instrumental in the founding of the city of Luanda and its development into a major slave port. By the 1610s, some of them were bartering Brazilian manioc for African slaves (Hodges and Newitt 1988: 10).

As we have seen, tomeans had begun allying with mainland Africans to source their slaves. David Birmingham notes that the earliest populations of Luanda included Jewish men from Portugal, Madeira, and Brazil who usually took Africans as wives and laid the foundations of Angola's modern Luso-African population (Birmingham 1981: 81). Large Portuguese-based merchant families financed local *asentistas* in the city. Gonzalo Nunes Sepulveda, a Lisbon-born New Christian, established himself in Luanda in 1604 as a slave merchant and remained active there for two decades until retiring to Seville (Boyajian 1983: 51). Between 1607 and 1614, a contemporary, Duarte Dias Henriques, farmed the cherished Portuguese Crown monopoly for slaves exported from Angola (Drescher 1993: 118). During this period, more contingents of so-called *degredados* were sent by the government to Angola to bolster a white presence. Fairly or not, numerous local African rulers blamed the Kongo-Angolan wars on meddling Jewish merchants, prompting Kongo's King Alvaro II (r. 1587-1614) at one point to propose their expulsion (Birmingham 1981: 81).When Bishop Francisco de Soveral was sent to São Tomé in 1623, he was instructed to "eliminate the many Jews there" and on the mainland (see Garfield n.d.: 17).

From the second decade of the seventeenth century, Luanda's slave exports boomed while the violence of slaving moved steadily inland (Miller 1991: 142). Slaves were obtained through war and tribute as well as through trade. Periodic droughts led to famine and yielded still more slaves. Maize, or corn, an imported American Indian crop, became an African food staple and triggered agricultural and demographic revolutions that only contributed to the growing volume of slaves (McCann 2005: 23).

Jan Vansina seems to blame the near-total breakdown in Kongo in the 1620s on the Portuguese authorities and their African allies. Clearly, they precipitated its disintegration by provoking rebellions and wars which were rekindled and led to the destruction of the Kongo monarchy in 1665 (Vansina 1966: 139).

These events on the mainland reverberated on the offshore islands. Religious and ethnic tensions periodically erupted in violence on São Tomé. Already by the mid-sixteenth century the island had become a complex, racially mixed, and rigidly stratified society of affluent and poor landowners, with a few Old Christian families possessing most of the wealth. Sugar was the mainstay, but competition from the Americas was cutting into profits. Periodic slave uprisings of mulattoes, supported clandestinely by New Christians, began in the 1570s and continued for several decades (Hodges and Newitt 1988: 21).

Operating from interior bases, the rebels continually harassed the plantations. Jews and New Christians may have supported the rebellions because, though some had grown prosperous, they could never escape their Jewish ancestry in the minds of others. Thus, New Christians were frequently made scapegoats for the island's problems and were accused of disloyalty. Garfield believes that most accusations of "New Christian-ness" were politically motivated and had nothing to do with religion per se (Garfield 1990: 649). He speculates that the Old Christians were envious of them because of the political power they exerted.

Sugar production dwindled steadily and many planters emigrated. Ultimately, dozens of them transferred their activities to the coastal plains of tropical Brazil while acquiring their slaves from São Tomé through such middlemen as the Jewish broker Luis Gomez Barreto. Inevitably, São Tomé's role reverted from plantation production to an entrepot and collection point in the maritime slave trade to Brazil and other New World destinations. The golden age of São Tomé had passed.

The Amsterdam Factor

The persecutions of New Christians on the Iberian Peninsula had gathered momentum in the early 1500s and intensified in Portugal after 1536 in the reign of King Joao III (1521-57). The fearful Inquisition spread to Portugal in 1547, and soon large numbers of conversos were fleeing to other parts of Western Europe and the Levant. Some groups settled in the Low Countries, or Spanish Netherlands, from the mid-sixteenth century. Herbert Bloom asserts that Spanish and Portuguese Marranos transferred Mediterranean trade from Lisbon to Antwerp, a Flemish city controlled by the Spanish Habsburgs and emerging as a great entrepot for overseas bullion and Portuguese spices (Bloom 1937: 73). Philip Curtin reminds us that refineries and sugar distribution networks for northern Europe were also based in Antwerp. Initially, Iberian Jews were drawn to the city because of its role in international commerce (Curtin 1990: 52-53). Before long, Jews and Marranos became adjuvants for commercial banking there, and some of them helped to finance the early sugar trade with Brazil. But a local revolt against the Spanish occupiers led to the destruction of Antwerp's refineries and stimulated the dispersal of sugar refining to other cities, particularly to Amsterdam.

The revolt of the Netherlands against Hapsburg Spain in 1572 would change the entire course of world trade. After the Dutch won independence from Spain, they welcomed New Christian and Jewish refugees and took advantage of their global connections. Indeed, the proclamation of religious toleration of the United Provinces in 1579 emboldened Sephardic New Christians to return to openly professing their Jewish faith. Many of the crypto-Jews who subsequently settled in Amsterdam returned to their Jewish beliefs and customs and did much to revive organized Judaism.

For centuries Amsterdam had been a meeting place for merchants from the Mediterranean and northern Europe. And as early as 1520, a few Dutch merchants had secured the exclusive right (*asiento*) to trade with Spanish America. In any case, these new immigrants brought with them their much sought after business acumen and global contacts. They undoubtedly contributed greatly to Amsterdam's rise to supremacy in world trade and to the establishment of a new trading system oriented to Africa as well as to the Americas. This liberal and cosmopolitan city became a center for western Sephardic Judaism.

In 1580, all of the Iberian Peninsula was united under King Philip II of Spain, with Portugal in a subordinate position. By then, Brazil had become the most important source of sugar for Europe, displacing the Atlantic islands off the African coast. At the same time, the African interior, especially Angola, had become the major source of slaves destined for Brazil's plantations. And it was not long before Amsterdam superseded Antwerp as the greatest sugar-refining center in Europe. Raw Brazilian sugar arrived in Lisbon and then was transferred to Amsterdam for refining and transshipment throughout Europe. Jonathan Israel maintains, in fact, that it was Jews who introduced the Dutch to the Brazilian trade (Israel 1988: 24).

David Eltis explains that the Spanish and the Portuguese had banned the enslavement of American Indians, and thus the demands for labor were equally acute in both the Spanish and Portuguese New World colonies (Eltis 1993: 1424). As that demand grew, the Spanish in 1595 awarded a New Christian merchant, Pedro Gomez Reynal, the exclusive right, or royal license (asiento), to import African slaves to its American possessions. Contractually, Reynal agreed to deliver 38,250 slaves over a nine-year period, promising that all slaves would be "fresh from Africa" (Rotberg 1965: 138). It is said that this became a model for many such asientos that followed in the decades to come.

The diasporic Jews and New Christians could bring to the

Dutch not only capital but also their global connections. Joseph Miller says much of the financing for the trade expansion came from Portuguese New Christian families in the Netherlands who had relatives in various cities in northern Europe and in Brazil. Brooks adds that "Dutch vessels trading in the 1590s onward derived considerable advantage from business and family associations between the Jews who had taken refuge in Holland and Portugal" (Brooks 1993: 221). Family ties also played a big role in the development of the sugar industry. Fernand Braudel explains that "at the end of the 16th century the network of Portuguese Jews who controlled the sugar and spice trades and possessed ample capital furthered the success of Amsterdam" (Braudel 1979: 816). Diaz-Mas goes so far as to assert that by that time Jews enjoyed a near monopoly of sugar refining in Europe (Diaz-Mas 2000: 54). Though it was not until 1655 that Jews received permission from the Amsterdam authorities to actually own refineries, many New Christians were already in the business. By 1610, the Netherlands had already achieved dominance over sugar distribution in Europe and, as we will see below, was well on its way to controlling the Guinea gold trade of West Africa.

It must be remembered that the converso populations in Brazil, Angola, and Amsterdam grew after 1601 when Spain and Portugal, faced with heavy debts, gave New Christians the right to emigrate in return for a substantial cash payment. By 1606, Amsterdam could boast sizeable Sephardic Jewish and New Christian populations, and they gained in prominence during the period of the Twelve Year Truce (1609-21) when the Netherlands enjoyed unimpeded access again to the ports of Spain and Portugal (Boyajian 1983: 12). The Sephardic merchants, with their knowledge of Spanish and Portuguese and their skills in international finance, were able to take advantage of this new situation to expand their trade with the Iberian Peninsula—and beyond to colonial America. Lopo Ramires, a powerful figure in the Amsterdam sugar trade, was only one of many Jews who profited from this new opening.

The Sephardic community in Amsterdam, numbering nearly four thousand in 1636, was large enough to have its own synagogue (Forbes 1988: 49). As a wealthy, sophisticated community, Amsterdam was seen as the mother city for Sephardic congregations in the New World and Africa. Printing presses were established in the city, and books were distributed throughout the Sephardic world. The Sephardic population of the Netherlands was further augmented between 1645 and 1660 when hundreds of New Christians fled to Holland from Spain in the wake of a new Inquisitional assault.

The Truce between Holland and the then reunited Spain and Portugal enabled Dutch Sephardic merchants to expand their already lucrative Brazilian trade. During the Truce, the Portuguese community in Amsterdam increased both in value and in volume its trade with the Iberian world. A significant portion of Dutch-built and -operated vessels belonged to Portuguese merchants in Lisbon and Oporto who readily invested in shipping via Amsterdam agents. During this period of unprecedented opportunity, some Holland-based shippers shifted from commodity trade in West Africa to the slave trade. Many Portuguese Jews got into the slave trade with the Dutch partly because Jews were prohibited from Asian and African commodity trading (Miller 1996: 220).

Beginning in the first two decades of the seventeenth century, Amsterdam's profits from Brazilian sugar imports climbed dramatically. By that time, some Amsterdam and Pernambuco Jews exerted considerable control over sugar as financiers and merchants. Some, like Diego Nunes Belmont, had become involved in the slave trade as well (Israel 1985: 139).

The situation changed for the Dutch Republic from 1621 to 1647, when their ships and cargoes were excluded from Spain—and from Portugal as well until the latter separated from the Spanish Crown in 1640. This exclusion presented both a threat and a challenge to the Dutch, and, with strong encouragement from Amsterdam's Jewish and converso communities, the government decided to seize Portugal's Brazilian possessions. The invasion plan was apparently devised by Portuguese merchants in Recife. The merchants convinced the directors of the DutchWest India Company that it would result in lower costs and greater profits. Thus, in 1624, a Dutch fleet captured Sao Salvador, and in 1630 the Dutch took Recife and the rich Pernambuco sugar region. Brazil was thus transformed into a Dutch colony and renamed "New Holland."

Converso involvement in the Brazilian sugar industry was already well underway. The industry's early development depended heavily upon Marrano initiative and technical skills. From the late fifteenth through the sixteenth centuries, a New Christian coastal presence was well established. For more than three decades before the Dutch conquest of Pernambuco, Amsterdam's Sephardic merchants had been trading with converso kinsmen in Brazil, partnering in hundreds of sugar-related ventures (Ebert 2003: 52-68). Long before 1630, Portuguese crypto-Jews were able to circumvent Spanish embargoes on Dutch shipping by sending Brazilian sugar to Lisbon, which was then reexported to co-religionists in Hamburg, Germany, where it was repackaged and sent to its final destination in Amsterdam for refining and retailing into European markets. Moreover, by the time the Dutch seized northern Brazil in 1630, two-thirds of the large plantation owners were allegedly Marranos, and they also possessed in whole or in part a significant number of sugar mills (Cayetana 1989: 76).

Certainly as a result of the Dutch takeover, the Sephardic Jewish presence in Brazil grew substantially. The Dutch authorities extended to them their pledge of religious freedom, and, as David Brion Davis notes, Brazil was "one of the few spots in the world where some Marranos could recover their Judaism and where Jews could freely practice their religion while engaging in a wide range of vocations" (Davis 1994: 16).

From the late 1630s, Jews in Brazil became important suppliers of African slaves on credit to plantation owners. Salo Baron asserts that Jews, commanding considerable capital resources, were in fact among the major retailers of slaves in Dutch Brazil between the conquest in 1630 and 1654. C.R. Boxer observes that Catholic planters borrowed heavily from the Jews to buy slaves imported from Angola. And while the Dutch West India Company maintained a monopoly on the shipment of slaves across the sea, Jews supplied capital to plantation owners enabling them to buy them in Brazil auctions in hard cash. Boxer adds that local plantation owners acquired Angolan slaves on credit or on the installment system at exorbitant rates (Boxer 1952: 199). "The natural result," Boxer explains, "was that all the Catholic Brazilian planters were deeply indebted either to Hollanders or to Jews and had no prospect of ever paying off their debts. Their only hope of solvency lay in the expulsion of the 'heretic intruders'" (Boxer 1952: 199-200). Arnold Wiznitzer argues that Jews were less important as plantation owners than as "financiers of the sugar industry, as brokers and exporters of sugar, as suppliers of Negro slaves on credit" (Wiznitzer 1960: 70).

Once the Dutch had taken Brazil from the Portuguese, it was clear that they would have to seize their African holdings as well in order to control the source of labor for Brazilian plantations and mines. The issue was a hotly debated one as the Protestant Dutch had been reluctant to become directly involved in slave trading. The Dutch West India Company since its founding in 1621 had resisted it. Now, the pressure had become too great and its former policy was abandoned. Already in 1635, the Dutch West India Company began to purchase for the Brazilian market slaves along the West African coast, initially seeking slaves along the so-called Slave Coast of modern Togo, Benin, and western Nigeria. Then, in 1637, a fleet captured the key Portuguese base of Elmina on the Gold Coast. Interestingly, it was an expedition organized in Recife, Brazil. Quickly, the Dutch seized other Portuguese forts along the Guinea coast and inched southward down the coast of Loango (Israel 1995: 35). In 1641, they captured the great slave port of Luanda and much of the colony of Angola, thereby solidifying their control over the major sources of slaves for the New World. Indeed, by 1642, the Dutch West India Company had almost complete control over the Guinea coast of West Africa and most of West Central Africa, thus enjoying a vast trading empire on both sides of the Atlantic. By 1670, this carrying trade—largely a company monopoly—was exporting more than 3,000 slaves annually from the Loango coast alone.

The Company almost immediately became dependent on Jewish commercial expertise in Angola. From the early sixteenth century, Christian-Portuguese and Dutch traders who ventured out to West Central Africa were accompanied by Jews or crypto-Jews expert in negotiating trade agreements. In the late sixteenth century, the most famous of these was the Angolan trader Duarte Lopes, who, during his slave trading forays into the Kongo interior, developed a deep knowledge of the culture and history of African societies. Eventually, Lopes gained favor in the Kongolese court and became a key adviser who urged the king to sever the country's destructive ties with the Portuguese and establish a direct link with Rome's Holy See (Thomas 1997: 132). Unfortunately, the initiative failed to materialize; nevertheless, Lopes represents only one of many examples of the extent to which Europeans were able to gain access to the inner circles of African governments.

Jews, Conversos, and the West African Trade

While the Hollanders may have been relative newcomers to the West African trades, the Portuguese were old hands. According to George Brooks, from about 1500 to 1630, New Christian merchants from Portugal, Spain, and, much later, the Netherlands played a major role in the commerce of the Upper Guinea coast. They invested capital and did considerable business there. Indeed, in the early sixteenth century, the Portuguese monarch sold at public auction contracts for exclusive trading rights in certain regions, with the bidders agreeing to pay an annual rent in return. Many of the contracts went to New Christians, Brooks maintains. One of them, Mestre Filipe, rented the Gambian trade from 1510 to 1514 and played a significant role there in stimulating trans-Atlantic trade (Brooks 1993:178). Later, in 1612, the Dutch West African trade would be pioneered by a Portuguese-born Amsterdam Jew, Jacob Peregrino.

Clearly, Jewish as well as New Christian factors were operating in Senegambia and Upper Guinea by the opening of the seventeenth century. In 1601, the Portuguese Crown had issued an order allowing Jewish merchants and *lancados*, based mainly on Cape Verde Island, to settle and trade along the Senegambian and Upper Guinea coasts. (*Lancado*, a Portuguese pejorative term meaning "outcast," was affixed mainly to those who had committed petty crimes or were religiously persecuted by the Catholic authorities.) It was not long before hundreds of Jews were acting as trade factors along the coast and even up country among the Wolof and other African communities. Along with the conversos, they traded for gold, wax, gum, ivory, and slaves. In time, New Christians and conversos in Senegambia began to work closely with Iberian Jews in Holland in their attempt to unite against growing competition from English and French counterparts. Indeed, strong commercial ties developed between Sephardic Jews in Holland and New Christians in West Africa. Some Amsterdam Sephardic Jews even outfitted ships in the early 1600s for the West African trade.

By the 1620s, Jews were numerous enough in West Africa to have established a synagogue at Rufisque in Senegal and at Joal.

Inevitably there were religious tensions between Jews and Christians, but in time all the foreign populations mixed with the local Africans and produced a richly textured creole culture. A Catholic-centered Luso-African population would emerge by 1700, by which time nearly all traces of Judaism had disappeared. Still, some Jewish families based in France continued to do business in West Africa. The Abraham Gradis family, of Portuguese origin though domiciled in Bordeaux, France, enjoyed a monopoly over French commerce at Goree in Senegal from the mid to late eighteenth century and held an interest in the French slave trade (Stein 1979: 159).

Portugal broke with Spain again in 1640, ending a joint monarchy that dated back to 1580. The secession led to a revival of trade with the Dutch, but it also renewed Portuguese interest in retaking Brazil. The process of reconquest gained traction in 1645 when Catholic Portuguese planters in northern Brazil, accusing Jews of having engineered the Dutch invasion a decade and a half earlier, rebelled against the Portuguese Jews and Dutch West India Company officials. The rebellion spread across New Holland's plantations, devastating many of them and driving Jews and Dutch officials from much of Brazil, save for Recife and a few other coastal ports. When Recife finally fell in 1654, Jews and Protestants were given three months to leave the country.

Following the expulsion of the Dutch from Luanda in 1648 and then from Brazil in 1654, the Catholic planter families in Pernambuco maneuvered to have their members and friends appointed as military governors in Angola. These relatives and associates in turn allied themselves with the local and deeply entrenched Luso-African families, many of whom were descended from earlier Jewish settlers and traders who had fled the Inquisition or the law—the so-called *degredados*. Boxer observes that some crypto-Jews began to serve on the municipal council after the recapture of the city (Boxer 1969: 282). Thus, the

Luanda-Recife slave trade connection was preserved and, over time, greatly expanded.

The loss of Brazil may have been a setback for Dutch Sephardic Jewry, but it must be weighed against the end of the Eighty Years War between Spain and the Netherlands. Indeed, the Spanish-Dutch Peace Treaty of 1648 restored commercial links, and Spain agreed to allow Jews who were Dutch subjects to trade with Spain and Spanish America legally through Christian factors, or agents, residing in Spanish ports. After this time, the Dutch developed a new and cordial relationship with Spain, one that became extremely favorable for Dutch Sephardic Jewry (Israel 1992: 191).

The Dutch soon became chief carriers for the Spanish empire. Spain simply lacked the ability to supply the West Indies with enough slaves and even to control the slave trade. The intensity of the two countries' interconnection was revealed in 1662 when the Dutch negotiated their first asiento with the Spanish, enabling them to legally convey slaves to the Spanish colonies. The relationship was strengthened in 1664 when the king of Spain appointed Manuel de Belmonte, a Jew of Spanish origin, his Agent-General in Amsterdam for the procurement of slaves for the New World (Davis 1994: 16). By then, some Portuguese Jews had heavily invested in the West India Company (Swetschinski 2000: 117). Moreover, writes J.E. Inikori, by 1670 the West India Company was exporting nearly three thousand slaves annually from the Loango coast some three hundred miles north of Luanda. It was a slave source pioneered by the Dutch more than three decades earlier in order to supply Brazil's plantations and mines (Inikori 1982: 202).

Between 1680 and 1696, the lucrative asiento fell to a New Christian, Jean Barroso del Pozo. In the 1690s, another converso, François van Schoonenbergh, proved key in arranging for the slaving asientos that enabled the Dutch to supply America with African slaves. Thus, the Spanish Caribbean was opened up to seemingly unlimited trade possibilities, and this opening ultimately shifted the center of gravity of global commerce to the West Indies.

The Curaçaoan Factor

Not surprisingly, while some Jewish and New Christian refugees from Brazil returned to Amsterdam and continued their association with the city's sugar interests, many others moved northward into the Caribbean, especially to the Guianas, Guadeloupe, Martinique, and the Dutch base on the tiny island of Curaçao (see Benjamin 2002: 95). They brought with them sugarcane treatment techniques and expertise in overseas trading and investment. These Jews and conversos offered production technology, financial resources, and extensive family contacts with relatives on both sides of the Atlantic. For centuries, since their expulsion from the Iberian Peninsula, many Jewish merchant families were interlinked professionally and personally across the globe. Amsterdam Jewry and Jewish communities in the West Indies were closely connected through business, religion, and marriage. Jonathan Israel observes that from the mid-seventeenth century, Spanish and Portuguese communities "had forged vigorous and enduring links with the Caribbean, Brazil, North America...and western Africa" (Israel 1992: 365). Sephardic Jews in America and Africa collaborated not only with their fellow New Christians in Lisbon, Madrid, and Antwerp but also with Spanish and Portuguese merchants in Amsterdam, London, Hamburg, and other western European cities.

After the expulsion of the Jews from Brazil in 1654, the center of Jewish and converso commercial activity in the Carribean shifted to the tiny Dutch island of Curaçao. Within a few decades, Curaçao would have the largest Jewish community in the New World and the first synagogue in North America.

Though Jews first settled there in 1634, their population greatly swelled two decades later, after the fall of Recife. Under Curaçao's first governor, a Jew named Samuel Coheno, Jews were welcomed to the island and allowed the same complete freedom of worship that they enjoyed in Amsterdam. It was not long before the tiny semi-arid island would become a key transit point for African slaves bound for much of the Caribbean basin.

Curaçao's central position in the sugar and slave trades further benefited from the English takeover of Spanish Jamaica in 1655. Since the early part of the century, the English had been expanding into the Lesser Antilles, planting mainly tobacco with limited numbers of white indentured servants from the British Isles. With Jamaica now in British hands, the Spanish contractors (*asentistas*) would secure the majority of their slaves from Dutch Curaçao.

Eventually, lured by the English and French who desperately needed labor and expertise, Jewish and converso trade networks were extended to include non-Hispanic Caribbean islands as well as English colonies on the North American mainland. John Edwards notes that, from the 1660s, "Amsterdam Jewry maintained considerable influence over the 4,000 or so Sephardim who lived throughout the West Indies" (Edwards 1988: 170). Before the mid-seventeenth century, African slaves were destined almost exclusively for Spanish America and Brazil. Now they were being imported into the West Indies in rapidly increasing numbers.

Thus, the Amsterdam-oriented Jewish, converso, and Protestant refugees from Brazil were partly responsible for the seventeenth-century sugar revolution in the West Indies and for the dramatic expansion of the Atlantic slave trade into that region. Without doubt, Jewish refugees from Brazil played a significant role in instructing the English and French in sugar production techniques and in setting up some of the first sugar refineries.

By the 1670s, the Amsterdam-Lisbon-Recife connection was

ultimately displaced by the Amsterdam-Antwerp-Curaçao link. It should be remembered that in 1675 the Dutch secured the asiento from Spain (Blakely 1993: 116). Eli Faber says that "Sephardic communities on the islands of Jamaica, Barbados, Martinique, Nevis, and Suriname became part of a network that reached back to Amsterdam from Curaçao" (Faber 1992: 22). Many Dutch Jews on Curaçao also collaborated with conversos in Cartagena, Colombia, and Maracaibo, Venezuela.

From 1696 to 1701, Spain gave its asiento to the Portuguese Royal Guinea Company to supply African slaves to all its American colonies. Salo Baron notes that in the 1690s, a Curaçaoan Jew, Manuel Alvares Correa, served as an important intermediary between the Dutch and Portuguese West Indies companies for the purpose of shipping slaves from Africa to Spanish Mexico via Curaçao (Baron 1975: 247). In addition, a major Portuguese merchant, Andrew Lopes (also known as Andreas Noguera), was active at this time in the slave trade between Africa and Mexico and was known to have introduced other Jews to the trade in the 1690s. Gedalia Yogev observes that Lopes was an agent of the Portuguese Royal Guinea company, which acquired from the Spanish Crown a slave asiento. Lopes, who was a successful slave trader with excellent connections, was instrumental in organizing the subsequent transport of slaves from Africa to the Americas. It should be noted, however, that Spain did not renew the asiento in 1701, perhaps because of this Jewish involvement (Yogev 1978: 36).

Conversos were also found to be slave trading along the west coast of South America. The unification of Portugal and Spain from 1580 to 1640 gave the former access to Spanish American colonies and silver production. Already the Peruvian viceroyalty had been making huge demands for African slaves needed to labor in the silver mines of Peru and the gold mines of Chile. And by 1640, Lima alone could boast of an African slave population of nearly 20,000. Manuel Bautista Perez, the spiritual leader of Lima's secret Jews, was a major trader in human cargoes in Peru in the early seventeenth century. This Lima-based merchant obtained African slaves in the Caribbean from his own extended family members and sold them to Spanish Peruvian planters and miners. He was also involved in contraband trade and was eventually arrested and executed (Bowser 1974: 58-59).

Jewish-converso involvement in the slave trades began to diminish in 1701 when the Spanish slave trade asiento passed from Portugal to France and then to England by the Treaty of Utrecht in 1713. The Curaçaoan slave trade consequently declined, and the Dutch West India Company shifted its focus to Suriname. Suriname became the company's chief slave trade destination and represented more than 60 percent of its global slave trade until 1738 when the firm, no longer enjoying a legal monopoly, ended its role as a carrier of and trader in slaves altogether. However, as we have seen, Jewish involvement in Suriname's slave plantation economy was quite extensive, with at least 115 of the 400 or so plantations under the ownership of Jews (Israel 1985: 177). But in terms of slave trading, the handwriting was already on the wall for the Dutch West India Company and its clients. In 1672, the heavily capitalized Royal African Company received a charter in England and by 1700 had already established a strong presence in West Africa, exporting more than 140,000 slaves to British possessions in the West Indies. As a formidable sea power with a mammoth merchant marine, England had in the early eighteenth century begun to surpass the Dutch Republic in total shipping tonnage. Though some Jews shifted their business to London, they failed to gain the influence they had enjoyed in their heyday in Amsterdam.

Nevertheless, Curaçaoan Jews apparently did not end their slave trading activities. They remained leading shippers, ship owners, and marine insurers until well into the eighteenth century. And Jewish brokers on Barbados and Jamaica became active with the English traders. Also, in the 1750s we see Abraham and

Jacob Franco and others shipping slaves to Puerto Rico on specially chartered vessels out of England.

After they obtained the coveted Spanish slave trade asiento, the British displaced the Dutch in the eighteenth century as the world's greatest sugar importer and slave trading nation. The Atlantic slave trade continued to flourish; in fact, its volume did not peak until the decade of the 1780s. Nevertheless, from the 1730s, the involvement of Jews and conversos rapidly diminished into relative insignificance.

Unlike in the Atlantic world, Jews and conversos played no visible role in the slave trade of the Indian Ocean. While some scholars have asserted that during the eighteenth century approximately a quarter of all Dutch East India Company stockholders were Jews and still more may have been New Christians, there is little if any evidence that these two groups were actually participants in slaving and slavery. Clearly, a slave-worked plantation economy emerged in the East India Company's Cape Colony, and by 1795, when the company surrendered its possession to the British, there were no fewer than 17,000 slaves, most of whom originated mainly from southeastern Africa, India, and the Indonesian archipelago. Nevertheless, after the Fourth Anglo-Dutch War of 1780-84, the company's monopoly on slave trading in the Indian Ocean was broken forever (Eldredge and Morton 1994: 14).

CHAPTER FOUR

Jews and the Rise of South Africa

The Jewish Diaspora/Migration Routes

The Early Entrepreneurs

Jewish involvement in South Africa reaches far back into the country's history, possibly to 1484 when Abraham of Bija and Joseph De Lomega conveyed information to King John II that a new route to the Indies could be found by sailing down the west coast of Africa and circumnavigating the continent. They could bypass the Muslim-dominated eastern Mediterranean, including Egypt, and establish direct contact with the suppliers of eastern spices and luxury goods. By eliminating the Muslim middlemen of the Levant they might enhance their profits and improve the terms of trade. The Portuguese, already probing into sub-Saharan Africa with maps drawn mainly by Jewish and New Christian cartographers, were intrigued enough to dispatch Vasco da Gama, who succeeded in rounding the Cape of Good Hope in 1497 and sailing into the Indian Ocean. Two navigators of Jewish birth are said to have accompanied him: Gaspar da Gama and Joao Nunez (Walker 1957: 14-16).

This was the first documented European voyage into the Indian Ocean, and it followed one undertaken by a royal Chinese fleet less than a half century earlier. The latter began in China and reached the east coast of Africa. Unfortunately, the emperor was unimpressed and the project was terminated (Snow 1988: 21). China's involvement in Africa would not resume for another 500 years. Still, South Africa may have been spared from one alien people only to be confronted by another.

Jews are not heard from again in southern Africa until after 1652, when the Dutch East India Company established a refreshment station at Table Bay at the base of the African continent. Though the royally chartered Amsterdam-based company had Jewish shareholders since its inception in 1602, it was dominated by directors who adhered to the Dutch Reformed Church, a rather doctrinaire Protestant Calvinist denomination. Not surprisingly, all company employees at the Cape had to be Protestants. Those few of Jewish birth were constrained to accept Christian baptism or leave the firm. The policy remained in force until 1803, when the Dutch Batavian Republic granted freedom of worship to everyone. The British maintained that policy after assuming full control of the Cape Colony several years later (Elphick 1979: 116-69r).

From then until about 1831 a small trickle of observant Jews began to arrive, many of them sailing over from the tiny island of St. Helena, a British outpost in the South Atlantic. Before Britain's seizure of the Cape Colony, St. Helena had served as a vital though totally inadequate refreshment station for English ships passing between the Far East and the British Isles. Among the first Jewish arrivals in Cape Town, the capital and largest city, was Saul Solomon in 1806; he became an early English-speaking leader in the development of Cape Town's infrastructure.

The Solomon family was followed two years later by a surgeon named Dr. Siegfried Frankel who established a small medical practice. He is believed to be the first observant Jew to settle at the Cape and was the first Jewish medical doctor in the country's history. Interestingly, Jews did not immigrate within a larger group until 1820, and then as members of the government-sponsored Albany Settlement on the far-eastern Cape frontier. Among the predominately Scottish settlers in this scheme was Benjamin Norden, who eventually moved to Cape Town, involved himself in city affairs, and in 1841 founded South Africa's first Hebrew congregation, the so-called Society of the Jewish Community, or "Hope of Israel"—in Hebrew, *Tikvath Israel* (Saron and Holtz 1955: 9).

Samuel Rudolph, an American émigré, ran the services for a handful of worshipers. Eight years later the congregation was large enough to build a synagogue and engage a rabbi. In the early decades, its membership reflected the makeup of the colony's Jewish population, which was overwhelmingly German and English. There is no evidence of discrimination in those early days, and Jews readily assimilated into the Cape's predominantly English colonial culture (Shain 1994: 12).

Jews were among the earliest whites to conduct trade up the east coast into Zululand. Nathaniel Isaacs arrived in 1825 and for a few years dealt with two powerful Zulu kings, Shaka and Dingaan. He was followed in 1834 by Jonas Bergtheil, who stayed on for years and was an important player in the economic development of Britain's new colony of Natal. By 1848 he had become a controlling director of the powerful Natal Cotton company (Muller 1969: 188). In 1857, Bergtheil became a member of Natal's first legislative council, even before any Jew had been elected to Parliament in London.

These early entrepreneurial pioneers were followed in 1859 by brothers Elias and Aaron de Pass, who established a number of whale- and seal-oil processing plants as well as repair yards for passing ships. Aaron's son David became a pioneer sugar planter who in the 1880s laid the foundations of Natal's vibrant sugar industry, which became a major generator of wealth in the early twentieth century (A. Arkin 1984: 58).

In 1835 many thousand Boers, or white *voortrekkers*, migrated northward out of the Cape Colony in search of new lands for their livestock and in reaction to a growing English presence in their lives. Most were poor illiterate debtors and lived precariously on leased land of marginal fertility. This epochal "Great Trek" resulted in the establishment of several non-viable interior republics, notably the Orange Free State and the South African Republic, or Transvaal (Etherington 2001: 243-61). Their constitutions excluded Africans—or kaffirs as they were derisively called—as well as women of all races.

Jews recognized that these impoverished farmers (Boers) desperately needed household wares and farm implements, and they responded by traveling from farmstead to farmstead selling goods from the tailgates of their wagons. These *smous,* or itinerant peddlers, accumulated capital, which, in the absence of banks, they lent to the Boers or invested in small retail shops for themselves. Interestingly, by 1850 German-Jewish families could be found in almost every Free State hamlet. They also opened businesses in the major frontier market towns such as Grahamstown and Graaff-Reinet. Without these rural stores the white farmers would have been hard put to survive.

In those days, Jews enjoyed wide acceptance and respect in the Boer Afrikaner communities, where they were viewed as fellow believers in the Old Testament. Nevertheless, Jews perceived of themselves and were perceived by others as a distinct group within the greater white Protestant Christian community. Along with Catholics, they were officially barred from military service, from public schools, from holding public office, and from standing for election to the all-white legislature or Volksraad. However, exceptions were often made, and Jews would become politically prominent in the Afrikaner republics long before the Anglo-Boer Wars. A Dutch Jew served as the state public prosecutor for the Transvaal in 1869, and a decade earlier the Free State capital, Bloemfontein, was laid out by the government's surveyor general, a Jew named Gustave Baumann. Isaac Baumann, a relative, became two-time mayor of Bloemfontein and a director of the National Bank (Rosenthal 1966: 314).

South Africa's Jewish population grew slowly in the first half of the nineteenth century and only gradually radiated from Cape Town. By 1860 there were approximately sixty-five Jewish families in the Cape Colony. But Jews always seemed to be innovators in business. In the 1860s in Port Elizabeth the Mosenthal brothers from Germany laid the foundations of the country's mohair industry by setting up marketing centers for merino and mohair fleeces throughout the Cape Colony. Soon, even greater Jewish fortunes would be made on the interior highveld—but by co-religionists from another part of the European world.

Generally, nineteenth-century South African Jews were not deeply involved in agriculture and livestock or in rural land ownership. Nor did they employ large numbers of Africans. A major exception to this is ostrich husbandry. Oddly, in the 1880s a number of Russian Lithuanian families settled in the southern Cape village of Oudtshoorn and developed an enormously profitable export industry in ostrich feathers. By the turn of the century Max Rose gained prominence as the "Ostrich King of South Africa." He and others exported their feathers to Europe's leading couturiers and milliners in an age when feathered hats and bonnets were all the rage in high society. Remarkably, until the outbreak of the First World War, feathers were the country's fourth largest export commodity in terms of earnings. By then, Oudtshoorn had a sizeable and prosperous Jewish population and was known as the feather capital of the world (Coetzee 2000: 88-89).

Before the 1880s, South Africa's Jews numbered fewer than four thousand and were predominantly well-assimilated, well-educated Ashkenazic middle-class merchants and artisans of English and German extraction (Hoffman and Fischer 1988: 2). They were centered in the Cape Colony in and around Cape Town and Port Elizabeth. Then, beginning in the last two decades of the nineteenth century, southern Africa experienced unprecedented waves of new immigrants, almost entirely Yiddish-speaking Ashkenazics from eastern Europe. Most of them originated from an area of Czarist Russia known as the Pale of Settlement situated between the Black Sea and the Baltic, which included Russian Poland, southwest Russia, and the Baltic Lithuanian provinces. These desperately poor peasant refugees from a massive Czarist pogrom came overwhelmingly from small Lithuanian villages, or *shtetls*. The economics of these tightly knit communities rested on micro enterprises, artisanal and mercantile in nature. They migrated first to London in hopes of continuing on to New York, but a significant number moved on to South Africa after having failed to secure passage to America.

The Lure of Diamonds and Gold

Significantly, their arrival in South Africa roughly coincided with the discoveries of diamonds in Kimberley (1867) and, after 1886, of gold on the Witwatersrand, or "Rand," as it was popularly known. In many respects, the size of South African Jewry would be influenced by the mineral discoveries and the wide range of employment and goods and services needed by the burgeoning extractive industries and the communities that mushroomed around them. Rosenthal notes that Jews were among the first at the diamond fields, as diggers as well as traders and artisans. Initially, the immigrants—referred to as *Litvaks* (a Yiddish word meaning Jews from Lithuania)—took advantage of these opportunities by entering the service and provisioning sectors as purveyors of hardware for the diggers, working as small shopkeepers, and petty traders, boot makers, tailors, and wagon operators transporting fortune-seeking miners and mining supplies from Cape Town and Port Elizabeth to the interior diamond fields and on to the emerging city of Johannesburg on the Rand (Rosenthal 1970: 412).

In these booming new centers of mineral extraction the Litvaks encountered slightly earlier arrivals of German and English-speaking Jews who had already been developing much of Kimberley's infrastructure, including hotels and bars. Others had arrived with European-honed skills in diamond cutting and stock brokerage. The Jewish population mushroomed and a synagogue was built in 1872. Remarkably, by then South Africa had surpassed Brazil as the world's largest diamond producer (Hull 1990: 62-64).

Nearly all the diamonds at Kimberley were extracted from a huge hole where hundreds of prospectors, Africans as well as Europeans and Americans, held individual titles and worked the pit with primitive tools. This chaotic and uneconomical situation would soon change. In 1873, a London-born Jewish cockney, Barney Barnato, journeyed to Kimberley, went into diamond brokerage, and began buying up the small claims (Shimoni 1983: 194). It was a timely action, for in 1885 a railway was extended from Cape Town to Kimberley, allowing for the transport of more and heavier materiel (De Kiewiet 1957: 122-23).

By 1888, Barnato had succeeded in bringing nearly the entire Kimberley mining complex under his personal control (Herrman 1930: 228). But not for long. Owning the mine was one thing, operating it was another. More capital was needed to acquire the heavy machinery to cost-effectively operate it. In less than a year, Barnato was challenged by Alfred Beit, a new arrival of Hamburg Jewish background. Beit and Cecil Rhodes, another hugely successful Kimberley diamond entrepreneur, turned to the House of N.M. Rothschild & Sons in England. The Rothschilds were the richest Jewish family in Europe. In 1889, with their funds as well as capital from earlier profits at Kimberley, they acquired nearly all the shares in the De Beers mine and formed the De Beers Consolidated Mines Ltd. (Beyers 1977: 48). Faced with this challenge and with the opportunity to become even richer, Barnato—who controlled a vast array of diamond mines himself—agreed to amalgamate them in return for substantial equity in Rhodes's and Beit's new entity. For his agreement, Rhodes rewarded Barnato with one of four life governorships of the mammoth new firm. Overnight, De Beers Consolidated made Rhodes and Barnato the two leading businessmen in Africa and put them in control of the world's largest diamond mining monopoly (Rotberg 1988: 210-12).

The final process involved the monopolization of the overseas marketing of diamonds so as to assure price stability in an otherwise volatile trading environment. To achieve this, a group of Kimberley Jews, led by Barnato and the Mosenthal brothers, created in the same year the first "diamond syndicate" to purchase and market De Beers diamonds (Herrman 1930: 236). Thus, Kimberley's diamond barons, who were by then predominantly Jewish, gained a monopoly over the extraction, processing, and marketing of De Beers diamonds. Henceforth, diamond supplies were artificially controlled so that consumer demand would always outstrip marketable supply. Arkin notes that the marketing of precious stones "was largely controlled by syndicates of German-Jewish gem experts" (A. Arkin 1984: 58). It was a monopoly that made an enormous fortune for the Kimberley men and which endured for more than a century. So in that small southwest corner of the Orange Free State, Jewish financiers led the way in transforming the diamond industry into a vast monopoly of global proportions. For the first time, South Africa attracted substantial foreign capital and produced real wealth.

And that was just the beginning. In 1886, gold was discovered on the Witwatersrand, or "white water reef," in the South African republic of Transvaal, another impoverished and landlocked rural Afrikaner state. A new frenetic rush of prospectors ensued, and from the barren veld emerged almost overnight a huge mining city, called Johannesburg. Many Kimberley Jews, with venture capital and entrepreneurial experience gained from their diamond digs, trekked northward to seek new fortunes. Within a year they founded Johannesburg's first Jewish congregation. Together with Cecil Rhodes and a number of other gentiles they were among the earliest providers of startup capital on the Rand. They also helped to lay down the essential financial institutions that nourished the infant extractive industries and the municipal infrastructure of Johannesburg.

In 1887 Jews were instrumental in establishing the Johannesburg Stock Exchange chaired by Randlord Harry Solomon. Many of the brokerage houses listed on the exchange in the 1890s were Jewish-owned—so many that the trading room closed annually on Yom Kippur. Barney Barnato headed the powerful and today venerable Johannesburg Consolidated Investment Company. Otto Pollak in 1890 founded one of the largest stock brokerage houses in the city, which by its centenary in 1990 had become the largest in South Africa. Another brokerage giant was H. Eckstein & Co., whose partners included Alfred Beit and Lionel Phillips, also of Jewish Kimberley fame.

Phillips became pioneering president of the Johannesburg Chamber of Mines. While the brokerage houses attracted investors for the mining firms, the Chamber of Mines served as a lobby on their behalf and as a mechanism for recruiting labor and keeping miners' wages low. To achieve their goals, the companies recruited widely throughout southern and central Africa for African laborers. Portuguese Mozambique became one of the major sources, thanks in part to the recruiting efforts of Lionel Cohen, who was based in Lourenco-Marques.

Jews not only raised capital and labor for the mining companies, they also became its key directors. Among the most prominent in the early years were the brothers George and Leopold Albu (DeKock 1972: 9-10). In 1895, with participation from the House of Wernher Beit, they founded the General Mining Group, a conglomerate that in the twentieth century evolved into gargantuan Gencor, South Africa's second biggest mining house and the world's largest exporter of steam coal. Another major player was the ebullient Lithuanian immigrant Sammy Marks. As we shall see, Marks was a rich and powerful Transvaaler who controlled the highly successful African and European Investment Company (Mendelsohn 1991: 37).

Jewish Randlords and Uitlanders

By 1898, the little hinterland South African Republic (SAR) had risen almost phoenix-like to become the world's largest gold producer, exceeding the United States and Australia. An impressive fifteen of the twenty-five gold barons, the so-called Randlords, were of Jewish ancestry. They exerted enormous influence in the financing of the mining companies, in their ownership and management, and in the corridors of government in Pretoria, the SAR capital. They also forged parliamentary allies in Cape Town, capital of the administratively separate Cape Colony. In sum, from the last quarter of the nineteenth century they and their associates in the United Kingdom and Europe would play a disproportionate role in the implantation of industrial capitalism in the entire region of southern Africa.

It is worth reflecting here that prior to the Transvaal gold rush, the South African Republic was a poor landlocked entity consisting mainly of non-literate Africans of diverse cultures and languages and semi-literate white Afrikaans-speaking Boers. The indigenous Africans who made up the overwhelming majority of the population did not enjoy citizenship, voting rights, or individual property ownership. Unmistakably, power in both the Orange Free State and the South African Republic rested entirely on an elected white male-only legislature, the *volksraad*, with their respective presidents holding considerable executive authority.

Before the mineral revolution, Bloemfontein and Pretoria, the capitals of the Orange Free State and the SAR respectively, were small dusty farming communities, and Johannesburg did not even exist. Nearly all whites were members of the tightly knit Dutch Reformed Church, whose leaders were politically influential. It was a religiously and politically conservative society, patriarchal, racially prejudiced, and agrarian-oriented. Banking was practically non-existent, and capitalism had not taken deep root. As we have seen, Jews as artisans and peddlers provided essential imported goods, were few in number, and were treated with respect. Most of them were not religiously observant, but they had mastered Afrikaans and lived peacefully and symbiotically on the veld among the independent-minded Boers.

This bucolic self-sustaining way of life was abruptly and profoundly challenged by the diamond and gold discoveries and the massive influx of English- and Yiddish-speaking *uitlanders*, or foreigners, who in the perception of the Afrikaners conveyed an ethos that was intensely profit-motivated, generally secular, and less socially disciplined. The Transvaal government of President Paul Kruger was of two minds about them. On the one hand Kruger viewed the Jewish and non-Jewish immigrants as a threat to the traditional Afrikaner way of life. On the other, their entrepreneurial activities brought dramatic economic development and, through taxes and duties, much-needed revenue to state coffers. His response was to restrict their voting rights while encouraging their businesses by granting monopoly concessions to key sectors of the economy, like mining, water, transport, electrical power, and liquor.

After the discovery of gold in the Transvaal and the extension of the railway to Johannesburg, many recent Lithuanian Jewish immigrants with little money to invest in mining opened small businesses which ranged from houses of prostitution to canteens selling food and liquor. Charles van Onselen notes that Jews were the first to recognize the profitable role liquor could play in this burgeoning population of African migrants (van Onselen 1982: 6). Many of the Litvaks already had prior experience in the liquor business in eastern Europe and readily applied their skills to the local scene.

Already by the late 1880s hard liquor had become a hugely profitable enterprise, and the Lithuanian émigré Sammy Marks emerged as one of the Transvaal's so-called Liquor Kings. Marks had made his first fortune in the 1870s during the Kimberley diamond rush. In 1883 he moved to Pretoria and opened the Hatherly Distillery. To win support from the Afrikaner political elite, he helped to finance their military operations against the Pedi kingdom, an area coveted by the expansionary Boer farmers. In return he secured a monopoly concession over liquor distilling, and after the discovery of gold on the Witwatersrand in 1886 his enterprise boomed. As the number of miners on the Rand rapidly escalated, especially African miners, their demand for spirituous beverages soared. With time, workers' precious wages were being wasted on alcohol consumption, which in turn contributed to violence and lawlessness.

By 1895, alcoholism had become a major problem in the segregated African workers' compounds, as the infamous Hatherly Distillery was turning out nearly 400,000 gallons of liquor annually (Van Onselen 1982: 53). Marks had gained near-total control over liquor production in the Transvaal as well as in Portuguese Mozambique, where so many of the miners were recruited.

By this time numerous illicit liquor syndicates held monopolies over distribution in the miners' compounds. Nathan Friedman and Smoel Nathanson were described as the kingpins of this destructive trafficking. In 1897, the Randlords finally prevailed on Kruger, whose own government had profited from the liquor revenue, to institute prohibition. By then, Sammy Marks, who some liked to call the "uncrowned king of the Transvaal" (van Onselen 1982: 74), had diversified into commercial farming and coal, which found great demand from the mining houses. In years leading up to the South African War (Anglo-Boer War), Marks and other kingpins allegedly lent money to hard-pressed Afrikaner farmers and government leaders and in return gained unprecedented access to the corridors of power in Pretoria (Mendelsohn 1991: 56).

By then a number of Jews were serving as key advisers to the Kruger regime. Benison Aaron chaired Kruger's campaign finance committee in Johannesburg, and Alois Nellmapius worked closely in his cabinet (Greenstein 2002: 32). Sammy Marks, whose businesses depended on both Cape and Transvaal government support, had for years given personal financial aid to Kruger. Van Onselen indicates that through gifts and business loans, Marks made Kruger a wealthy man. It also may have enabled him to be a major power broker in Pretoria during the crucial years before and after the war. In appreciation, Kruger gave generously to Jewish charities and courted local Jewish capitalists (Shain 1994: 21). Clearly, some Transvaal Jews played an important role in sustaining the Afrikaner regime in the crucial years leading up to the Second Anglo-Boer War.

Jews, British, and Afrikaners

From the early 1890s, the clouds of war had begun to gather in the Transvaal. Since the first Anglo-Boer War in 1881, the imperialist-minded British had exercised only a vague suzerainty over the South African Republic. Through Rhodes's prodding and sometimes direct involvement, Britain had extended its control over independent African kingdoms to the north and west as well as along the coast in order to encircle the Afrikaner republics and prevent them from gaining independent access to the sea and potentially to other European states, particularly Germany (Rotberg 1988: 155).

Since the discovery of gold and diamonds, the Afrikaner states were seen to be of great strategic value. While prime minister of the Cape in 1895, Rhodes staged his own raid on the Transvaal hoping to provoke a uitlander uprising against the Afrikaner regime. It failed, and he had to pay a hefty ransom for some of his captured mercenaries. This abortive and illegal Jameson Raid also forced him to resign from Cape government in disgrace.

The Jameson Raid only heightened Boer anger and suspicions

of British imperialist intentions and added fuel to a nascent Afrikaner ethnic nationalist consciousness. Britain accused President Kruger of intransigence over their demand to open the franchise to the uitlanders and reduce taxes and duties on the rapidly growing white non-Afrikaner population and their businesses. They saw the oligarchic regime as unwilling and unable to meet the demands of the burgeoning economy. But clearly the imperialists had another agenda, and that was to consolidate the prospering Afrikaner republics and their own coastal colonies of the Cape and Natal into a unified entity firmly within the British Empire. If the Afrikaners would not comply peacefully, the British would preemptively invade and take them by military force.

South African Jews, especially those in Cape Colony, generally favored the imperialist goals, reasoning that a unified South Africa would lead to larger markets, freer trade, and closer ties to overseas markets and financial institutions and investors. In the Transvaal, most of the Randlords—Beit and Phillips leading the way—tacitly or openly sided with the British in hopes of eliminating a government in Pretoria that was becoming too heavy handed, incompetent, and xenophobic. On the other hand, mining magnate George Albu and the irrepressible Sammy Marks remained formally neutral while being quietly sympathetic to and sometimes cooperative with their Afrikaner friends. Though Marks and his associates had become rich through Afrikaner concessions and loan arrangements, they also needed the goodwill of the Randlords who bought their coal. Thus, full partisanship was out of the question.

President Kruger was strongly influenced by his Jewish friends and advisers, who seemed to encourage his intransigence and further polarize the already divided white community. Jewish-owned or controlled newspapers played a role in molding public opinion on the issues and did much to heighten local tensions. Emmanuel Mendelssohn, owner of the influential

Standard and Digger's News, characterized the Randlords as greedy and arrogant, and he enthusiastically embraced Kruger. In contrast, the Jewish-owned *Cape Argus* tended to favor British intervention.

In frustration, the British escalated their demands until Pretoria was forced to declare war in 1899. The ensuing Anglo-Boer War (also known as the South African War) was a drawn out and costly conflict for both sides. It was also seen as a David and Goliath affair, with a jingoistic and belligerent Britain unilaterally invading a country under false pretenses. Many Johannesburg Jews, faced with economic near paralysis, receded to the coastal cities or left South Africa altogether. In 1902, only after the Boers resorted to guerrilla tactics and the British responded with a scorched earth policy and incarceration of Africans and Afrikaners in brutal concentration camps, did the Afrikaners surrender.

Jewish Political Leadership and the Union of South Africa

The postwar period was a turning point for Jews throughout South Africa. Britain's political and economic reconstruction of the country gave them an unprecedented opportunity to become politically involved, especially at the municipal level. Between 1902 and 1910, when the two colonies and the defeated republics were welded into a Union of South Africa, Jews quickly and quietly assumed high positions of leadership in the major towns and cities as mayors and councilmen. Some of the important mayoralties went to Harry Graumann in Johannesburg in 1909 and to Felix Charles Hollander in Durban (Greenstein 2002: 24-27). Sir Matthew Nathan became governor of Natal; Adolph Schauder became a Port Elizabeth councilman and later its mayor; Harry Solomon, former chair of the Johannesburg Stock Exchange, became a member of the Transvaal Legislative Council; and Morris Alexander of Cape Town entered Parliament in 1908 and served for more than four decades. He was joined in 1914 by Morris Kentridge, who became the first Jewish Labor Party member. When the postwar Union of South Africa was launched in 1910, five Jews were elected to the first Parliament, and all were members of the ruling Unionist Party, which tended to represent the industrial sector and to favor British supremacy in the new Union of South Africa (Saron 2001: 112).

In the 1920s and '30s some Jews became active in the tiny Liberal Party, but their only parliamentary members were those elected to represent Africans who, from 1936, were effectively disenfranchised by being barred from standing for election to the national legislature. One of the most outspoken "Native Representatives" in the Senate was Leslie Rubin, a brilliant Cape Town lawyer and outspoken civil rights advocate. Rubin and a few other white Native Representatives were lone voices in the House and Senate for the "non-white" population.

Though whites never comprised more than 12 percent of South Africa's population, their political monopoly of power was expanded in 1959 when the Promotion of Bantu Self-Government Act eliminated Native Representative seats for the so-called Bantu. This effectively ended all African participation at the national level of government. Total white domination of parliamentary power was ensured in 1970 when "Coloreds" (racially mixed peoples) were also deprived of any of form of legislative representation.

Though Jews as a tiny minority in the country tended not to stand for elective office and enjoyed little direct participation in the public sector, they did wield an awesome degree of informal power behind the scenes far out of proportion to their numbers in the population. At their peak in the early 1970s, South African Jews numbered nearly 120,000, or some 3 percent of the white population, yet their share of per capita wealth, their contribution to the nation's gross domestic product, and their participation in the business sector were considerable (Dubb 1994: 4). Many enjoyed easy access to the highest levels of government, and, as we've seen, even before the turn of the last century and the South African War (1899-1902), some of the nation's largest and most strategically important industries were financed, owned, or controlled by certain Jewish individuals or extended families. It should also be noted here that from the late nineteenth century Jews tended to live in the urban areas. By the onset of World War II, roughly 80 percent were urbanized and concentrated in Durban, Cape Town, and Johannesburg. And at that time, fully 17 percent of Johannesburg's white population was Jewish (Shain 1994: 19).

Generally, Jews—especially first- and second-generation Lithuanians and Latvians—made impressive economic gains during the era of the Union of South Africa. They took full advantage of South Africa's vast natural resources and consumer base to expand markets not only throughout the country but into neighboring British-ruled colonies and protectorates as well. They accumulated enough wealth to send their children on to higher education for professional studies.

Indeed, by the 1930s Jews had attained a higher educational and occupational status than any other white group. Large numbers earned degrees in local colleges and overseas and had begun to distinguish themselves in most professions, especially law, medicine, engineering, and accountancy. The second generation of these Baltic Jews moved away from Yiddish, mastered English (and some Afrikaans), and rapidly assimilated into the white population. With the exception of those who took up residence in rural communities in the Transvaal and Orange Free State, where Afrikaans predominated, they tended to identify with English speakers. And by the 1950s most Jews were almost indistinguishable from the rest of the white population.

Jews and the Industrialization of the Country

Clearly, by the 1920s and early '30s, Ashkenazic Jews had achieved important positions in key sectors of the economy. In mining, Ernest Oppenheimer was clearly the most outstanding success story. Oppenheimer arrived from Germany in 1902 to manage the local office of A. Dunkelsbuhler, a London diamond-buying firm which had been in Kimberley since 1872. Dunkelsbuhler was Oppenheimer's uncle, and it was not uncommon for Jews to employ family members or immigrants from their communities back home in Europe (Pallister 1988: 49).

By 1890, A. Dunkelsbuhler had become an influential member of the Diamond Syndicate. Oppenheimer did well in the firm and used his financial success and experience to construct his own diamond empire. Then in 1917, he founded the Anglo-American Corporation with startup capital from the J.P. Morgan interests in the United States (Hull 1990: 126). Twelve years later he secured additional financial backing from the giant Rothschild Group in order to acquire a controlling interest in De Beers. Finally, in 1935 he formed E. Oppenheimer & Son Ltd. to direct Anglo-American and its rapidly expanding corporate empire. In the same year he converted to Christianity like a number of prosperous South African Jews at the time (Innes 1984: 101-104).

As we shall see later in the narrative, anti-Semitism in South Africa was on the rise, and Jews' loyalty to the British Empire was questioned. Those who had the influence and connections made bids for knighthood and became outspoken champions of British causes. Their children were sent to leading English boarding schools and universities in South Africa and overseas. Many became fully acculturated and acted more British than their counterparts in England. This quest for Anglicization was motivated in part by a desire to distinguish themselves from the poorly educated and impoverished eastern European immigrants flooding into South Africa in the wake of the Nazi Holocaust.

By the late 1930s, Ernest Oppenheimer had gained almost complete control not only over De Beers but of the hugely profitable and monopolistic London diamond syndicate, the Central Selling Organisation (CSO), as well. As the Second World War approached, Oppenheimer's Anglo-American Corporation had become the largest corporate entity in South Africa, and its member companies were a major force in the economic, political, and social life of the country (Pallister et al. 1988: 67). Ernest Oppenheimer was clearly South Africa's richest citizen and the most powerful businessman in southern and central Africa. And during the war years when the Allies desperately sought the region's strategic minerals, Oppenheimer's cooperation was crucial and assured (Hull 1990: 149).

Jews were also to be found playing cutting-edge roles in other critical economic sectors. As the century opened, many of the country's major newspapers fell under the ownership or editorship of journalists of Jewish ancestry. In 1903, Lionel Cohen assumed directorship of the *Rand Daily Mail*, one the country's highest-circulation and most influential English-speaking dailies (Kaplan and Robertson 1991: 215). The Jewish journalist Sarah Goldblatt in 1913 was working closely with C.J. Langenhoven—a leading Afrikaner intellectual and nationalist—as editor of his Afrikaans language newspaper, *Het Zuidwester*.

Arguably the most powerful media mogul in the country before the Second World War was Isadore (I.W.) Schlesinger, a New York– born Jew of Hungarian parents. Schlesinger immigrated to South Africa in 1894 and became the uncrowned king of mass media communications until his death in 1949 (Kaplan 1986: 133-34).

Early in the century he made a modest fortune selling real estate and insurance. He was not alone. Jews in Cape Town and Johannesburg were becoming major owners of hotels and urban real estate. Schlesinger did even more. In 1904 he formed his own life insurance company, American Life, which served over the years as a key generator of capital for his manifold enterprises (Hull 1990: 162-63). In the 1920s, his sprawling estate, known as Zebediela, was the largest single-owner citrus fruit farm in the world.

Schlesinger also achieved fame as the developer of an extensive chain of cinemas throughout the country under an umbrella company, African Consolidated Theatres, Ltd. And through it he monopolized the distribution of American films across all of southern Africa. More than anyone else Schlesinger brought the popular image of America to Africa. In 1930 he founded the African Broadcasting Company, but six years later the government purchased it and transformed it into the mammoth South African Broadcasting Corporation, popularly known as the SABC. Through his huge holding company, African Consolidated Investments Corporation, Schlesinger made substantial investments in advertising, real estate, life insurance, and other sectors. By 1940, his vast corporation controlled more than eighty companies producing an impressive portion of the nation's goods and services.

Jews were also pioneering in the fields of beverages, mass-production textiles, furniture, and general department store development. Early in the century, the ubiquitous Sammy Marks laid the foundations of South African Breweries. In the 1920s Gus Ackerman, Sam Kirsch, and Leon Segal created the first chain store group in South Africa, and in 1931 Max Sonnenberg founded the Woolworth's department store chain, which eventually had outlets in major cities throughout the country. Later, Jews were also responsible for opening Greaterman's and O.K. Bazaars stores. Both became giants of the retail sector. Phillip Frame, a Polish immigrant, founded what evolved into the mammoth Consolidated Textile Mills and was also the architect of the extensive Frame Group of Industrial Organizations.

The Roots of Modern Anti-Semitism: The Lithuanians and Latvians

As the twentieth century progressed, Jews were not only becoming a major presence in the economy but were growing rapidly in number as immigration escalated. On a countrywide basis, their numbers exploded from approximately four thousand in 1880 to thirty-eight thousand by 1904 and fifty thousand in 1911. Just after the Boer War, Transvaal Jews comprised nearly five percent of the total white population. The majority of these arrivals came from eastern Europe, mainly Lithuania, and as we have read they were uniformly poor, semi-literate, and Yiddish-speaking (A. Arkin 1984: 60-65; Dubb 1994: 37).

The dramatic influx of unassimilated Jews began to weaken the equilibrium that had existed between the Jewish community and the English and Afrikaner populations. Most of the newcomers did not mix easily with the well-established middle class of acculturated Jews who had begun to meld into the wider white population. This new wave of strangers especially alarmed the white Afrikaners, who had been devastated by the Boer War and felt vulnerable as they moved into the urban areas in search of non-farm employment.

The clouds of anti-Semitism had already begun to gather in the Cape and Natal in 1902 when legislative efforts were made to restrict eastern European immigration on the grounds that Yiddish was not a European language that could qualify for the new literacy standard (Shain 1994: 58). Within four years, Jewish agitation in the Cape and in England succeeded in repealing it. Moreover, the 1906 Aliens Act barred those who lacked the financial means of supporting themselves.

Some scholars have observed that when Jews begin to present themselves as economic competitors, anti-Semitic feelings tend to re-emerge. Certainly in the case of South Africa a critical shift in attitude occurred in the 1930s. Late in the previous decade,

Jewish success in business and politics had become quite visible and had begun to attract envy and resentment. Predominantly English-speaking non-Jews in the upper socio-economic strata perceived that some Jews were monopolizing key sectors of the economy, thus edging out competitors. On the other hand, poor whites, particularly the Afrikaners, saw the new wave of eastern European immigrants as competitors in an ever-tightening blue-collar job market. As long as the economy remained relatively strong, as it did through much of the 1920s, such sentiments remained beneath the surface. However, events in South Africa and abroad in the 1930s changed all that (Cohen 1984: 8-10).

A hint of things to come surfaced in 1930 when the Union government published the Quota Act, which placed an immigration limit for eastern European countries (Sichel 1966: 15). Europe had fallen into deep economic depression, and many of the unemployed were seeking a new life elsewhere. The act had the almost immediate effect of reducing immigration from that region to a trickle.

By contrast, Jewish immigration from Germany had been extremely modest until the Nazis came to power in 1933 and began harassing Jews and enacting blatantly anti-Semitic legislation. Hitler's enactment of the odious Nuremberg Laws, which deprived Jews of their citizenship and led to the confiscation of their properties and businesses, added enormous pressure to leave the country. Between 1933 and 1936, more than six thousand German Jews immigrated to South Africa (Campbell 2000: 101). In 1936 alone, 2,549 Jews arrived: the largest number of Jews ever admitted in a single year (Dubb 1984: 24-26). By then, the country's Jewish population had climbed to ninety thousand, nearly five percent of the total white population and fully seventeen percent of the white population of Johannesburg, where the majority of Jews had been concentrated for more than half a century. Of the total, 46,697 were South African-born (Shimoni 1983: 66). Significantly, since the 1870s the overwhelming majority of South Africa's Jews were urbanized or at least concentrated in the cities and major market towns.

These statistics alarmed the government, which in 1937 countered with a harsh Aliens Act that was explicitly designed to curb the flow of Jewish refugees. It worked. German-Jewish arrivals fell dramatically to 238 in less than a year. Henceforth, every alien immigrant had to be screened by an autonomous Immigrants' Selection Board, the test of entry determined by the applicant's potential assimilability and employability.

By then anti-Semitism had broken to the surface in South African society, not only among Afrikaners in the rural areas of the Transvaal and Orange Free State who saw the small Jewish shopkeepers and traders as obstacles to their own economic advancement, but also among unemployed Afrikaner youth in the urban areas. Many perceived that jobs in trade and industry were falling into the hands of the new immigrants. Shain has noted that "Jews were associated with hegemonic English culture and as such posed a threat to traditional...Afrikaner rural values" (Shain 1998: 69).

Afrikaner ethno-nationalism was also growing and climaxed in 1938 with nationwide celebrations marking the centenary of the Boers' Great Trek. At a time of depression-induced fears and insecurities, Afrikaners were countering with a deeper ethnic self-consciousness which found inspiration in German Nazi ideology of racial purity and the exaltation of the German *volk*, or people. Anti-Jewish sentiments rapidly permeated leadership circles as well as the rank and file of mainstream Afrikaner nationalism. Dutch-born H.F. Verwoerd, editor of *Die Transvaaler*, a leading Afrikaans daily, was one of many outspoken sympathizers of Hitler's National Socialism. He criticized Jewish "over representation" in key economic sectors and suggested that quotas be placed on Jews in those sectors until they reflected the demographic realities of the white population. Reverend D.F. Malan, a power within the Reformed Church, warned Jews that they were "guests" of South Africa, not citizens who deserved to be treated equally. As minister of the interior, Malan helped to push through the 1930 Quota Act (Walker 1957: 627).

Interestingly, both men served as prime ministers in the post–World War II period and became Judeophiles. However, in the late 1930s it was politically correct to be Judeophobic. Anti-Semitism was tolerated then, and it assumed a virulent form in two youth-oriented paramilitary Afrikaner organizations modeled after similar groups in Nazi Germany: the *Ossewa Brandwag* (Oxwagon Sentinel) and the Greyshirts. At intimidating mass rallies and marches, both organizations called for racial purity and the expulsion of Jews from the country. They supported Verwoerd's contention that since Jews were such a tiny minority they should be limited to holding only 5 percent of jobs in commerce and secondary industry (Shain 1994: 146-48).

Newell Stultz argues that anti-Semitism didn't become explicit in National Party thinking until the late 1930s, when some party leaders had clearly fallen under the influence of Aryan theories of German Nazism (Stultz 1974: 44). Nevertheless, overt anti-Semitism dissipated rapidly when South Africa entered the war on the Allies' side. After the war, revelations of the genocidal atrocities committed by the Nazis against the Jews seemed to have deprived South African anti-Semitism of what little moral force it had possessed in the decade before. Moreover, South Africa's economy and job market improved for almost all whites, and anti-Semitism withered in almost direct proportion.

Hermann Giliomee concludes that the anti-Semitism of the National Party in the 1930s was "opportunistic rather than deep rooted." The economy was weakening, Afrikaner unemployment was soaring, and a scapegoat was desperately needed. The Jews were an obvious choice, as they were a cohesive, highly visible, economically successful group, and many were enjoying a conspicuously affluent lifestyle (Giliomee 2003: 96).

If South African Jews were generally successful in business

before the war, they prospered even more afterwards. Immigration resumed anew, and by 1946 Jews numbered 104,156, or 4.4 percent of the country's white population (Dubb 1984: 27-29). Many of the arrivals were highly skilled and turned their knowledge to the country's continuing economic development. More will be said of this later.

The Rise of Zionism

Running concurrently with anti-Semitism were Jewish feelings of Zionism. Indeed, throughout the twentieth century Zionism figured largely in the consciousness of South African Jewry. It is often noted that South African Jews have been among the most ardent Zionists in the world. Perhaps this has to do with the Lithuanian immigrants who had already embraced the notion of an exclusively Jewish homeland before their departure for Africa. Certainly Lithuania is considered the cradle of world Zionism, and as Jews left Europe in huge numbers they carried their Zionists sentiments with them.

The South African Zionist Federation was founded by eastern European immigrants in 1898, scarcely a year after Theodor Herzl had convened the first Zionist Congress in Basel, Switzerland (Frankenthal and Shain 1993: 5). Southern African Jewry responded to his call with immediate enthusiasm, and by 1905 more than sixty Zionist societies were flourishing between Cape Town and Bulawayo in Southern Rhodesia.

In time, the Zionist movement gained crucial support from an unlikely source: the Afrikaner leader Jan Christian Smuts (Shimoni 1980: 65). Smuts, a hero of the Boer War and the First World War, befriended Dr. Chaim Weizmann, who inherited from Herzl the mantle of leadership. Ingham asserts that Smuts was instrumental in 1917 in securing the Balfour Pledge from the British government. Smuts visited Palestine in 1919 and gave his unqualified support for it as the future national Jewish homeland (Ingham 1986: 165-67). Through his efforts, it was endorsed by the League of Nations in 1922, and four years later Smuts's PACT government passed a resolution formally supporting the creation of a Jewish State of Israel.

It is questionable whether Smuts's motives were entirely driven by Judeophilia. He saw a need for the British to have a presence in the region in order to safeguard its position in Egypt and the Suez Canal. A pro-Western European state in the eastern Mediterranean would be a vital bulwark. In any case, Smuts continued his enthusiastic support for the Israeli cause through the decades and pressed it again at the close of the war in 1945.

Another reason for his support of Zionism may have stemmed from the strong financial backing he received from wealthy Jews at home and abroad for his personal political agenda. For years before and after the war, Smuts served as South Africa's prime minister, and he and his United Party consistently won strong support from the Jewish electorate.

Ernest Oppenheimer, himself a member of Parliament from 1924 to 1938, was an ardent supporter of Smuts and his desire to keep South Africa firmly within the British Empire (Hocking 1973: 182). Jews overwhelmingly voted for Smuts in the 1948 all-white elections. This is not surprising considering the National Party's anti-Semitism of a decade earlier. Smuts lost that crucial election to the segregationist and racist Daniel F. Malan, but in the decade ahead, Malan and his party initiated a policy of rapprochement. Jews were admitted to membership in the National Party, and in 1953 Malan made his much-celebrated journey to Israel (Shimoni 1980: 213). South Africa became the first country in the world to extend formal recognition to the new country. Such gestures did much to allay South African Jewish fears of Afrikaner nationalism and to somewhat moderate their criticism of Malan's racist policies at home. While Jews didn't flood into the National Party's ranks, their financial contributions to it grew. Many Jews, worried over postwar labor militancy and black migration into the urban centers, bought into the party's clarion call to unite against the "Black Threat" to white supremacy.

As the twentieth century progressed, South Africa's Jews became more self-confident and more activist in promoting their own interests. They were also becoming more concerned with secular and cultural issues. In 1903, leading Jews in the Transvaal and Natal formed a Jewish Board of Deputies, which they modeled after its parent body in London. A similar chamber was formed in Cape Town a year later (Kentridge 1953: 94).

In the early decades, the board concerned itself primarily with issues of immigration and naturalization. It successfully lobbied for the repeal of the 1902 immigration law that had discriminated against Yiddish-speaking immigrants (Shimoni 1983: 49). The organization was greatly strengthened in 1912 when the Cape Town and Johannesburg units were merged into a unified, countrywide entity, the South African Jewish Board of Deputies. Over the years, the board grew in stature and influence in the corridors of political power. Already by the mid-1920s, it had become an umbrella organization for more than three hundred and twenty Jewish organizations nationwide. Nevertheless, until the 1980s it steadfastly maintained its controversial policy of non-interference in political issues except where Jewish concerns were directly affected (Joseph 1988: 85). As we shall see later, this official neutrality brought it under increasing attack when it failed to take a stand against apartheid.

Jews and South African Culture

From the early twentieth century Jews had been constructing a strong civil society for themselves. They would establish a wide range of philanthropic, cultural, and welfare organizations, including Hebrew day schools, nursing and retirement homes for their elderly, and orphanages. B'nai Briths sprang up in their communities as well as numerous literary societies. By the 1930s, printing presses were turning out a huge number of works in Yiddish as well as in English. Jews had also begun to excel in sports, and in 1935 South Africa sent its first team to the world Maccabi Games in Palestine (Goldman 1984: 174-77).

Jewish intellectuals were assuming important positions in academic disciplines. Max Gluckman and Meyer Fortes became giants in the field of anthropology and wrote many pathbreaking works on traditional African societies. From the 1930s, British colonial authorities north of the Limpopo were interested in applying the new science of social anthropology to the improvement of African welfare. Most of Gluckman's research was undertaken in the British protectorate of Northern Rhodesia, though his influence was international. Fortes did cutting-edge fieldwork in East and West Africa as well. By the 1930s, Jews were being admitted to faculties at the prestigious English-speaking Universities of the Witwatersrand and Cape Town. Jack Simons, a pioneer in African studies at the University of Cape Town, was among them.

The Early Quest for Social Justice

From the early years of the twentieth century Jews cultivated a keen interest in issues involving social justice, and they were the spearheads of so-called South African liberalism. As targets of discrimination themselves, they became associated with Africans and Indians in their struggles for civil and human rights. One of the earliest manifestations of this tendency is found in Natal and involves the activities of Mohandas Gandhi, a young lawyer from India who arrived in South Africa in 1893 to defend a group of Indians who were being discriminated against by the white local authorities. Gandhi stayed on for decades after the trial, and in the first year following the trial he founded the Natal Indian Congress (Davenport and Saunders 2000: 276-77).

While in South Africa, Gandhi turned out an impressive number of newspaper articles addressing such issues as government restrictions on Jewish immigration and the importance of non-violent resistance. His thought-provoking essays attracted a number of Jewish intellectuals, including Henry Polak, a successful attorney for the Transvaal Supreme Court who offered pro bono defenses for Indian passive resistors. He was joined by a young Jewish scholar, Sonja Schlesin, who contributed key organizational skills. Indeed, for years thereafter, Schlesin served as Gandhi's personal secretary, and Polak provided desperately needed capital and wise counsel. In 1903, he helped Gandhi launch a newspaper, *Indian Opinion*, then contributed articles and served as its editor. For years, *Indian Opinion* gave voice to aggrieved Indian merchants in Natal and the Transvaal. Hermann Kallenbach, a well-known architect, added additional visibility to the growing number of highly educated young Jewish professionals who worked closely with Gandhi in those formative years (Hotz 1969: 6-11).

In 1906, Gandhi introduced his passive-resistance philosophy of *satyagraha*, or soul force. And three years later he published his seminal work, *Indian Home Rule*, which enunciated his goal of "an exploitation-free society in which the ordinary individual can claim and defend his rights." Though Gandhi returned permanently to India in 1915, his ideas on non-violent resistance left an enormous impact and legacy on Jewish thinking and in the minds of leading African nationalists across the continent (A. Arkin 1983: 32-35).

Gandhi's ideas could not have been planted at a better time in South African history. From the end of the First World War, the country would experience a revolution in manufacturing similar in impact to the revolution in mining half a century earlier.

Between 1922 and 1929 the nation's annual growth rate averaged 7.6 percent, due largely to the advance of secondary industry. The factory system was expanding dramatically as large companies were established to mass-produce vehicles, footwear, textiles and garments, appliances, food, and the like. Most of these enterprises were labor intensive, but labor was disorganized and easily exploitable. South African industries became notorious for their poor wages and dismal working and living conditions, especially for Indian and African laborers. By the same token, enviable profits accrued to the owners, a disproportionately large number of whom were of Jewish ancestry. As the postwar economy expanded, the income gap between whites and everyone else only widened.

While most Jews, especially those of English and German extraction, pursued careers in business—leaving the public sector to gentiles—a significant number pioneered in the field of labor relations and organization and became activists in left-wing politics. South Africans of Lithuanian and Latvian origin were particularly prominent, probably because it was in their European homeland that Marxian socialism took its early rooting. If, as we've seen, these Baltic countries were cradles of Zionism, they were also breeding grounds of socialism and communism. And the Jewish émigrés were its prime conveyors. Indeed, they were among the first whites to become involved in labor mobilization, and much of it was through the South African Communist Party (SACP), which was founded in 1921 out of an amalgam of several socialist organizations, principally the Jewish-dominated Durban Marxist Club, the Jewish Socialist Society, and the International Socialist League (Walshe 1971: 95). The SACP's Jewish members consisted of a fair number of lawyers and intellectuals, and they tended to provide the key leadership of these radical organizations from their inception.

One of the Communist Party's first forays into labor politics involved the Industrial and Commercial Workers' Union (ICU), founded by Clements Kadalie, a Malawian, in the 1920s. Jews enthusiastically embraced the fledgling African union and drew extremely close to its leadership (Roux 1978: 153-97). Indeed, the ICU's first constitution was written by a Cape Marxist, and some of Kadalie's closest advisers included Jewish labor activists Helen Joseph and Leon Levy. Attorney Emanuel Gluckman provided important legal advice as the union came under attack from the government.

Thus, Africans at crucial moments reached out to Jews in their quest to be organized into unions. In 1927, SACP member Bennie Weinbren was instrumental in establishing the first African industrial union. A year later the South African Federation of Non-European Trade Unions was founded with Weinbren as its first president. Another major figure in the early labor movement was a Latvian émigré named Solly Sachs. Sachs, an ardent socialist with extraordinary organizational and negotiating skills, took a keen interest in the plight of white workers, and in the early '30s he became general secretary of the (all-white, predominantly Afrikaner) Transvaal Garment Workers' Union (GWU). Through a series of strikes Sachs was able to win major wage and benefits concessions from the mainly Jewish employers (Roux 1978: 256).

Predictably, the mainstream Jewish as well as non-Jewish business community generally treated Sachs and the other labor leaders as pariahs and accused them of hatching communist conspiracies aimed at empowering blue-collar workers and destabilizing the country. Sachs, like many of his early Marxist-Leninist contemporaries, tended to see the struggle in South Africa as one between capitalists and workers, not between whites and blacks. Imbued with the paradigm of universal class struggle, they placed less emphasis on race and ethnicity and endeavored to bring non-whites into their activities and organizations (Frankental and Shain 1993: 6). In later years, much of the liberation-style rhetoric of African nationalist leaders was framed in a language learned during their time in training under Jewish Marxists. In sum, an argument can be made that Jews played pivotal roles in laying the foundations of modern unionism and nationalism in South Africa. Clearly, many of the trade unions today are directly descended from those constructed by Jews decades ago.

Another giant of organized labor in the 1930s and '40s was Max Gordon (Roux 1978: 313). A Trotskyite like most of his fellow organizers, he became secretary of the African Laundry Workers' Union in Johannesburg in 1935. Within three years he would also organize bakers and printers into unions and provide the groundwork for the African General Workers' Union (Leatt and Kneifel 1986: 143). In 1938 he combined them into a joint committee under his paternalistic control (Walker 1957: 658). Much of the credit for the massive expansion of African trade unions during the war must go to Gordon. In the '40s, he created numerous African trade unions and provided them with essential leadership training. Nevertheless, in the final analysis Gordon became disillusioned with unionism after Africans tired of his overbearing approach and yearned to free themselves of white hegemony altogether.

South Africa's communists may have championed the cause of blue-collar workers, but by the late 1930s they were deeply divided over their loyalty to Stalin and the central committee of the party in Moscow. The brutality of Stalin's regime and his harassment of the maverick Leon Trotsky caused many South African communists to leave the party or to be expelled from it. From that time onward, tensions persisted within the party between the hard-line Stalinists and the moderates.

An interesting former party member was Latvian-born Hyam Basner (Roux 1978: 294-96). In the late 1920s he fought to protect African tenants against provisions of the Urban Areas Act. After he broke with the SACP in 1939 he devoted his energies to assisting the African National Congress (ANC) in organizational reforms that eventually enabled it to become a more populist movement. In 1947 Basner resigned as a Native Representative in the South African Senate, and fourteen years later he exiled himself to Ghana where he became an influential adviser to Kwame Nkrumah in the development of his pan-African programs.

Another prominent Latvian-born unionist and SACP leader was Rachel "Ray" Alexander Simons. As a youth Ray was involved in the Latvian Communist Party, and when she immigrated to South Africa in 1929 one of her first moves was to join the SACP. While in the Cape Province mobilizing workers in a wide number of trades, her name became synonymous with the Food and Canning Workers' union, which she founded in 1941. Like most Jewish labor union activists, Ms. Alexander recruited workers from all ethnicities and both genders (Gastrow 1987: 4). In 1954 she worked with Helen Joseph, Florence Mkhize, and Lilian Ngoyi to establish the Federation of South African Women, which for years would champion women's rights in the workplace.

Also among the SACP's distinguished members was Rowley Israel Arenstein, a highly regarded Durban attorney who served as a major legal adviser to the South African Congress of Trade Unions (SACTU) in Natal province. In the 1950s Arenstein befriended ANC president Albert Luthuli and became a confidante and legal adviser to him. Some argue that he influenced Luthuli in his passive resistance approach to the struggle for African civil rights. Like Basner, he opposed armed struggle as being contrary to Marxist principles.

After the Second World War, white veterans returned to their mining and manufacturing jobs, while many Africans—who had replaced them during the war—were fired or demoted. This led to severe labor tension and a number of outbursts, including the mammoth African Mineworkers' strike of 1946. Jews, notably Hilda and Lionel Bernstein, played a significant role in its organization and implementation.

Zionism Redux: Flirting with the Israelis

Another immediate and perhaps broader post-war concern for South African Jewry was Zionism and the creation of a Jewish state in the Middle East. Since 1922 the Jewish community had been making substantial public- and private-sector investments in the British Mandate of Palestine, especially in housing for the steady stream of Jewish immigrants from Europe (Gitlin 1950: 234). In 1935, in an act of solidarity, they contributed a team of athletes to the world Maccabi Games. In 1948, during the first Arab-Israeli war, they sent nearly a thousand volunteers after first clandestinely shipping weapons (Saron 2001: 233). By the time of Israel's independence in that year, no other Jewish community in the world was contributing as much, per capita, to the creation and support of the new Zionist nation.

After the Second World War, white Afrikaner nationalists began to seek a rapprochement with South African Jews, who by then had become an economic powerhouse. Within a year after the National Party came to power, Rev. Dr. D.F. Malan, hitherto a Nazi sympathizer and now prime minister, hailed Israel's independence and extended de jure recognition. In 1951 he was instrumental in lifting the ban on Jewish membership in the Transvaal National Party, and two years later he made an official visit to Israel, the first head of government in the world to do so.

Afrikaners, with fresh memories of the Anglo-Boer Wars, were only too happy to see the "Anglos" defeated by Jewish "freedom fighters." They also saw in the new state the fulfillment of Old Testament prophesies. They compared their own history of the divinely sanctioned Great Trek into a hostile interior in the 1830s and their subsequent covenant with God with that of the Old Testament story of the Jewish Exodus to a Promised Land in the Middle East (see Akenson 1992: 151-79). Some historians argue that by combining the two narratives they sought moral and religious justification for their own occupation and control of territory inhabited by other peoples.

As black African nationalism swept across the African continent and the era of decolonization and independence unfolded, Israel sought to build political and economic ties with the new nations of the Third World as well as to win international acceptance for itself (Caterdal 1991: 72). In 1962, Israel sided with the United Nations on a sanctions vote against South Africa, and four years later it supported a resolution calling for an end to South Africa's mandate over South West Africa (Namibia).

Then came the Six-Day War in 1967 and Israel's seizure of Arab lands in the Middle East. South African Jews had made the largest financial contribution of any community in the world to this conflict and its aftermath. Not surprisingly, it was not long before South Africa would join Israel as a pariah state in the world community.

The war was a turning point in the restoration of bilateral relations between what were seen as two alien "settler states." With encouragement from many in the Jewish community, trade and cultural relations between the two countries grew robustly. This accelerated after Israel's Yom Kippur War in October 1973, which led nearly every other African country to break relations with the Zionist state. When two years later the United Nations General Assembly passed a resolution equating Zionism with apartheid, the two countries deepened their ties, especially in the areas of arms trade and the sharing of nuclear materiel and technology.

By 1986, South Africa had become Israel's best single purchaser of its arms, some of which were used against African liberation forces north of the Limpopo River (Reiser 1989: 141). South African Jews and the apartheid state itself also began to make huge investments in Israel's military-related industries. In a kind of quid pro quo, Israel bought into South Africa's segregationist ideology of separate racial and ethnic development when, from the late 1970s, it invested in the ethnic black "Bantustans." In terms of international trade and the need to mitigate sanctions, South Africa began to use Israel as a backdoor into Western markets. Sensitive exports first went to Israel, where they were re-packaged and forwarded to other countries under different labels.

Navigating in Treacherous Waters

As the twentieth century proceeded, mainstream South African Jewry navigated warily among the many -isms: Zionism, African nationalism, Afrikaner nationalism, socialism, capitalism, and communism. Along the way, the Jewish community became deeply divided politically, even though few Jews entirely lost their common emotional tie to their biblical Middle East origins. In the 1960s and '70s, in the wake of growing government repression of non-whites, especially in the aftermath of the Sharpeville Massacre of 1960 and the Soweto Rebellion of 1976, many younger Jews made their *aliyah* (a term referring to Jewish migration to and permanent settlement in Israel) and became citizens. At the other end of the pole were young Jews who joined the South African Defence Force and fought against guerrillas of the African liberation movements in Namibia and Zimbabwe.

Significantly, the powerful and venerable South African Jewish Board of Deputies (SAJBD) remained staunchly Zionist while refusing to take a stand against apartheid, perhaps for fear of polarizing its membership or alienating the country's ruling elites (Cohen 1984: 12-16). The post-Sharpeville era was a prosperous time for Jewish businesses, as real national growth rates fluctuated between 5 and 7 percent. Many key ANC leaders were either in jail or in exile and seemed to pose little threat to the business community. It wasn't until after the Soweto Rebellion of 1976 and rising economic uncertainties that the Board leadership occasionally voiced mild criticism of the regime. And not until 1982 did it speak out against the detentions without trial of apartheid opponents (Shain and Frankental 1997: 54). Nevertheless, when the U.S. Congress passed its Anti-Apartheid Act in 1986 and comprehensive economic sanctions became a reality, the Board of Deputies began to lobby Americans to oppose such penalties, warning they would destabilize the weakening economy. Yet unlike many Christian clergy—notably the Afrikaner iconoclast Reverend Beyers Naude and the African Desmond Tutu—the rabbinate were uniformly silent or equivocal as the country began to slide further into chaos.

Jews as Philanthropists and Business Innovators

Through their uncommon vision and philanthropy, secular and observant Jews and people of Jewish heritage would endow numerous schools, libraries, museums, hospitals, and cultural centers. One encounters their names on public buildings and not-for-profit institutions throughout South Africa. Some scholars suggest that Jewish philanthropy was rooted in the culture of the European shtetl, where *tsdokeh,* or charity, was a cardinal virtue, second only to scholarship as a source of social esteem.

As we've seen, Jews had acquired a huge stake in the country's economic development and had begun to play vital roles in the private sector far out of proportion to their numbers in the total population. Indeed, from the end of the Second World War they and the Afrikaners had been the most economically successful and had taken the most advantage of the manifold human and natural resources that the country had to offer. Still, it began to weigh on the conscience of Jews and Christians alike that whites were in many respects the chief beneficiaries of a patently unjust system called apartheid. But the business community was divided philosophically. Some bristled at the cumbersome state bureaucracies and at the racial restrictions placed on occupational mobility, while others feared that the dismantling of the framework of white supremacy would destroy the economy and erode their quality of life. It was only when the economy began to decline after the mid-1980s that business leaders became more reformist and more outspokenly critical of the apartheid superstructure.

Jews can take a large share of credit for transforming South Africa into the economic giant of sub-Saharan Africa and for giving its white minority population one of the highest standards of living in the world. As new generations of businesspersons came forward, new innovations came with them. Harry Oppenheimer succeeded his father, served in Parliament, gave huge sums of money to charitable organizations, and greatly expanded the vast Anglo-American group of companies into the country's biggest multinational corporate entity and De Beers into the world's largest cutter and private marketer of industrial and gem diamonds. In the field of chain-store retailing, Gus Ackerman's son, Ray, took over Pick n' Pay in the 1960s and transformed it into a retail giant of over two hundred stores. He also pioneered the development of hypermarkets (one-stop shopping) in the mid-1970s with the opening of the gigantic Eastgate mall outside Johannesburg.

From the 1890s, Jews maintained their leadership in food processing, laying the foundations of what became in the mid-twentieth century the mammoth Premier Group and Tiger Oats, Ltd. These two entities have been responsible for processing a substantial proportion of the country's low-cost food staples, and their products are found in nearly every South African home. In the field of life insurance, there is perhaps no peer to Donald Gordon, of Lithuanian Jewish heritage, who revolutionized the country's insurance industry after founding Liberty Life in 1957 (Kaplan 1986: 211). Real estate and hotel development were also of considerable Jewish interest. In the early 1980s, Michael Rapp and Donald Gordon conceived of the huge Sandton City shopping complex, which quickly moved the center of gravity of Johannesburg business towards the suburbs. Also in that decade, real estate mogul Sol Kerzner created the opulent hotel and casino complex called Sun City in the apartheid Bantustan of Bophuthatswana. There, whites and blacks could mingle in a multiracial setting beyond the rigid structures of segregation (Berger 1986: 195).

Novelists, Writers, and Artists

Olive Schreiner, of Jewish heritage and one of nineteenth-century South Africa's greatest novelists, was a key figure in the development of modern Anglophone literature in the country. Her novel *The Story of an African Farm* (1883) had an enormous influence on South African Jewish writers for many decades thereafter (Kanfer 1993: 146). In the twentieth century, Lithuanian-born Sarah Gertude Millin was a prolific liberal novelist of international standing in the 1920s and '30s who late in life sympathized with apartheid, according to her biographer Martin Rubin (Rubin 1977: 20). Decades later, Nadine Gordimer became the single most famous and respected figure in South African fiction and in 1991 won a Nobel Prize for literature. Her many works addressed issues of racism and its dehumanizing effects on South African society. South African–born and educated Dan Jacobson also achieved international fame as a novelist and essayist, even though most of his adult life was spent abroad (Leverson 2000: 60-75). Jews were also prominent in the field of journalism. Anton Harber in 1985 launched the *Weekly Mail,* which soon became South Africa's most outspoken anti-apartheid newspaper.

Beyond literature, Jews distinguished themselves in other cultural realms as well. From the mid-1970s, Johnny Clegg blended Zulu pop and rock to produce wildly popular Juluka music albums that subtly criticized apartheid and contested the notion of culture as something fixed in its parameters. Then there was Barney Simon, who more than any other figure in the country's history advanced the cause of indigenous African theater. A founder of the famous Market Theatre, in the 1970s and '80s he produced many plays that critically addressed issues of apartheid in human lives. He also achieved high recognition for his many media scripts. Finally, in painting, Irma Stern (1894-1966) won world recognition for her works, which today are in major galleries and private collections.

Jews as Defenders of Civil Liberties

A modern history of South African Jewry would be grossly incomplete without noting the pivotal role that some courageous Jews played in defending civil liberties and in advancing the post-1948 anti-apartheid movement (Shain and Mendelsohn 2000: 11-14). There are several strands to the story. Some fought for social and racial justice within the system as jurists, journalists, and members of Parliament, while others became leaders of radical political organizations such as the South African Communist Party (SACP) and the African National Congress (ANC) and ultimately faced harassment, imprisonment, and, for some, dismemberment and death. Nearly all of them may have been motivated by the Jewish notion of *tikkun olam* (world repair) or the "duty of social activism," even though a significant number were secular and alienated themselves from the Jewish community at large. Mainly of Lithuanian birth or ancestry, they idealistically embraced Marxian socialism, which they perceived as fundamentally non-racist, anti-capitalist, and oriented towards a classless secular society.

A turning point came in 1948 with the publication of the Fagan Commission Report, authored by the highly respected Jewish jurist Henry Fagan (Moodie 1975: 63). The report touched off an intense pre-election national debate by asserting that the National Party's (NP) goal of total segregation in South Africa was both impractical and impossible. It concluded that the demographic shift of the Bantu population from the countryside to the urban centers was unavoidable and irreversible. The NP then used this report to raise fears of a black menace and treated the trend as a kind of Trojan Horse phenomenon that would eventually overwhelm the white minority population. In short, the NP won the election that year and immediately launched its program of "apartheid."

In the decades ahead, an avalanche of legislation extended and entrenched racial discrimination and segregation in all spheres of life. This patently retrograde policy mobilized a portion of the Jewish community to become more actively involved with African, Indian, and "Colored" anti-apartheid movements. In 1952 the regime's draconian laws helped to spark the Defiance Campaign, which was brutally put down by government force (Walshe 1971: 402-405). Gradually, trade unions were weakened, occupational discrimination was more deeply institutionalized, and most forms of protest and strikes were illegalized or severely restricted. These harsh and arbitrary measures were effective in that the National Party increased its legislative majority in the elections of 1953 and 1958.

Initially, some Jewish leaders opposed the ANC's adoption of civil disobedience, fearing it might push the government towards more repressive measures and lead to a violent revolution and race war. In 1959, Helen Suzman, a descendant of Lithuanian Jews and a member of Parliament, broke from the mainstream opposition United Party to form the Progressive Party, which for decades hence would keep non-violent anti-apartheid liberalism alive. With courage and perseverance Ms.

Suzman became the lone voice of multiracialism in the national legislature. An internationally respected champion of equal justice for all races, she retired from Parliament in 1989 after 36 years of service and 28 honorary doctorates from leading universities. She died early in 2009.

Others had already become more militant and impatient and gravitated to the Communist Party and the various African trade unions as members and key organizers. Lithuanian-born attorney Joe Slovo, an avowed Stalinist and general secretary of the South African Communist Party, was instrumental in drafting the Freedom Charter, which was adopted by the ANC in 1955 (Karis and Gerhart 1977: 205). It introduced a non-racial ideology into the liberation struggle by proclaiming that "South Africa belongs to all who live in it, black and white." The Charter remained the benchmark of opposition to apartheid into the 1990s and gave the liberation struggle a necessary moral force. In 1985, in recognition of his huge role in the anti-apartheid movement, Slovo's African compatriots made him the first white ever to serve on the all-powerful National Executive Committee of the ANC.

After the Suppression of Communism Act of 1950, the Communist Party was banned, and Marxian Jews were forced to resign from all legislative bodies and from the civil service. Radical Jews henceforth began to work covertly with black African nationalists with the intention of undermining the government through peaceful demonstrations, bus boycotts, and strikes.

The Sharpeville Massacre of 1960 and the intensification of police suppression that followed further radicalized the activists and forced many either into exile or into underground cells. As civil liberties continued to erode in the name of fighting terrorism, the liberation struggle shifted from a strategy of civil disobedience to violent confrontation (Gerhart 1978: 242-52). Joe Slovo with Nelson Mandela and Walter Sisulu became intimately involved in the formation of *Umkhonto we Sizwe* (Spear of the

Nation), which functioned as the armed wing of the ANC. Another Jewish activist, Ronnie Kasrils, took leadership of Umkhonto's military intelligence entrusted with sabotage. Ben Turok also assumed a strong leadership position in the organization. Frankel notes that the structure and terminology of Umkhonto was adapted from the Irgun, Menachem Begin's Jewish underground movement that fought the British in Palestine in the late 1940s.

The anti-apartheid campaign was severely weakened in 1963 when police raided the joint headquarters of the ANC and SACP in the Johannesburg suburb of Rivonia. Many Africans were arrested along with five whites, all of whom were Jews. At the Rivonia trial the following year, a prominent Jewish attorney, Percy Yutar, acting as Transvaal state prosecutor, argued that the defendants were guilty but recommended a charge of sabotage rather than treason (Frankel 2000: 187-98). Consequently, the judge spared the lives of Mandela, Sisulu, and most of the others by giving them life imprisonment on Robben Island.

At the treason trial and in numerous other trials from the late 1950s, Jewish lawyers courageously defended both victims and opponents of apartheid. Isie Maisels led the defense team for the 1958 treason trial and won acquittals, while Arthur Chaskalson, a human rights lawyer, founded the Legal Resources Centre in 1978 to challenge apartheid laws. Albie Sachs and Ruth First, Slovo's wife, were also vocal defenders of human rights; it cost Sachs a limb, and First her life.

Jews and the Post-Soweto Era

The Soweto Rebellion of 1976 furthered polarized the Jewish community. Most individuals moved to the political left, while significant numbers threw their support to the ruling National Party. Indeed, in elections the following year, over 70 percent of

Jewish voters in many urban districts supported the Nationalists as the party best able to fight terrorism and black militancy. In the late 1970s many Jews accepted the government's pledge to "reform" apartheid, and most of those in the business community, beleaguered by wildcat strikes and worker boycotts, entered into a formal dialogue with the regime. In 1979, the government gave black workers the right to organize and bargain collectively. But that vital concession only raised worker expectations and motivated them to escalate their demands.

By the early 1980s resistance had become more widespread, and it seemed evident to a growing segment of the Jewish population that apartheid was tearing the nation apart and moving it towards civil war and economic chaos. Black township violence, work "stay-aways," and consumer boycotts were reducing worker productivity and corporate profits. In 1980 alone, black unions called 207 strikes, costing industry 175,000 man-days. And from 1985, a growing number of key foreign companies were leaving the country.

To the north, the four-centuries-old Portuguese Colonial Empire ignominiously ended with the establishment of Marxist-led Angola and Mozambique. And just across the Limpopo River the white Rhodesian regime of Ian Smith had capitulated to the liberation armies of Robert Mugabe and Joshua Nkomo. The liberation struggle in Namibia was also well under way.

In South Africa, local government in the racially segregated black townships was collapsing in the face of resistance from a number of mass movements. Thus, vast sums of public funds had to be spent fighting so-called terrorists both at home and across borders. South Africa was geopolitically encircled and internationally isolated. And across the nation the newly formed Congress of South African Trade Unions (COSATU) rapidly gained in strength and militancy on the shop floors of white-owned factories and in the streets. The South African business community also feared that ever-growing pressures for comprehensive international sanctions would adversely affect their own trade, finance, and ability to borrow money to meet its mounting debts. By 1987 leading members of the Jewish and Christian business community opened their own dialogue with exiled members of the African National Congress in Zambia in hopes of avoiding a bloody upheaval. For Jews, it was a question of ensuring their own survival in an increasingly hostile and dangerous country.

Jews and the Post-Apartheid World: Exodus Redux?

The deteriorating events of the 1980s and early 1990s accelerated the exodus of whites from the country, especially professional Jews with skills that were in need overseas. The release of Nelson Mandela from prison in 1990 and the official end of apartheid were greeted by most Jews, especially the youth, with relief. However, it only temporarily slowed the exodus. Indeed, between 1980 and 1990, South Africa would lose more than 26,000 Jews, declining from nearly 118,000 to about 92,000 (Dubb 1994: 37). Many of them took with them critical skills. Already by 1990, fully 17,000 South African Jews had settled in Israel alone (Kaplan and Robertson 1991: 256).

South African President F.W. de Klerk and his Nationalist Party were growing alarmed by the loss of Jewish talent and capital. In the early 1990s, he tried to gain the support of the Jewish community by taking a pro-Israel stance and paying a state visit to Tel Aviv. In 1993, he appointed the first Jew in South African history to a cabinet post (Goldberg 2002: 46). His overtures were too late and gained little traction.

Most South African Jews warmly welcomed Mandela's release and his elevation in 1994 as the country's first African head of state. The ANC had unequivocally emerged as the pre-eminent force of South African politics. Nevertheless, some Jews were of mixed mind over the ANC electoral landslide, for it raised fears of a one-party state dominated almost entirely by a movement that almost since its founding had taken an anti-capitalist, Marxist-tinged stance. Not surprisingly, in elections that year only one in nine Jews cast their vote for the ANC, while over half voted for the more centrist Democratic Party headed by Tony Leon, a fellow Jew who garnered 80 percent of their vote (Shain 2002: 106-107). By then, it was estimated that the country's Jewish population had fallen below 65,000 and was declining at a steadily accelerating rate.

The communal violence, crime, and insecurity that both preceded and followed the transformation to African majority rule only accelerated the exodus of Jews, especially professionals in early middle age with portable skills. By 2005, possibly fewer than 25,000 Jews remained in the country, and of those a large percentage were elderly and/or people with fixed assets that could not easily be liquidated. Since the 1980s, rural Jews, always a minority, have been drifting to the cities, mainly Cape Town, leaving behind abandoned enterprises and empty synagogues.

Demographically, significant changes have occurred since the end of official apartheid and the commencement of African majority rule. Political upheavals and rapid social and economic change have fueled Jewish anxieties over their future in South Africa and have contributed to a revival of Orthodox Judaism and a renewed search for spirituality. Some observers suggest that overall Jews who have remained in South Africa have become more Jewish in both their identity as Jews and in their religiosity. Indeed, a return to a more observant lifestyle has been noted by a number of scholars. This "born-again" Judaism is most profoundly revealed in the growth of the Lubavitch Hasidic and Ba'al Teshuva movements. The latter term translates loosely to "those who have returned to Orthodox Judaism" and has found wide favor among the youth.

Obviously, Zionism—which in its heyday was practically the civil religion of South African Jewry—has lost some of its former power over the country's foreign policy with regard to Israel and the Middle East. Many Jews still seem to identify closely with Israel, and its president was invited by Mandela to his inauguration in 1994. Since then trade and diplomatic relations have remained positive. In 1999 President Mandela visited Israel, and in 2004 Israel's then deputy prime minister, Ehud Olmert, returned the gesture. Bilateral trade remained strong, and in 2007 South African exports to Israel increased by 14 percent, while imports grew by 24 percent. A survey of South African Jewish opinion in the late 1990s revealed that 87 percent of respondents held a special attachment to Israel, and fewer than 1 percent expressed negative opinions about the country and its policies..

Since black majority rule in 1994, Africans have made an effort to involve Jews in shaping the country's future. The late Joe Slovo became a member of Nelson Mandela's cabinet, and the respected jurist Arthur Chaskalson was appointed the first president of the Constitutional Court, where he was joined in membership by civil rights attorney Albie Sachs. The court was established to interpret, protect, and enforce the new post-apartheid constitution. The constitution contains a Bill of Rights thanks in part to Mr. Sachs, who persuaded the ANC to support it.

As the twenty-first century opened, many radical Jewish leaders in the old liberation movement had either gone into retirement and/or distanced themselves ideologically from their earlier Marxist orientation. Late-middle-age Jews still enjoyed a strong presence as scholars in leading educational institutions, while others remained in senior positions in the legal professions. Statistics suggest that younger people with skills in the health professions have been emigrating at an accelerating pace. Many owners of profitable businesses continued to operate them but have acceded to governmental affirmative action pressures to bring significant numbers of Africans into management positions. The Mandela and Mbeki governments have been quite accommodating to the private sector and have refrained from nationalizations or confiscations of private property. Economically, South Africa has posted high annual GDP growth rates since majority rule but has not succeeded in reducing extremely high unemployment rates among Africans.

Jewish emigration did not end with the end of apartheid, and most Jews face their personal and collective future with a mixture of equanimity and uncertainty. Feelings of vulnerability today seem less inspired by anti-Semitism than by worries over personal security in an age of escalating crime. Fortunately, there have been no major outbreaks of anti-Semitism since the fall of apartheid.

Aliyah (migration to Israel) has increased gradually, with little indication of a stampede. In July 2008, the South African Zionist Federation in Israel and the Jewish Agency for Israel sponsored their first organized aliyah from South Africa with one hundred people. It will probably not be the last.

CHAPTER FIVE

Jews and Judaism in Central and Eastern Africa

Countries in Central and Eastern Africa with Jewish Populations in the Late Nineteenth and Twentieth Centuries

New Immigration from Eastern Europe

South Africa was a springboard for European Jews seeking business opportunities north of the Limpopo River. Not surprisingly, they were predominantly of Lithuanian and Latvian backgrounds, and from the early twentieth century they became an important catalytic force in the economic development of colonial British East and Central Africa. Ashkenazics were instrumental in laying the foundations of the major colonial towns and cities of Kenya and Northern and Southern Rhodesia, contributing to their governance as mayors and municipal councilors.

In the early decades of the century they opened businesses in the urban centers as jewelers, tailors, pharmacists, butchers, brewers, and hoteliers. In the rural areas they operated general merchandise outlets that catered to white settlers and Africans alike. They were among the most passionate promoters of private enterprise, taking early leadership positions in chambers of commerce. Jews founded some of the first trading and transport companies and developed expansive networks of commodity production and distribution (Macmillan and Shapiro 1999: 291).

In Northern Rhodesia especially, the Susman and Diamond families led fellow Jews into cattle ranching, the abattoir business, and the marketing of beef to the labor-intensive mining industries of the Copperbelt and the Belgian Congo. Added to this were the great cattle routes they blazed to markets in Angola and South Africa. In Southern Rhodesia after World War II they gravitated towards light industry and developed some of the most successful textile, timber, and furniture enterprises in the colony. In South West Africa from the early 1920s, the Sam Cohen family distributed trucks, tractors, tires, and heavy earth-moving equipment to both the public and private sectors. And with their family's accumulated wealth, they invested in the extractive industries and in charitable causes (Gill 1956: 20-35).

The immigrants were initially young individual men escaping anti-Semitism and poor economic opportunity in their homelands. But before long they were joined by family members, and their subsequent business enterprises were built on tightly knit extended family networks. Most arrived either with little or no capital or represented more prosperous relatives with well-established business concerns in South Africa. Because in the early years the region had no banks or credit facilities, those with capital or who accumulated it early on lent it to their coreligionists on the basis of trust founded on family, kinship, and a shared heritage in the Baltic provinces of the Russian Empire. They readily mastered English, though the first generation found a degree of solidarity in Yiddish. Like their counterparts in South Africa, they tended to be fervent Zionists, and Zionist organizations were among the first social institutions they founded in their new communities.

Jews in Portuguese East Africa

In Portuguese Mozambique, however, the story takes a slightly different twist. A few Afro-Portuguese families of partial Jewish ancestry, like the da Silva-Portos and the Fonsecas, had been involved for centuries in the interior river valleys as *prazeros*, or plantation owners, trading in slaves and ivory. It was only after the conclusion of an Anglo-Portuguese boundary agreement in 1891 that European merchant capitalism began to enter the huge colony and spark its economic takeoff. To help pave the way, Benjamin and Leon Cohen were instrumental in forming the Camara do Comercio de Lourenco Marques, which was tasked with lobbying the colonial government to establish laws and business contracts favorable to European interests. With such a favorable business environment, small Portuguese Jewish communities emerged in the colonial capital of Lourenco-Marques and in the port of Beira, both of which by 1926 boasted tiny though flourishing synagogues (Penvenne 1999: 30).

Portugal, in its imperial, transcontinental dream of connecting its East African Indian Ocean colony with Angola on the Atlantic, had just been through a series of conflicts with interior African chieftaincies. In a vicious "pacification" program, the Portuguese authorities used African warlords to conquer on their behalf and rewarded them with their plunder. Carl Wiese, a Berlin merchant writing in 1889, observed the near-genocidal raids: "In their bloody raids whole regions are devastated just as if a violent hurricane had passed over them...the men are killed or sold and women and children who escape death are exchanged with the Arabs for powder or trade goods or go into productive slavery" (Newitt 1981: 52).

Once the vast inland territories had been seized and the expanding colony's international boundaries had been delimited, the mainly South African-based entrepreneurs sought to exploit the region's rich natural and human resources. The Arab and Swahili slave traders were expelled, and ties were broken with some of the very chiefs who had collaborated with the colonial authorities. Then, with scant financial resources of its own, the colonial government welcomed private companies and gave out huge land concessions as an incentive. Christians and Jews alike responded. One of the earliest Jewish pioneers was Carl (or Carlos) Wiese, who began as an ivory trader, forged alliances with important Afro-Portuguese families, and later secured several mining concessions from the colonial authorities in Beira. He was followed by Albert Ochs, a Belgian Jew who had made a fortune in South Africa (Macmillan 1999: 6).

By 1895 Ochs had acquired a controlling interest in the fast-growing Mozambique Company, which held enormous land and mineral concessions between the Zambesi and Sabi rivers and westward to the boundary with Cecil Rhodes's British South Africa Company in Mashonaland. The government-chartered Mozambique Company was set up in 1891 as a counterbalance to the British South Africa Company, which had territorial designs on the backwater Portuguese colony.

Ochs quickly accumulated a fortune subleasing his lands to mining companies and levying punitive hut taxes on the African populations that less than a decade earlier had been conquered by Portuguese imperial forces. He also established commercial sugar plantations on the Zambesi while giving out land concessions to white immigrant farmers in the Manica highlands. Ochs sold out to British interests in 1910, but not before helping to lay the foundations for Mozambique's subsequent colonial exploitation and development. It should also be noted here that Jews in Beira were successful pioneers in the trading and transportation sectors. The most prominent among them was Yorkshire-born Julius Alston who in 1892 founded what soon became the huge Manica Trading Company (Kosmin 1980: 13).

In the twentieth century, Mozambique became a major labor pool for the mining companies of the South African Rand. Jewish firms based in the Mozambican capital—notably Breyner & Wirth—participated in the recruitment process. Still, the Portuguese colony never attracted many Jewish entrepreneurs, and throughout the twentieth century the Hebrew community remained miniscule and nearly invisible (Penvenne 1995: 30).

The Lemba: The Earliest Jews of Southern Africa?

It is quite conceivable that the Bantu-speaking Lemba peoples who today live along the border separating Zimbabwe and South Africa are the oldest community of Jews in southern Africa. In the early 1990s geneticists discovered that approximately 9 percent of Lemba males carry a DNA signature that is characteristic of the *cohanim*, a priestly, hereditary caste arguably descended from Aaron, brother of the biblical Moses (Parfitt 1992: 344-45; Parfitt and Egorova 2006: 70-73).

Dr. Tudor Parfitt of Oxford believes he has traced Lemba roots to Senna, a remote valley in southern Yemen on the Arabian Peninsula. Drawing on Lemba oral history and his own exhaustive fieldwork, Parfitt estimates that they migrated to southern Africa via the Indian Ocean and the Swahili coast of Tanzania or Mozambique about a thousand years ago. Lemba legends suggest that they may have been involved in the construction of such ancient stone-walled towns as Great Zimbabwe, though hard evidence is still lacking. Since at least the early twentieth century, the Lemba have progressively converted to Christianity, though many of their rituals still bear a strong resemblance to those of Judaism. They remain a population that essentially lives apart from their neighbors and has been largely endogamous for uncounted generations. Despite mounting evidence, the white Jewish communities of South Africa and Zimbabwe have been divided over accepting their authenticity.

The Modern Jewish Impact on Zimbabwe and Zambia

The Jewish presence and impact in what is today Zimbabwe and Zambia were considerably larger than in Mozambique, even though Jews never composed more than a tiny minority. They were among the earliest white settlers in the African empire of Matabeleland and were instrumental in its ultimate conquest by the British arch-imperialist and diamond and gold magnate Cecil Rhodes of South Africa. English-born Daniel Kisch came into Matabeleland in 1868, involved himself in gold mining, and for nearly five years served as personal secretary to its African ruler, Lobengula (Kosmin 1980: 2). In 1875 a German Jew named Augustus Greite and his family established an export business in ostrich feathers and ivory in Bulawayo, the Matabeleland capital. Bulawayo would soon become the center of Jewish activity in Central Africa. By 1894 the small Bulawayo Jewish community had formed a congregation, with one of its members serving as the city's first mayor.

For years, Cecil Rhodes had been determined to conquer the region, not only because he believed it held huge deposits of gold but also to fulfill his dream of a north/south British African empire extending from Cairo, Egypt, to Cape Town, at the tip of the continent. Rhodes also wanted to ensure that it would not fall under the expanding Afrikaner's South African Republic based in the Transvaal or face annexation by the Portuguese, who sought to construct a vast trans-African colonial empire.

In the late 1880s, the Mozambican authorities used the private armies of a slave and ivory trader of Goan ancestry to expand their control inland. The mechanism for imperial expansion would be a private chartered firm, the Mozambique Company. Alarmed by this trend, Rhodes obtained a British-government charter for his own corporation, the British South Africa Company, which conferred upon it the right to form an army and engage in treaties with African chiefs. The Portuguese were soon checkmated, and in 1890, Rhodes's newly chartered British South Africa Company sent a "Pioneer Column" of English-speaking Jewish and Christian families under military escort to occupy African lands north of the Limpopo River and to establish farms and businesses that might service the company's new mining operations (Wills 1964: 140-52; Kosmin 1980: 7).

The local King Lobengula of Matabeleland was alarmed by this illegal occupation and sought to ally himself with a Rhodes rival as a counterforce. A year later, Edward Lippert, a German Jew based in Johannesburg, took advantage of this situation. He met with Lobengula and his trusted friend and interpreter, the Christian missionary Reverend John Moffat, and persuaded the king to sign the so-called Lippert Concession. For a paltry thousand pounds sterling, Lobengula conceded to Lippert the sole right to issue land titles in his empire for a period of a hundred years. Lippert, originally posing as an opponent of Rhodes, then sold the concession to him for thirty thousand pounds. Rhodes and his British South Africa Company used the Lippert Concession in a brazen attempt to legitimize their control over nearly all the lands embracing neighboring Mashonaland (Rotberg 1988: 337).

This opened the floodgates to European settlement and to massive land transfers of dubious legality from Africans to Europeans. In 1893-94, Rhodes provoked Lobengula into war, which the latter lost. A futile rebellion between 1896 and 1897 ended African sovereignty altogether. By 1901 the white settler population of what came to be called "Southern Rhodesia" (now Zimbabwe) climbed to more than 11,000 out of a disenfranchised African population of well over half a million.

Already by 1897 Jews composed more than six percent of the new colony's two emerging cities, Bulawayo and the capital, Salisbury. And by the turn of the century they were prominent in such occupations as merchants, shopkeepers, hoteliers, auctioneers, and brokers (Kosmin 1980: 10).

The colony's most fertile lands were now held by the white minority. The dislocated Africans cried foul, and in 1918 the British Crown declared the Lippert Concession bogus and asserted sovereign rights to the lands. However, by then it was too late, as much of the concession had already been subdivided into white farms and mining complexes. In fewer than six years Southern Rhodesia (named after Rhodes) would become a full-fledged colony internally governed first by the company and, from the 1920s, by local white elites as a formal British colony. From the start, Jews were involved in municipal governance, and in the first two decades of white settlement some of the earliest mayors of the colony's two major cities—Bulawayo and Salisbury—were Jews.

Though Jews played pivotal roles in the development of British East and Central Africa, they were always a minority; the white populations were overwhelmingly Protestant Anglican, Presbyterian, or Dutch Reformed. This was partly due to stringent immigration laws that made it difficult for Sephardic Jews to enter, especially if they spoke *ladino* (a hybrid of Spanish and Hebrew), which was not on the list of acceptable languages. Most Jews were therefore Ashkenazic, because Yiddish was considered a European language (Kosmin 1980: 62). Nevertheless, in the 1930s, when the British Colonial Office considered allowing victims of the Holocaust to immigrate in large numbers to the Rhodesias—and though most local Jews were prepared to welcome them—the local whites, who by then numbered almost 135,000, successfully blocked it. This was at a time when some of Salisbury's most successful Jews were Sephardic Greeks who had been trickling in from the Mediterranean island of Rhodes since 1906.

In 1921 Southern Rhodesia had the largest Jewish population in East and Central Africa, yet even then it numbered only 1,289 (Kosmin 1980: 63). It peaked in the early 1960s at about 8,000 out of a total white community of approximately 225,000 and an African population exceeding 4 million. In Northern Rhodesia (today Zambia), Jews never numbered more than about 1,000, and in Kenya around 330. Even though Southern Rhodesia's Jews constituted no more than 5 percent of the white population in 1911, they had already accounted for nearly 40 percent of all retail business and would hold that margin throughout most of the century until black majority rule in 1980.

Until the 1950s, Jews in the Rhodesias maintained a low profile in central government affairs, though they followed politics closely and were avid voters. This changed somewhat after 1953 when Northern and Southern Rhodesia and British Nyasaland were merged to form the Central African Federation. A key architect in the merger, and the federation's prime minister from 1956, was Sir Roy Welensky, a self-educated Northern Rhodesian labor leader whose impoverished father was a Lithuanian Jew and whose mother was an Afrikaner convert to Judaism. Though Welensky believed in white domination and distrusted African nationalists, he favored the education of Africans and their limited participation in the political process (Rotberg 1965: 360-61). However, with uncommon prescience he warned that if the country fell too soon under African rule, economic turmoil and political disarray would surely follow.

During the federation's brief and politically tumultuous life— from 1953 to 1963—the economies of the three units flourished, especially that of Southern Rhodesia. Salisbury, the federal capital, grew rapidly and attracted Jewish and Christian immigrants from South Africa, Great Britain, and the United States. Welensky keenly supported white immigration and put his colleague Bennie Goldberg to work in the Department of Home Affairs to promote it. By 1961, the federation's white population reached 312,000 (210,000 in Southern Rhodesia alone). Unexpectedly, its African population grew even faster and exceeded 8 million (Kosmin 1980: 106-107).

Between 1958 and 1962 labor issues in Southern Rhodesia were handled in part by a remarkably liberal cabinet minister, Abe Abrahamson, who favored the formation of multiracial trade unions and the repeal of the odious Land Apportionment Act. Unfortunately he lost his position prematurely, as the white population moved steadily rightward and Africans became more militant in the workplace. The Central African Federation was meant to be multiracial and democratic, yet Africans remained effectively disenfranchised. For example, in a federal referendum of 1956, Africans cast 560 votes out of an electorate of 49,060 (O'Meara 1975: 60).

With a plentiful labor force, an expanding consumer base, and spiraling world demand for minerals, many white-owned businesses extended their operations throughout the federation. For example, Northern Rhodesia–based Susman Brothers & Wulfson established numerous subsidiaries and, according to Hugh Macmillan, eventually became one of the largest and most extensive family-based businesses in southern Africa (Macmillan 2005: 411). Early on they established a mutually profitable relationship with the royal Lozi family (Macmillan 2005: 15). Moreover, by 1912, the Susman brothers had established a 25,000-acre ranch outside Lusaka, the protectorate's capital (Macmillan and Shapiro 1999: 60).

In Northern and Southern Rhodesia, Jews had been acquiring vast tracts of farmland since the 1920s. Some family interests owned multiple farms totaling tens of thousands of acres. Enjoying easier access to capital than the surrounding African smallholders, they were able to purchase machinery and irrigation equipment to vastly increase agricultural efficiency and output. Thus, not only was the federation capable of providing a bounty of food for itself, but it became a major food exporter to all of southern and Central Africa. By the 1920s, Northern Rhodesian Jews, both as ranchers and cold storage owners, had become major suppliers of meat to the mining companies of the Copperbelt and those northward in the Belgian Congo. And within a decade they would diversify into textiles and timber.

On the other hand, Jews with marginal trading and farming enterprises in the rural towns were beginning to settle in the major urban areas as manufacturing and service employment grew faster there. While the mining companies were generally massive and foreign controlled, local capital from wealthy white Rhodesians had by the 1950s become a factor of major importance to the overall economy.

Control over agricultural land had been a burning issue in Southern Rhodesia since the British conquest, and it became even more so when the Land Apportionment Act of 1931 reserved more than half the colony's land for Europeans only (Gann 1969: 268-69). Consequently, many African peasant farmers were evicted from their ancestral lands and forced into communal areas of only marginal soil fertility, where few could exist much beyond bare subsistence. The regime had created a huge landless class of peasants juxtaposed against a tiny white gentry.

Not surprisingly, the federation was highly unpopular among Africans, who saw it as a vehicle for further local white aggrandizement and more intensive racial discrimination. Numerous racially discriminatory laws originating in white-dominated Southern Rhodesia were extended into the other political units of the federation. By 1961, income disparities had reached the point where the average annual income of whites was 1,266 pounds, while that of Africans a paltry 100 (O'Meara 1975: 158).

These inherent inequalities only fanned the flames of African nationalism in each of its three administrative components: Southern Rhodesia, Northern Rhodesia, and Nyasaland. Thus, in 1963, the British authorities in London dismantled the federation and within a year gave Northern Rhodesia and Nyasaland their independence as Zambia and Malawi, respectively. Southern Rhodesia, with its sizeable white population, reverted to Crown Colony status.

These seismic events added more fears and fuel to settler European nationalism, and in 1965 the white population of Southern Rhodesia unilaterally and illegally declared its own independence as the "Republic of Rhodesia." Intially, local Jewish businessmen and industrialists generally opposed the move for fear of losing their extensive trade and investment links to the British and Commonwealth economies. However, events after 1965 transformed their opposition into enthusiastic support.

Indeed, Rhodesia may have failed to gain international diplomatic recognition, but in the face of ensuing sanctions, the economy actually prospered as the government encouraged and protected a rapidly diversifying industrial sector. Jews and Christians alike benefited from this import-substitution–led boom. They were also quite successful in resorting to sanctions-busting tactics until 1975, when neighboring Mozambique became an independent Marxist state and closed its seaports to them. Moreover, from 1972 the African liberation forces expanded their guerrilla operations and randomly attacked white properties, especially commercial farms.

Anti-Semitism, never very strong after World War II, largely vanished as the white population in general became increasingly vulnerable and defensive. In the face of these cascading events, the once-robust economy began to decline and terrorist activity escalated in the countryside. White immigration practically ceased, and Jews soon joined other whites in their exodus from the strife-torn rural areas and began to hunker down in the cities.

Black majority rule was finally achieved in 1980 after protracted negotiations among the African nationalists, the British government, and the Rhodesian regime under Ian Smith. For the next seven years, the economy declined further in the face of a sanguinary civil war and the erosion of government services and infrastructure. Moreover, the Mugabe regime had begun to push its socialist agenda more vigorously.

Jewish emigration accelerated, and by 2007 only a tiny remnant of about 600 Jews remained, concentrated almost entirely in Bulawayo and Harare, the nation's capital. They were tenuously linked to each other by the dwindling Central African Zionist Organization and the Jewish Board of Deputies. In Zambia and Zimbabwe synagogues were closing in the 1990s for lack of rabbis, and by the early twenty-first century, many of the small Jewish businesses were shuttered or sold to local African entrepreneurs, while the larger ones with subsidiaries were unbundled and sold as separate corporate entities. A few enterprises remained in Jewish hands, but most of the former owners served as managers with residual equity. Under President Mugabe's land reform program, most white farmlands, taken from Africans during the colonial era, were confiscated and redistributed to Africans loyal to the regime. By 2008 nearly the entire white commercial agricultural sector had been extinguished.

Jews in East Africa: Kenya and Uganda

British East Africa was never a region of significant Jewish settlement, but at one point it came close to becoming a new African Zion. In 1902 the British had recently completed their costly Uganda Railway from Mombasa on the Indian Ocean across Kenya and on to Kampala near Lake Victoria in the just-created Uganda Protectorate. Nairobi was about halfway along the line and became a refueling and repair center for the passing locomotives. Sir Charles Eliot, Kenya's governor, convinced Joseph Chamberlain, Britain's colonial secretary, that white settlers were desperately needed to establish farms and businesses to generate freight revenue for the money-losing railway (Bennett 1963: 8). Already a small settler community of farmers was emerging in the temperate, malaria-free highlands of Kenya, but its growth was modest. Chamberlain approached Dr. Theodor Herzl, Europe's top Zionist leader, with the idea of establishing a 5,000-square mile-Zionist colony along the Kenya-Uganda border for refugees from anti-Semitic pogroms in Russia's Baltic provinces (Trzebinski 1985: 49).

Herzl greeted the "Uganda Scheme" enthusiastically, reasoning that it might be a prelude to an ultimate Jewish homeland in Palestine. He was also impressed by the tiny Jewish community in Nairobi, which by 1904 had founded the Nairobi Zionist Association. Lithuanian-born Abraham Block, who became an enormously successful hotelier and founder-patriarch of the Bock family enterprises in Kenya, would become mayor of Nairobi, Kenya's colonial capital (Trzebinski 1985: 46).

Though anti-Semitism was not visible at that time, the white settler community, which was almost entirely Christian and led by an aristocratic farmer, Lord Delamere, mounted an aggressive campaign against the scheme, arguing that the Jewish refugees had no capital to invest, knew little about farming, and would not fit in to an intensely Anglicized colonial culture (Bennett 1963: 12). Kenya's commissioner, Sir Charles Eliot, conceded and began to lobby officials in London. Dr. Herzl, despite heavy lobbying of his own among fellow Zionists, also met with resistance. Most of his Zionist followers complained that the proposed land grant was insufficient to maintain a viable colony. Thus, at the 7th Zionist Congress in July 1905, after acrimonious debate, a resolution was passed opposing the scheme and calling for a full-fledged colony in the "Promised Land" of Israel in Palestine. Herzl died shortly afterwards, and the idea of a Jewish homeland in Africa was never revived (Trzebinski 1985: 111).

Kenya proper also did not hold much promise for Jews. Retailing in Nairobi, Mombasa, and most major towns was dominated by Gujaratis from British India, and modern commercial farming in the highlands was monopolized by Lord Delamere and his clique of English gentry. The Indians would also dominate the textile industry for nearly three decades after the Second World War. On the other hand, in the port city of

Mombasa, Otto Markus, an Austrian Jew, had founded the East African Trading Company in 1904 and was among the first settlers to see the potential of cotton growing in East Africa.

The Block family patriarch, Abraham, went into farming, then ranching, and by the 1920s into the retail trade. In 1947 the family diversified into the hotel business and finally into finance and cinemas. Even before Kenya's independence and African majority rule in 1963, the Blocks had begun to build alliances with leaders in the African business community. By 1974, Abraham's son, Jack, held thirty-six places on the boards of foreign firms, thirty-three of which he owned partially or wholly (Swainson 1980: 206).

The small Jewish community was successful in building close ties between Israel and Kenya and with the white settler political and business elites. Issy Somen, a leading member of the Nairobi Jewish community, served as the city's mayor in 1955-57 (Lerman 1989: 99). And though diplomatic links with Israel were severed following the 1973 Yom Kippur War, they were restored a decade later, in part through mediation by some influential Jewish businessmen.

Unlike Kenya, British Uganda never had a significant foreign-born Jewish community, but it did benefit from an extremely farsighted Jewish colonial governor, Sir Andrew Cohen, who served from 1952 to 1956. Cohen, a Fabian Socialist, introduced sweeping reforms at local and central government levels that resulted in greater African participation. With uncommon vision he advanced African higher education and encouraged the development of Makerere College. Few colonial governors in postwar Africa worked as vigorously as Cohen did to prepare Ugandans for political independence (Apter 1967: 264-76).

Judaism did emerge nonetheless as an indigenous grassroots phenomenon. In 1919 a tiny group of Africans broke from their colonialist Christian church, rejected the New Testament, and embraced Judaism. These so-called Abayudaya did not claim a lineage to the Solomonic rulers of antiquity and did not even receive a Hebrew Bible until it was presented to them in 1926 by two itinerant European Jewish traders. Still, the community grew and by 1970 it boasted 30 synagogues and nearly 3,000 members. Then in 1972 Idi Amin, Uganda's mercurial Muslim dictator, banned Judaism, shut down over 30 synagogues, and demanded that all Jews in the country renounce their faith. In less than a decade Abayudaya's membership would fall to less than 500 in only 6 synagogues. Throughout this period of distress, the chief rabbis of Israel refused to recognize the community, and only since the mid-1990s has it begun to revive, thanks mainly to the efforts of a small group of American Jews (Ross 2000: 15-55).

It is worth noting here the origins of Amin's anti-Semitism and its regional implications. Sudan, an Arab-ruled country, lay just to the north of Uganda and south of Nasser's Egypt. Since the Suez crisis of 1956, the Israelis had hoped that if they successfully encouraged a civil war in Sudan, Egypt might be diverted from future military confrontations with Israel.

After Uganda gained independence from Britain in 1964, Israel began to train the national army and covertly used the country as a conduit for arms shipments to secessionist rebels in southern Sudan. Idi Amin, an officer in the army and from a Muslim tribe along the border with Sudan, became their point man. In 1971, Uganda's president Obote attempted to stop the arms trafficking but was overthrown by Amin in a coup that won the tacit support of Israeli intelligence. The scheme backfired when the Israelis refused Amin's request for more military support for his own forces. Enraged, Amin became a sworn enemy of Israel and developed an anti-Semitic rhetoric. Israeli military instructors were sent packing, and the embassy was shut down. The confrontation came to a head in 1976 when Israeli special paratroopers rescued 105 hostages of an airliner hijacked by PLO terrorists at Uganda's Entebbe International terminal. Eighty-three of the freed hostages were Israeli citizens. The mission, code-named Operation Entebbe, caught the Uganda dictator unawares and humiliated him internationally.

Jews and Judaism in Ethiopia

The largest and most enduring Jewish community in East and Central Africa was to be found just north of Kenya in Ethiopia. Until quite recently Ethiopian Jewry represented one of the oldest diasporic communities in the world. Called today the Federal Democratic Republic of Ethiopia, the nation embraces nearly 450,000 square miles and is about three times the size of California. Known as Kush in biblical times and as Abyssinia in the Middle Ages, Ethiopia is one of the oldest civilizations in the world, and until 1974 it had one of the most enduring regimes. Its peoples, whom the ancient Greeks called "Ethiopians," meaning people with burnt faces, are Afro-Arabian and their culture has strong Semitic characteristics.

Peoples of Semitic origin crossed the Red Sea in early antiquity and settled in northern Ethiopia. A Semitized group, known as the Amhara, established a dynamic kingdom centered on the city of Aksum (or Axum), Ethiopia's capital at the time. Sabean, a Semitic tongue, merged with the local Cushitic language to form Ge'ez, which became the classical language of the Ethiopian state and later the language of their Coptic Christian Church. Aksum, on the other hand, evolved into an important crossroads of civilizations. A great cosmopolitan entrepot, the city was a corridor for trade between Africa and Asia, sitting as it did at the center of a vast network of trade routes.

Over the last four centuries, the tiny Jewish element in the population became increasingly isolated. Until the nineteenth century, they knew nothing of the Talmudic traditions that had informed Judaism for more than two thousand years. Their communities possessed the Torah but never acquired the Talmud or the medieval commentaries that shaped modern Judaism. Save for their religion, the members of the Beta Israel (House of Israel) community were almost indistinguishable from other Ethiopians. Landless for the most part, they evolved into occupational castes. *Falasha*, a pejorative word used by others to describe them, derived from an ancient Ge'ez term meaning "stranger" or "exiled one." Interestingly, the word doesn't appear in written records until the reign of Amda Sion (or Seyon) (1314-44), suggesting that before then they enjoyed a somewhat higher status in the larger Ethiopian society (Shelemay 1986: 20). More will be said of this later.

These hapless Falasha were almost all artisans and non-landowning farmers. Long separated from world Jewry, they were exceedingly poor and quite isolated. They resided in scattered villages mainly in the northwest highlands near Lake Tana and in the remote Semien Mountains farther north. In such a setting they were able to maintain deep Judaic traditions, and their faith certainly exerted a significant influence on broader Ethiopian culture as well.

Though they shared the same physical traits and language as their neighbors, they were seen by themselves and by everyone around them as a distinct people. The Beta Israel, as they called themselves, recognized the Old Testament and adhered to the five books of Moses. They had no rabbis but did follow priests, monks, and nuns. They observed Passover and worshipped in synagogues, or *mesgids*. Still, they never commemorated any post-exile holidays such as the feasts of Purim or Hanukkah, though they paid strict attention to laws of cleanliness and purity (Wagaw 1993: 18). They observed Mosaic dietary strictures and consumed no raw meat. Their religious works were written in Ge'ez and later in Amharic. Until recently, they were the only Jews who offered animal sacrifices for the forgiveness of sins. Each family had its own *cahen* who dispensed sage advice on religious issues and doctrine. Families were uniformly monogamous and patriarchal (Salamon 1999: 20).

Many fascinating and somewhat enigmatic historical streams make up the core, or essence, of Ethiopian Judaism. Their origins are shrouded in myth, legend, and controversy. Though most researchers agree that the Beta Israel are indigenous Agaw people, there is no consensus on the source of their Jewish beliefs and customs. Some scholars question whether the modern Beta Israel are in fact descendants of early Jewish immigrants or were simply shaped by some external Jewish influence. Indeed, did the Beta Israel's religious institutions derive from an early Jewish source, or are they an outgrowth of Christian Ethiopian canons?

Most Beta Israel assert that Ethiopia was Jewish before it was Christian and that chronicles suggest that Judaism was widespread in the country for at least thirteen centuries before the advent of Christianity. They claim that their ancestors actually came from Palestine with a legendary leader named Menelik, and they proudly see themselves as the direct ethnic and religious descendants of the original Jewish immigrants to Ethiopia. Thus, they perceive of themselves as the authentic descendants of ancient Israel and the Mosaic Law. They see themselves as exiles from Israel and as aliens in Ethiopia.

Serious scholars question whether the Beta Israel are indeed descendants of ancient Jews, and there continues to be heated controversy over the issue. James Quirin believes the Beta Israel were formed from a combination of influences, including some from Jews after their defeat by the Christian state (Quirin 1992: 12-19). Other scholars speculate that their faith may have trickled down from Elephantine via the Nile River valley and Meroe in the fifth century BCE after the destruction of their temple. Perhaps, then, the Elephantine Jews fled southwards into Ethiopia. Steven Kaplan questions this, noting the absence of any direct evidence of an ancient link between the Elephantine

Jews and the Ethiopians. Still, he concedes that the Beta Israel and Elephantine communities are "almost unique among Jewish groups in their practice of sacrificial ritual outside the land of Israel" (Kaplan 2000: 60). It is also known that the Egyptian Ptolemy Lagos (ca. 300 BCE) settled Jewish prisoners of war from Israel along the modern Egyptian-Sudanese border.

On the other hand, there is a school of thought that looks to southern Arabia for Ethiopia's Judaic heritage. It holds that southern Arabian Semites may have come into the Horn of Africa in the pre-Christian era, and thus the indigenous population's conversion came at the hands of émigré Jews from Yemen on the Arabian Peninsula. Surely there was considerable interaction between northern Ethiopia and southern Arabia as far back as the first millennium BCE. James L. Newman muses that Semitic populations may have been in Ethiopia as early as 4,000 years ago and that they settled among the Cushites of Eritrea and Tigray (Newman 1995: 90). They may have been followed by the Semitic Sabeans about 2,500 years ago. Clearly, tantalizing similarities can be found between Ethiopic and ancient south Arabian languages, and thus we must take Arabian influences into consideration.

There is compelling evidence of repeated migrations of Semitic-speaking peoples from the Arabian Peninsula as it dried up over the last two millennia. From about the sixth century BCE, southern Arabians set up small trading depots on the Eritrean coast in search of ivory as a commodity to enhance their Indian Ocean trade (Connah 1987: 80-87). Yet even before this, agriculture was well established and vital cereal crops were being cultivated with plows and marketed for export overseas. Thus, Judaism may have reached Aksum from Yemen through trade via Red Sea ports like Adulis.

There is a growing consensus that some Cushitic Agaw converted to Judaism and later embraced Christianity and that they were a major source of Jewish customs in mainstream Ethiopian

Christianity. David Kessler asserts that there indeed exists a strong Judaic component in Ethiopian Christianity, and that Judaism strongly influenced Ethiopian culture from the very first centuries of the Common Era. He hints that it may have derived from a pre-Christian Jewish presence in Aksum. A group of Agaw converts to Judaism may have brought it to that ancient cosmopolis (Kessler 1982: 63-73). Could it also be that many Agaw resisted converting to Christianity in the fourth century when it became one of Ethiopia's state religions?

The eminent Ethnomusicologist Kay Kaufman Shelemy goes so far as to speculate that the Agaw were a heretical, Orthodox Christian-influenced sect that did not emerge until the fourteenth century (Shelemay 1986: 17-23). There seems to be an emerging consensus that in a cultural sense Ethiopian Jews were a product of events that took place during the fourteenth and sixteenth centuries.

Such vexing questions as when Jews or Judaism arrived in Ethiopia and from exactly where may never be fully answered or resolved. Yet advances in DNA research techniques and fresh archeological excavations in the Horn of Africa may provide important new clues just as they have for the enigmatic Lemba of Zimbabwe and South Africa.

What is certain is that various key aspects of Judaism have been practiced in Ethiopia for a very long time, as mentioned in the Book of Isaiah and in other early texts and testimonies. It may be adduced that Aksum was probably founded by Semitic-speaking immigrants from southeast Arabia (modern Yemen) who settled among the Agaw. Aksum was a cosmopolitan enclave on the periphery of the Hellenic world, and its seaport entrepot was Adulis. This great international port of antiquity was the commercial link between the Mediterranean Basin, the Nile, the Red Sea, and the Indian Ocean, and it attracted peoples from throughout the ancient world (Connah 2001: 106). By at least 800 BCE, Semitic peoples were migrating from southern

Arabia to Africa via the 20-mile strait of Bab al-Mandab. They introduced new architectural forms, dietary requirements, literacy, and the Sabbath. They also penetrated the interior northern and central highlands and interacted with the Cushitic Agaw. Here we find hints of the presence of Jewish Aramaic loanwords in the Ge'ez Bible. By the first century CE, these migrants had fused with local Cushites and laid the foundations of Aksum.

The Ptolemaic rulers of Egypt encouraged Red Sea trade, and Aksum may have emerged in response. By the second century CE, Aksum had become the most important commercial center in northeastern Africa outside Egypt. Stanley Burstein notes that it was one of the major sources of gold for the Roman Empire in late antiquity (Burstein 2000: 91). And it would achieve distinction as a city of monumental architecture, with multistoried funerary monuments and very substantial buildings of superbly dressed stone masonry. Aksum minted its own coins which, according to Richard Pankhurst, "carried representations of the sun's disk and the moon's crescent, the symbols of ancient South Arabia" (Pankhurst 1998: 26). Its hinterland offered perhaps the largest supply of ivory in the ancient world, along with tortoise shell and rhino horn. As we've seen, its main outlet was the port of Adulis, which inevitably attracted Jewish, Greek, and Persian merchants. By 400 CE, Aksumite and Adulisite traders could be found in markets as far afield as Ceylon and India.

Aksum's King Ezana converted to the Monophysite doctrine of Christianity in about 340 and adopted the new faith as an official state religion. He may have done this to increase Aksum's trade with Roman-held Egypt. In any case, the new church was placed under the patronage of the Coptic Patriarchate of Alexandria.

From that time, rulers at Aksum began to use the word "Ethiopia" for their country. Today, Ethiopia is considered the longest-lived independent Christian kingdom in world history. After his conversion, Ezana went on to expand his realm, first by conquering Meroe, a city on the Nile that for centuries had traded intensively with Aksum.

Not long afterward, the Judaized Agaw were forced to migrate across the Abyssinian plateau to the east and west of Lake Tana, a region that became their heartland for centuries thereafter. There they developed a defensive policy of self-segregation and ultimately became an inward-looking community. Those who stayed behind and converted to Christianity held steadfastly to many of their Judaic beliefs and rituals and fused them with Christian doctrines.

Ethiopia reached its peak of power in the sixth century with the conquest of southern Arabia and its assertion as a Christian state. Early in that century they defeated the Himaryike ruler and enslaved thousands of southern Arabian Jews, taking many of them back to Ethiopia. Aksum's rule on the Arabian Peninsula was short-lived, however, for in 570 a Persian expedition evicted them. The Persians proceeded to overrun all of Arabia and eliminated the last vestiges of Aksum's influence. Aksum's international trade was further weakened by Persian control over Palestine and Egypt in the 620s. Things got even worse when the Arabs occupied Egypt in 645. Aksum's contact with Greek-speaking traders declined, and the old sea routes to Byzantium were forever severed (Marcus 1994: 9; Burstein 2000: 20).

The kingdom's fortunes fell further at the hands of local Beja rebels who preyed upon caravans. Then in about 710, Adulis itself fell to the Arabs, leaving interior Aksum landlocked and isolated from the rest of the world. Christians and Jews were forced to look inward, and in that extreme isolation the two monotheistic religions borrowed heavily from each other.

A powerful syncretic element, one which gave a sense of nationhood to all Ethiopians and bound them to the ruling lineage, was the great national epic the *Kebra Nagast* (Book of the Glory of Kings). The legend embedded in this remarkable book is an integral part of the master narrative of Jews, Christians, and

Muslims alike. Its official adoption by the Ethiopian monarchy resulted in a fundamental reconstruction of the identity and self-image of a new nation in the making. And it enabled the Ethiopian Jews, especially, to identify directly with ancient Israel, the birthplace of their religion. For them, the legend explains that Ethiopia had superseded Israel as the new Zion and that Ethiopian Jews were ipso facto the new Israelites.

The *Kebra Nagast* is undoubtedly a composite work, distilled from a cornucopia of oral traditions, completed in its final version sometime in the fourteenth century, and appropriated by the Christian Amharic ruling caste to authenticate and legitimize its own authority. Though historically unproven, it has enormous salience for all Ethiopians.

As the story goes, in about 950 BCE, Sheba, Queen of Aksum, visits King Solomon, ruler of Jerusalem. She bears him a son, Menelik, who is the first born of Solomon's three sons. Sheba and Menelik return to Aksum, though he eventually revisits Jerusalem to meet his venerable father and to be crowned king of Ethiopia. Note here that the utilization of the Solomonic lineage would serve to legitimate the Ethiopian monarch from that time onward. To continue, Menelik returns to Aksum, but not before snatching the sacred Ark of the Covenant from the Temple. The Ark, which henceforth is situated in Aksum, reputedly contains the Ten Commandments. Menelik settles in his homeland of Ethiopia, and thus an Amharic Semitic family is enthroned with Aksum as the New Jerusalem, the Holy City and political capital of Ethiopia. Thus, the heritage of Zion is transferred from Jerusalem to Aksum, the new Zion (Levine 1974: 105).

The epic asserts that the ruling dynasty of Ethiopia is directly descended from the Israelite kings of the Old Testament. According to Steven Kaplan, the legend became "the basic metaphor for legitimacy and authority within Ethiopian culture" (Kaplan 1993: 652). Ken Blady adds, "To legitimize their claim to rule by divine right the Amharic Christian elites perpetuated a historical fiction that they were descended from an uninterrupted line of kings whose lineage traced back to Menilek I [sic], the offspring of the mythical union of King Solomon and the Queen of Sheba." He concludes, "By aligning themselves with the House of Israel they could trace their lineage from Shem rather than from Ethiopus, the offspring of the accursed Ham" (Blady 2000: 348). The Ethiopian Christian elites thus embraced the Judaic concept of the covenant and, as will become evident, retained it for many centuries after Ethiopia became a thoroughly Christian state.

Not long afterward, this master narrative or national charter was modified to exclude the local Jewish community. It was Menelik, after all, who embraced the God of Israel. And, according to Donald N. Levine, by capturing the Ark he could now escape the Old Testament Curse of Ham by claiming descent from Solomon and David (Levine 1974: 105). So those Ethiopians who embraced Christianity—notably the royal family—were God's Chosen People, not the Jews. Excluded were any suggestions, based on earlier oral traditions, that the Aksumites may actually have adopted the core ideas of this great epic from the Judaized legends of a South Arabian kingdom during the Aksumite occupation of Yemen in the late sixth century.

Evidently, the final revised chapters of the *Kebra Nagast* cast the Jews as wicked and cursed and unworthy of any leadership positions in the country. The ruling Christian dynasty seemed to paper over the contradiction of claiming Israelite descent while scorning and de-legitimizing Ethiopian Jews.

Since Ethiopia's transformation into a Christian kingdom, successive rulers used the faith as a rationale for territorial expansion. From the tenth century, Judaized Agaw resisted Aksum's advance and began to carve out their own independent kingdom in the northwest. The ensuing turmoil resulted in a seizure of power by an Agaw-speaking Christian prince in 1137 and the establishment of a Zagwe dynasty, which governed for about 130 years (Pankhurst 1998: 45-46).

Though the Zagwe re-established links between the Holy Land of Palestine and the Ethiopian Church, they were unable to contain Islam, which by the mid-thirteenth century was winning converts in communities east and north of the kingdom. And while many Christian Ethiopians saw Islam as an alien religion—as a faith of nomads and merchants—others saw in it new opportunities for trade.

In 1270, central power was usurped by Yekunno-Amlak, an Amharic prince from the province of Shoa who claimed descent from Solomon and Sheba (Pankhurst 1998: 72). The *Kebra Nagast* would henceforth be used to restore and revive the Solomonic dynasty. His grandson, Amda Sion (1314-44), using the *Kebra Nagast* narrative as a nation-building tool, extended the Christian kingdom's southern and western boundaries at the expense of non-Christian populations. It was during this time that the Jewish minorities came under official demonization. In the fourteenth and fifteenth centuries, Jews are depicted in the chronicles of the Solomonid monarchs as "renegades" and "crucifiers" who were acting in concert with Muslim enemies of the Christian state.

Sion (otherwise known as Seyon) proclaimed himself founder of the new Ethiopian state and gained recognition by his Amharic followers as the great "Christian Proselytizer" and the "Pillar of Zion." John Iliffe notes that he crafted an expansive bureaucratic empire and created a vast evangelizing expanse for the Ethiopian Church (Iliffe 1995: 57-60). Eventually, the church as an institution became a major owner of land in the country and extracted wealth—feudal style—from the peasants who worked it. Typically, most farmers were transformed into tenants on the lands of their ancestors. In the process, the Christian clergy became chief beneficiaries and acquired prosperity and power. Their patrons, the Solomonic dynasty, were rewarded by their loyalty while acquiring legitimacy and a portion of lands' bounty. Sion's well-provisioned armies, in "crusade" mode, defeated numerous Muslim sultanates as well as the fledgling Jewish mini-states in the north. Now, Jews could only retain their lands if they converted to Christianity. Most did not and consequently lost control over vast expanses of valuable agricultural lands.

Land became the crucial index to wealth, status, and power in Ethiopia. And now that Jews had lost their holdings, they gravitated towards the crafts and became artisans—many as weavers and potters. But as Pankhurst observes, pottery making was a poorly compensated, isolated, and despised occupation (Pankhurst 1992: 226). In effect, the Jews were condemned to a life of relative poverty and remained an underclass in society until well into the twentieth century.

Attacks upon their communities and their faith only contributed to their retreat into geographical isolation. They developed an ideology of self-segregation and became "strangers" in their own country, mainly in order to reduce the threat of forced religious and cultural assimilation. They refused to eat food prepared by non-Jews, and consequently their travel was severely limited (Blady 2000: 361). Local Christian communities began to see these strange people as possessing supernatural powers, especially the blacksmiths and goldsmiths who had to mix fire and water in their smelting process. Jews were also stigmatized as *buda* (evil-eyed), with power to turn themselves into flesh-eating hyenas and prey upon the population at night. Indeed, they believed Jews could transform themselves into many malevolent shapes and behavioral patterns (Salamon 1999: 8). Faced with constant humiliations, the Beta Israel began to see themselves as aliens, as a people of the dispersion. And not surprisingly, the first references to the term *Falasha* are to be found in the royal chronicles of Sion in the fourteenth century.

The status of Jews deteriorated further under Emperor Yeshaq (1413-30 or 1412-27), who launched a policy of progressive disenfranchisement. Many of those who refused to pay tribute to him were sold into slavery and ended up in Arab households in the Muslim Middle East (Kessler 1982: 75).

The persecution was intensified during the reign of Zara Yakov—also called Yakob—(1434-68), who punished the Jews for giving refuge to one of his rebellious sons. This is curious because Yakob's mother was a Falasha (Pankhurst 1998: 100). Interestingly, oral traditions suggest that it was the son who, while in hiding, introduced monasticism to the Jewish people. Christians viewed Zara Yakob as the founder of the first Ethiopian empire, which he formed by melding a fractious church and state and extending his domain to the borders of the Red Sea and Eritrea (Blady 2000: 358). But he also acquired the appellation of "Exterminator of the Jews." He reputedly accused blacksmiths and goldsmiths of sorcery and had many of them tortured and executed.

Clearly, by the mid-fifteenth century, the Beta Israel had emerged as a distinct inward-looking group and were evolving into a caste within the dominant Christian Ethiopian society (Quirin 1992: 29). According to Hagar Salamon, physical contact with non-Beta Israel people was forbidden, because they did not follow the rules of purity practiced by those of Judaic faith (Salamon 1999: 21). Because of this practice, non-Jewish Ethiopians called them *"attenkun"* (touch-me-nots). According to Teshome Wagaw, their self-imposed segregation bred deeper suspicion and mistrust among the general populace (Wagaw 1993: 13).

Between 1380 and the early 1600s, Jews and the Christian state engaged in periodic warfare. In the early sixteenth century the conflict escalated during the reign of Sarsa Dengal (1563-97) when Ethiopia had to face growing threats to its territory from Muslim jihadists. At that time, Ethiopia was a feudal state centered in the northern-central highlands and comprising heterogeneous populations sharing similar cultures and language.

Following the Ottoman Empire conquest of Egypt in 1517 the Turks set their sights on the Red Sea and western Indian Ocean. But after a prolonged struggle, the Portuguese were able to maintain their Indian Ocean bases. Nevertheless, Ottoman-Portuguese rivalries in that region had a devastating effect on Ethiopia's international trade. And from 1526, Ethiopia became the target of attacks from an alliance of mainly Somali-based Muslims with Turco-Egyptian backing. However, the Muslims found Ethiopia's rough, mountainous terrain logistically difficult, and it left them exposed to guerilla attacks by Ethiopian armies and mercenary Portuguese musketeers.

Exhausted, the Ottomans concluded a peace in 1589 and Ethiopia remained under Christian rule for another 385 years. However, during the conflict, some Jews allied with the jihadists and were collectively accused of treason. Dengal used this as a pretext for eliminating almost all of the remaining independent Jewish kingdoms and destroying thousands of Judaic holy texts (Levine 1974: 77).

Things got even worse after the first Muslim episode. Susneyos III came to power in 1606-07, and during the 1620s he destroyed many Falasha villages and ordered the execution or forced conversion of its inhabitants to Christianity in retaliation for their support of a pretender to the throne. It was clearly an act of genocide, and by the end of his reign in 1632, the Falasha states in the Semien region of northern Ethiopia were entirely destroyed and their populations dispersed. If it were not for the protection afforded by their own monks, the religion itself might have perished.

The Muslim threat returned shortly afterward, and Susneyos converted to Roman Catholicism in hopes of enlisting military support from Spain. After he established contacts with the Vatican, Jesuits were allowed to enter the country. Before long, they began attacking Ethiopian Christianity for its use of so many Jewish rituals. A Jesuit writing at the time complained:

"The Christianity professed by the Abyssinians is so corrupted with superstition, errors, and heresies, and so mingled with ceremonies borrowed from the Jews, that little besides the name of Christianity is to be found here; and the thorns may be said to have choaked [sic] the grain" (Rotberg 1965: 127).

Surely there was some truth to this allegation. Ethiopian Christianity had become quite syncretic. Many Ethiopians were celebrating two Sabbaths: the Jewish Saturday and the Christian Sunday. They also observed many Jewish dietary taboos. And for centuries circumcision had almost universally been practiced by Jews and by Christians and Muslims. Thus, Ethiopians recoiled from such attacks by the Jesuits and fiercely resisted a Catholic bishop's orders in about 1620 to prohibit male circumcision (Marcus 1994: 40). The Jesuits were finally expelled in the 1630s, and Ethiopian contacts with Europeans virtually ceased for more than 150 years.

It was also at this time that Gondar was founded as a permanent seat of government, thus ending a long tradition of constantly rotating capitals. Jews by then were widely recognized for their artisanal abilities and were engaged in the new city's construction as skilled carpenters and masons (Quirin 1992: 101; Blady 2000: 359). Indeed, most of the city's castles, palaces, bridges, and walls were conceived and built by Jews in the employ of the state. Gondar's population grew rapidly and may have reached seventy thousand by the end of the eighteenth century, making it the leading city of the country (Marcus 1994: 41). Yohannes became emperor in 1667, and within a year he began a policy in Gondar of separating Muslims and Jews from the Christian population (Pankhurst 1992: 100).

Though Gondar itself was vibrant, the empire was gradually collapsing as warlords gained strength in the provinces and challenged central authority. By 1770 Ethiopia was a state in name only. In the so-called Age of the Princes (1755-1855), the Beta Israel became progressively marginalized and impoverished and lost their right to own land. From 1769 to 1855 Ethiopia was reduced to little more than a series of independent provinces that only paid homage to the emperor out of loyalty to age-old traditions and to the royal family's historic ties with the church.

Only the church, with its powers of patronage and its literate clergy, seemed to hold the people together. In spite of this erosion of central power—or perhaps because of it—the Beta Israel endured. Scottish traveler James Bruce encountered a number of Beta Israel communities on his visits to Gondar between 1770 and 1771 and commented on their distinctiveness and their isolation (Wagaw 1993: 14-15). Before this, Ethiopia and its Jews were almost totally unknown to the Western world and the kingdom existed largely in fantasy and myth.

Things began to change for Ethiopia from the second half of the nineteenth century. In 1855 Tewodros (Theodore) II came to power and began a campaign of national reunification. He persuaded the church to recognize him as "King of Kings" and "Emperor" of all Ethiopia, which enabled him to break the power of the provincial nobility and appoint his own governors. The incorporation of new territories opened up opportunities for the expansion of Christianity. In 1860, he allowed the London Society for the Promotion of Christianity Among the Jews to establish bases in the countryside in an effort to win more converts from among the Jewish minorities. Pastor Henry Aaron Stern, one of several missionaries of Jewish ancestry, became an active proselytizer. Jewish converts were sometimes employed by missionary societies to spread the Gospel, because it was assumed that their Jewish coreligionists would be more prepared to listen to them (Summerfield 2003: 30). The Beta Israel grew alarmed over their success and resorted to legal means to discourage their evangelistic militancy. Though Emperor Theodore won some support from the Christian community, he also made many enemies, and his suicide in 1868 brought most of his bold initiatives to a halt.

After the Suez Canal in Egypt was opened in 1869, international maritime traffic on the Red Sea skyrocketed, and northeastern Africa suddenly became strategically important to the Western imperial powers. It also attracted the attention of European Jews, who grew alarmed over the inroads that Christian missionaries were making among the dwindling Ethiopian Jewish population.

Joseph Halevy, a Sephardic teacher and noted Semitist from Turkey, visited Ethiopia in 1867 as an emissary of the Jewish philanthropic organization L'Alliance Israelite Universelle (AIU) (Parfitt 1999: 1). Halevy was the first European Jew to make personal contact with Ethiopian Jews in modern times (Isaac 1992: 408). The AIU, arguably the first modern international Jewish organization, called for a worldwide alliance of Jews. Though it was a French organization, it sought to raise the moral and intellectual status of all Jews in the diaspora. We will learn more about them in our next chapter.

Halevy was shocked by the way the Beta Israel practiced Judaism, and he recommended the opening of a school where Hebrew could be taught and then used as the medium of instruction. Halevy affirmed the Beta's Jewishness but was unable to overcome the AIU's concern that the "falashas" were practicing a non-Talmudic form of Judaism. Undeterred, Halevy would devote years to finding ways of connecting the Beta Israel, or falasha, to world Jewry.

An important break in this quest came in 1904 when one of his students, Jacques Faitlovitch, journeyed to Ethiopia under a grant from Baron Edmond de Rothschild (Semi 1998: 147; Parfitt 1999: 1). His overall goal was to counteract Christian missionary activity among the local Jews. Faitlovitch stayed on and worked to build an intelligentsia knowledgeable in traditional Orthodox Judaism and motivated to go out and regenerate isolated and poorly educated communities in the hinterlands (Semi 1998: 193). As Kaplan put it, Faitlovitch also "attempted to create a

Western-educated elite capable of interacting on a more or less equal basis with their foreign Jewish counterparts" (Kaplan 1992: 155). As a Zionist, he taught them to perceive of themselves as a diasporic community oriented towards Israel as the Promised Land. He promoted, though never proved, the thesis that they were a pre-Talmudic lost tribe that wandered into Ethiopia in antiquity. In 1924, Faitlovitch opened a Hebrew school in Addis Ababa while also making provisions for some of his students to travel abroad for advanced studies (Corinaldi 1998: 175). The school, which received considerable support from American Jewry, was a teachers training institute with a curriculum firmly rooted in Hebrew. Faitlovitch also founded the "Society for the Dispersal of Israel" in Tel Aviv in hopes that it would bring the existence of the Ethiopian Jews to the attention of the rabbinical authorities (Grinfeld 1986: 30).

Faitlovitch continued to work with the Beta Israel until his death in 1955. Over the course of his years of labor he succeeded in bringing the Beta Israel into the mainstream of Jewish history and making them visible to Jewish communities overseas. In 1921, the chief rabbi of Palestine called upon world Jewry to support an Ethiopian aliyah (immigration to the Promised Land) (Isaac 1992: 408). At that time, his appeal fell largely on deaf ears, although it did have the unwelcome effect of fueling the controversy over their claim to authenticity as true Jews.

Unquestionably, European visitors found the Beta Israel communities in Ethiopia extremely weak and disunited. The Great Famine of 1888-92 caused major demographic and religious disruptions. Jews were denied plows and oxen, and by 1893 nearly 40 percent had died of starvation. In 1894-95, they had to contend with a rinderpest epizootic that decimated their herds of cattle and made it difficult for them to follow their rites of animal sacrifice (McCann 1995: 121). Many of their religious leaders, especially the monks, abandoned their work and entered secular employment in order to survive.

This was also a time of dramatic transition in the nation's development. Menelik II reigned as king of Shoa province from 1865 to 1889 and as emperor of Ethiopia from 1889 until 1913. His reign witnessed the beleaguered nation's reunification, modernization, and territorial expansion (Pankhurst 1965: 2-4). With modern imported weapons, Menelik's highly disciplined armies pushed southward to the shores of Lake Rudolph in East Africa and eastward into the Ogaden and Tigray. He reduced the powers of the feudal lords and centralized the government. Internationally, he is best known for defeating the imperialist Italians at the Batttle of Adowa in 1896 and preventing the takeover of Ethiopia by Western powers (Pankhurst 1965: 9-10). Indeed, Ethiopia became the only sovereign African nation, excluding Liberia, to preserve its independence during the infamous European scramble for and partitioning of the African continent in the late nineteenth century. Menelik also saved Christianity and Judaism from extinction by repulsing Islamic jihadists who were expanding from their Sudanese redoubts.

Menelik's modernization program was extended under Haile Selassie, the nation's last monarch, who ruled from 1930 until his assassination in 1974 during a Marxist military coup. Selassie referred to himself as the "Lion of Judah" and boasted of being the 225th emperor in direct line from Menelik I.

In 1935, the Italians under the fascist Benito Mussolini reinvaded Ethiopia and occupied it for nearly six years until they were expelled by a British expeditionary force during the Second World War. Initially, many local Jews had welcomed and supported the Italians because the fascists pledged to protect their religious interests and refrained from articulating a policy of systematic discrimination (Summerfield 1999: 52). Moreover, these were hard economic times, and many Jews viewed the Italian army as a job opportunity. By 1940, however, nearly everyone had switched to the resistance (Summerfield 1999: 56). In 1941, Haile Selassie triumphantly returned from exile and re-established his government and the nation's sovereignty.

Life for Jews after the war did not measurably improve, and international Jewry remained divided over how to respond to the deplorable condition of their coreligionists in Ethiopia. In 1954 the Jewish Agency's Department for Torah Education and Culture in the Diaspora opened a school in Asmara for thirty-three young Jews. In the same year some students were sent to study in Israel. Nevertheless, Israel and the Jewish Agency were ambivalent about allowing Ethiopian Jews to participate in aliyah. The Americans were generally more supportive, and the American Association for Ethiopian Jews, founded in New York in 1969, became early champions of the cause.

Selassie and Israel drew closer together in the late 1960s over their common fear of hostile Muslim neighbors. In 1967, with Israel's support, he launched a costly and ultimately military offensive against secessionist guerrilla movements in Ethiopia's territory of Eritrea, a land—formerly part of Italian East Africa—acquired by Ethiopia in the early 1960s (Ottaway 1990: 103; Makinda 1987: 39). The war with the Eritrean liberation movements raged on even after the emperor was pressured by the Organization of African Unity (OAU) to break relations with Israel in 1973 (Pankhurst 1998: 265).

Ethiopian Jewish interest in immigrating to Israel became greater in the 1970s and '80s after a number of traumatic events. Jews were especially hard hit by a severe famine that spread across the country between 1972 and 1974 (McCann 1995: 143). It was a catastrophe that contributed to the overthrow of the Selassie government and its replacement by an intensely ideological Marxist military regime. This was followed by years of civil war and population displacements that weakened and demoralized Ethiopian Jewry.

Momentum for emigration was building in Ethiopia, while in Israel the debate escalated over the old question of whether the Beta Israel qualified as authentic Jews under the 1950 Law of

Return, which asserts that all Jews have a right to immigrate to Israel (Corinaldi 1998: 175). But are these impoverished Africans indeed original Hebrews from ancient Israel or simply recent converts? It was noted that the Beta Israel had the Torah but had never acquired the Talmud or the medieval commentaries that shaped modern Judaism.

Finally, after long debates among Israeli theologians and politicians, a breakthrough came in 1973 when the chief Sephardic rabbi of Israel recognized the Beta Israel as authentic Jews and supported their right to immigrate. Two years later, the Ashkenazi chief rabbi and the Israeli minister of the interior agreed that Ethiopian Jews were eligible for aliyah under Israel's Law of Return (Corinaldi 1998: 176-77).

After the 1974 military coup, the new urban-oriented government under Haile Mariam Mengistu declared Ethiopia a Marxist state and issued a proclamation abolishing private land ownership. Also, religious organizations of every faith came under attack. The land confiscations placed an incredible hardship on the Beta Israel, as they were overwhelmingly rural people who drew their sustenance from the soil. Then in 1977 some Jews were grudgingly allowed to emigrate under an arms deal between the government and Israel (Westheimer and Kaplan 1992: 23). Desperate for weapons after the Soviet trade in arms collapsed, Mr. Mengistu sought to use Jews as bargaining chips to obtain an arms agreement with the Israelis. Still, only 121 Jews were actually able to leave before the agreement fell apart months later. In 1982, the U.S. State Department reported that many Jews in Ethiopia had been arrested and tortured in a general crackdown on all religious organizations.

Life for everyone became more precarious with extensive crop failures in 1983 and early 1984. Many thousands of Jews and others sought succor as refugees in neighboring Kenya and Sudan. The cumulative effects of repression, drought, food shortages, and loss of land and livestock only intensified the urge to leave Africa and to secure ultimate refuge in Israel. Pressure began to build in the U.S. Congress to work with Israel in support of a massive airlift. Thus, in November 1984, at the height of a raging famine and with many Jews in refugee camps in Sudan, Tel Aviv launched a secret rescue, code-named "Operation Moses." It was funded mainly by the United Jewish Appeal, with coordination and implementation by the U.S. Central Intelligence Agency (CIA) working covertly with Mossad, Israel's counterpart. The secret airlift was briefly suspended after it was divulged to the press and then resumed in March 1985 as "Operation Joshua."

Aliyah continued in 1989 after brutal government "villagization" projects had disrupted Jewish life, and diplomatic relations were established between the governments of Ethiopia and Israel. Snubbed by Russia's President Gorbachev, Mengistu decided to accept military assistance from Israel, hoping that its arms and its counterinsurgency skills might still enable the Ethiopian army to defeat the Eritrean liberation forces (Henze 1993: 67). Emigration restrictions were consequently eased, and in May 1991 "Operation Solomon" resulted in the evacuation of another 14,500 Ethiopian Jews within the span of about thirty-six hours (Westheimer and Kaplan 1992: 32; Cohen 1998: 17). Paul Henze asserts that Israel then deposited $35 million in an Ethiopian government New York bank account as final payment for their release of the "Falashas" (Henze 1993: 69).

These dramatic rescue operations were unique in that never before had Africans been taken out of Africa not as slaves but to preserve their religious beliefs. And they entered another country—the so-called Promised Land— not as asylum seekers but as new citizens. Remarkably, between 1984 and 1992, at least 40,000 Ethiopian Jews left the nation of their birth and ancestry. Some perceived this massive aliyah in biblical terms, calling it the Great Twentieth Century Jewish Exodus.

The story does not end there. Mengistu's government was

overthrown in the spring of 1991 after seventeen years of military dictatorship, and civilian rule was restored. But the tiny communities of peoples of Jewish ancestry left behind continued to feel vulnerable and oppressed and appealed to Israel to accept them. This presented a new problem to the Israeli leadership, because most of the 21,000 to 30,000 remnants were *Falas Muras,* or people who had converted to Christianity only within the past generation or two. Nevertheless, by 1995, most of these people had been recognized as having Jewish ancestry and were eligible to perform their aliyah to Israel if they agreed to reconvert to Judaism. Nevertheless, the process of removal was painfully slow and dragged on for many years (Anon. Jewish Federation 2008: 1-2).

The fortunate Jews who made their aliyah to Israel had to begin life anew and struggled to redefine their self-image and identity. Those who possessed occupational skills needed for the development of Israel readily found employment or started their own enterprises. Others went into the military and police and advanced steadily in rank. However, the majority remained mired in poverty and found themselves ostracized and socially marginalized.

Arguably, for the majority of the more than 77,000 Ethiopian Jews residing—and enjoying citizenship—in Israel today, assimilation and acculturation have been difficult and only partial. For them, Israel has not yet become their Promised Land.

CHAPTER SIX

North African Jewry since the Seventeenth Century

Major Clusters of Jewish Population ca. 1950

Jewish and Muslim Coexistence in North Africa

Jewish families have been closely tied to North African Islamic rulers throughout most of the history of Muslim ruling dynasties. From at least the seventeenth century, Jews were indispensable to the functioning of North Africa's governments. Its monarchs relied on them to perform an array of key services as administrators, customs officials, tax collectors, treasurers, commercial brokers, physicians, and diplomats. They also played crucial roles in international trade and finance. They served as intermediaries between European Christian commercial interests and the ruling political and commercial elite of the various Mediterranean emirates and regencies.

In many respects, Jews were the "face" of Muslim North Africa in its dealings with the outside world. Yet, although they were integrally woven into the very economic fabric of the Arab and Christian worlds, most of these high-ranking Jews lived in ghettoes socially and culturally separated from Muslim society. They were simultaneously insiders and outsiders, visible and invisible, influential and insecure in their person and position yet extremely vital to the officials who entrusted them with awesome responsibilities.

Generally, the position of the Jewish elite was precarious, as they enjoyed no independent base of power or legitimacy. These courtiers were extremely vulnerable because their position depended on the will and whim of their sovereign. If their sultan, dey, or bey died, they faced the possibility of termination. The strength of the privileged Jewish families derived in many cases from the extent of their international commercial relations as well as from their ability to remain in a situation of trust with their overlord. Still, this coexistence rested on a condition of mutual dependence or symbiosis. As Daniel Schroter put it, "rulers often found it less risky to employ court Jews than members of the majority religion" (Schroeter 2002: 121).

It should be remembered that many rulers, especially in Algeria, Tunisia, and Egypt, were themselves nominally under authorities in distant Istanbul and were thus seen by the masses as foreigners from other regions of the vast Ottoman Empire. Jews and all non-Muslims were guided by certain rights and obligations embedded in Islamic law and custom. It may be recalled that as non-Muslim dhimmis they were subject to a special poll tax, they had to wear certain types and styles of clothing to distinguish them from Muslims, in most cities they were compelled to live in segregated quarters, they could not bear arms, and they were exempt from military service. They were barred from certain occupations, usually those that were the most lucrative, and they were constrained to act deferentially when in the presence of Muslims. Only a tiny minority were given special permission to own land or to live outside the ghetto (Meyers 1996: 87).

But along with these sometimes humiliating disabilities came certain rights and protections that their masters were compelled to honor. Jews were to be protected from physical harm, dispossession, and theft. They were also free to practice their own faith (Schroeter 2002: 7-9). Thus, they were in many respects internally self-governing—living within their own laws and answerable to the leaders of their own faith, whether they be rabbis or family patriarchs. Jews were free to convert to Islam, and many did to enhance their economic opportunities and avoid discrimination. On the other hand, it was a criminal offense to leave Islam (apostasy) and to revert to Judaism as crypto-Jews. Within these Islamically defined parameters, Jews and Muslims in North

Africa from the seventeenth until the mid-twentieth century lived in comparative peace. Surely, occasional pogroms and almost unrelenting discrimination generated tension and recrimination, but most of the time coexistence was the norm.

It needs to be emphasized that throughout this period the vast majority of North African Jews were illiterate and extremely poor if not indigent. Like their counterparts in Ethiopia, they followed a wide range of poorly paid arduous occupations, including weaver, tailor, cobbler, tanner, butcher, artisan, and manual laborer. Others were small shopkeepers and petty traders. Those in the cities rarely ventured beyond the *mellah*, or ghetto. Rural Jews tended to be itinerant, and like the *smouses* of South Africa they peddled their wares from village to village (Blady 2000: 298). They were often ill-treated, ridiculed, and held in contempt by their Muslim patrons. From the early nineteenth century an increasing number drifted to the cities and were forced to live in crowded and filthy squalor. There, many found no means of supporting themselves other than as beggars, pimps, and prostitutes.

Morocco: Jews and an Expanding Muslim State

The Sultanate of Morocco historically has held the largest proportion of Jews in North Africa, and it is here that we take up the story begun in an earlier chapter. Morocco began to open up to the West during the heyday of the Saadian dynasty under Sultan Ahmad al-Mansur (1578-1603). He was the most famous of the Sherifian-Sadid sultans. It may be recalled that in the historic Battle of the Three Kings in 1587 fought in northern Morocco, he defeated the Portuguese, seized their Atlantic coastal forts, and thus stanched further penetration of the sultanate by hostile Christian powers. The imperialist-minded sultan then turned southwards, and with imported European muskets and

Andalusian mercenaries he conquered the expansive Muslim Sudanic empire of Songhay in West Africa. This gave al-Mansur access not only to the valuable Saharan salt mines of Taghaza but to the even more valuable gold mines of the upper Niger. He then turned over the minting of gold coins to his Jewish officials, who in turn arranged for their export into Europe's money markets. With this highly valued currency, Morocco was able to vastly increase its international trade, a trade that was operated in large part by Jews acting on behalf of the sultan.

Al-Mansur's Jewish diplomats entered into negotiations with Queen Elizabeth I of England, an archenemy of Spain. Since the reign of Sultan al-Mahdi (1554-57), the two countries had been in regular trade contact, but now Morocco would boost its exports of saltpeter (used in making ammunition) and cane sugar, produced by Jews who managed plantations and mills owned by the sultan himself and worked by thousands of slaves under conditions often worse than those in the Americas (Gerber 1980: 13).

Domestic slavery had been deeply rooted in Moroccan society for centuries. Jews and Muslims alike held slaves and continued to do so well into the early twentieth century. Many Jews especially acquired slaves as payment from defaulted debtors. Though Jews rarely had more than a few slaves of their own, there were many exceptions. For example, in the nineteenth century the Bayruk family owned at least 1,500 slaves, and an Essaouira merchant housed numerous concubines.

By the opening of the seventeenth century, Jewish agents of the sultan controlled much of Morocco's international trade, especially with England, France, and the Netherlands. However, a new challenge came in 1603 when al-Mansur died and Morocco was plunged into a divisive succession struggle. His Saadian dynasty collapsed and after a period of turmoil was replaced in the mid-seventeenth century by the Sherifian Alawis who, like their predecessors, claimed descent from the Prophet

Muhammad. Alawi dynastic power—and indeed that of the central government itself—was consolidated by Sultan Ismail, who reigned from 1672 to 1727. His stellar military achievements were due in large part to a vast standing army of 35,000 to 45,000 black slaves (Schroeter 2002: 38).

The country may have been reunified under the sultan and his brother, but even Ismail's authority in the provinces was compromised by powerful coalitions of sufi religious orders and by fiercely independent Berber strongholds in the rugged Middle Atlas Mountains. Fortunately, the Jews managed to make themselves indispensable to the Sherifians, and anti-Semitism was largely kept under control by their new dynastic protectors.

Even before Ismail's accession to power the Jewish sugar merchants found themselves in growing competition from Brazilian and West Indian planters. Samuel Palache, a Moroccan Jew, engineered the first treaty between Morocco and a Christian country in 1610: an agreement with the sugar-refining Low Countries of Western Europe (Diaz-Mas 2000: 54). And from then until the 1680s Amsterdam's Sephardim and their Moroccan coreligionists enjoyed a fruitful trade relationship embracing a wide range of commodities. The Palache family remained close to the royal court, and from 1624 to 1642 Moses Palache served as the sultan's private secretary, handling highly confidential affairs of state (Bloom 1937: 81).

In the seventeenth century many of Morocco's preeminent merchants were Jews, and they nearly cornered the export of cloth, copper, pelts, and ostrich feathers, as well as the movement of gold currency into the major cities of Western Europe. They additionally sold grain to Oran and other Spanish bases in North Africa. Moroccan Jews were also widely known as expert gunsmiths, and their weapons were exported throughout the Muslim world as well as sold to local authorities. Indeed, the gunsmiths of Fez were chief purveyors to the Moroccan Royal Army in the eighteenth century (Cook 1994: 283).

Successive sultans granted the elite Jews a high degree of legislative and judicial autonomy because they were People of the Book; that is, they shared a common religious heritage based on early biblical texts. Until the era of French colonial overrule in the twentieth century, local Jews could use Spanish-based rabbinic law in many of their transactions.

Like the Solomonid dynasty of Ethiopia, the Alawid dynasty in Morocco would give the Muslim theocracy a political continuity and stability in which trade and markets could flourish in relative peace and security. Moreover, successive generations of certain Jewish families lived near the palace, and as a backbone of the civil service they were able to provide an essential continuity and institutional memory to the ruling dynasty. It is no wonder that in 2008 the Alawid family continues to govern the state as one of the longest ruling dynasties in the world.

By the time Sidi Muhammad III came to power in 1757 most of Morocco's international trade was in Jewish hands. Muhammad sought to further expand this trade in 1764-65 by building an entirely new port city, Essaouira (also known as Mogador), on the Atlantic coast, where he could more closely monitor and control the country's burgeoning commerce (Park 1996: 66). The sultan selected ten wealthy Jewish families from different towns throughout the sultanate and made each send a member to represent them in the new port. According to Schroeter, by 1780 the most active Moroccan merchants in the city were Jews (Schroeter 2002: 19). As enticement, he allowed them to wear Western clothing, send their children to schools abroad, and not have to live in a mellah.

It was not long before Essaouira emerged as one of Morocco's major trading entrepots. It was here that representatives from foreign merchant firms of the top trading capitals of Europe established themselves. And it was also here that traders of southern Morocco exported their goods to Europe. Essaouira eventually became the only Atlantic maritime port in Morocco where foreign trade was permitted (Schroeter 1988: 20).

Muhammad III soon cast his eyes across the North Atlantic for new commercial opportunities and turned to his own Jewish advisers to craft a visionary diplomacy and market approach. Many of these advisers were highly skilled in foreign languages and already enjoyed overseas connections in major markets. First they succeeded in signing a commercial treaty with France (Gottreich 2007: 7). Then, in 1777, through the intermediary Isaac Cardoso, a Jewish Moroccan merchant in New York, the sultan extended diplomatic recognition to the fledgling United States. Nine years later, an astonishingly liberal treaty was concluded giving United States consuls in Morocco extraterritorial jurisdiction over Americans there and placing commerce on a reciprocal most-favored-nation basis (Diaz-Mas 2000: 55). Finally, in 1789, President Washington and the sultan signed a friendship treaty, via the intercession of Isaac Pinto, a Tangier Jew with offices in New York City. It is a document still in effect today and is one of the oldest treaties between the United States and a foreign country.

No other country in the world had engaged so deeply and intimately with the new American nation. For Morocco it was a risky undertaking. It meant alienating the British and linking its own destiny as a mature and relatively prosperous state with a young developing country that at the time was small in population and poor in fluid resources. Yet it resulted in one of the most enduring bilateral relationships in modern world history.

Morocco's opening to the West as well as the position and condition of Jews was set back by a succession of religious fanatics. Sultan Yazid (1790-92) treated Jews harshly and ruled brutally. Mulay Sulayman, who came to power in 1792, was xenophobic in temperament and discouraged international trade out of concern over the growing cosmopolitanism of the Jews and their warm ties with Christian nations (Bar Asher 1986: 297-305).

The economy weakened and was further damaged by drought

and a devastating plague in 1799. The economic setback was particularly hard on Jews, who by then were becoming progressively urbanized. Indeed, Judeo-Berber refugees from the countryside flooded into the existing mellahs, which became increasingly overcrowded and unhygienic (Stillman and Zucker 1993: 64-65; see also Schroeter 2002: 90-91). In response, Sulayman in 1801 revived the practice of mellahization, a policy that, we might recall, was first implemented in Fez in 1438 after an anti-Jewish pogrom. More mellahs had been established in the sixteenth and seventeenth centuries in the imperial cities of Marrakesh and Meknes, respectively. Typically, they were located adjacent to the royal compound, or casbah, where the rulers could both protect their inhabitants from anti-Semitic mobs and control their activities.

Sulayman would establish new, distant ghettoes in all the major cities save Tangier (Bar Asher 1986: 309). In this international seaport city, Jews and other non-Muslims shared the same neighborhoods with no clearly demarcated boundaries. Still, nearly all the mellahs, most of which were sited in the least hospitable parts of the city, in time ultimately bulged with humanity and degenerated into squalid, disease-ridden enclaves. A few of the more successful Jews, notably those of Spanish heritage, escaped this suffocating form of segregation by converting to Islam.

Tangier was a star in Morocco's dealings with Europeans (Pennell 2000: 35). The sultans, fearful of excessive European interference, confined non-Muslims to this cosmopolitan seaport that bustled with expatriates from nearly every country in Europe. In 1826 Meir Cohan ben Maqnin, a Jew, became its chief of customs, serving at the convenience of the monarch. Two years later he was appointed Morocco's ambassador to Great Britain and did much to stimulate trade between the two countries (Serels 1991: 7; Schroeter 2002: 77-79). Jews living in Tangier were also prominent in global finance. According to

Mitchell Serels, Moses Pariente opened Tangier's first bank in 1840, making the city even more attractive to Jewish and Christian merchants. For a century hence the Banque Pariente served as one of the country's most important banking institutions (Serels 1991: 11).

Morocco's economy steadily weakened as the nineteenth century progressed and European traders and investors began to look eastwards toward Algeria and Egypt. Moreover, the Muslim theocracy felt increasingly threatened after the French had conquered its immediate neighbor, Algiers, in 1830. Before then, Morocco had no land borders with a Christian country.

The opening of the French-financed Suez Canal in 1869 diverted much of the Mediterranean trade toward Egypt. At the same time, Britain, France, and Spain became more interested in the strategic importance of the southern Mediterranean coast, particularly the approaches to the Strait of Gibraltar, the Mediterranean Sea's vital gateway. By the 1880s, France had become more imperialist, and its expanding Mediterranean and Atlantic coastal colonies, with railways reaching into the hinterlands, secured markets and diverted trade away from the historic and once-lucrative trans-Saharan routes that passed through Morocco. As customs revenues declined, so too did the state's ability to provide essential services to its population, especially in the area of public security. Centrifugal tendencies spurred on by Berber rebellions in the distant and mountainous northern provinces necessitated heavy military expenditures. At the same time, the beleaguered government struggled with only moderate success to reform itself and to modernize the country's antiquated infrastructure.

All this required money, and the people of Morocco recoiled at proposals for tax increases. Budget deficits ballooned in the face of weak government receipts. Thus, successive sultans became fatally reliant on the British and French for loans. Rising tension over unpaid debts led to a French bombardment of

Tangier, which by then was the sultanate's Mediterranean port of access for European merchants. French and British interference in Morocco's fiscal affairs grew, and in 1856 an Anglo-Moroccan treaty opened the country to free trade and linked it to a 10 percent customs duty. While this may have benefited some local Jewish and foreign nationals doing business in the country, it only angered the general populace, which had grown accustomed to relatively inexpensive imported goods.

British interest in the sultanate revived, especially after Sir Moses Montefiore's high-profile visit with the sultan in Marrakesh in 1863. Montefiore, a fabulously wealthy and politically well-connected British philanthropist, would travel the world promoting and defending the civil rights of his fellow Jews. He came to Morocco on a complaint and was able to extract from the sultan a royal edict that vowed greater security and respect for his Jewish subjects (Schroeter 1996: 106). No one is quite sure what the sultan received in return, but the situation of Jews in the country improved substantially (Gottreich 2007: 1).

French-Moroccan relations, on the other hand, seemed headed in the opposite direction. Since mid-century, France loomed ever larger in Morocco's internal affairs. Things came to head in about 1905 when imperialist Germany began to take an interest in the sultanate. A year later, an international conference was convened in the Moroccan city of Algeciras and resulted in a treaty whereby the European powers halfheartedly pledged to honor the independence and territorial integrity of Morocco and its sovereign and to preserve an "open door" in the sultan's dominions. This did not bode well for Morocco, because in the quid pro quo France and Spain were given the green light to take control of the country's military and financial affairs, and Germany was assured a substantial share in an international bank set up in Tangier to administer Morocco's finances. To add insult to injury, Tangier was designated an international free port.

Obviously, Morocco was becoming victim to Great Power rivalries that inexorably led in 1914 to world war. Moreover, during the reign of Mawlay Abd al-Hafidh (1908-13), Jews were becoming much more visible and influential in Moroccan politics. The European encroachment into Morocco only further destabilized things, culminating in a complete loss of sovereignty in 1912 after the humiliating Treaty of Fez, which bifurcated the country into a large French and a small Spanish Saharan protectorate. Tangier was left as a free port (Diaz-Mas 2000: 61). Though some Jews prospered in the teeming city-state, most continued to live in filth and abject poverty.

Between 1912 and 1934 the two European colonial powers engaged in costly and destructive military "pacification" campaigns against the indigenous populations. Under a colonial system of indirect rule, Louis Lyautey, the French governor (1912-25), ruled through the sultan, though clearly his authority had been vastly reduced to figurehead status.

Colonial policies in French Morocco largely benefited the local Jewish communities. The hated and demeaning institution of dhimmi was abolished, and Jews who could afford it were now free to live outside the mellahs. All occupations were open to everyone, and public schools adopted a modern French-centered curriculum. On the other hand, with the introduction of a Western secular legal system, the religious leadership and powers of both Jewish and Muslim communities were diminished. Additionally, the replacement of Arabic by Spanish and French as official languages of the respective protectorates brought Morocco more fully into the Western capitalist and cultural orbit. Colonialism wrought profound changes in nearly every aspect of Moroccan life. It also created a wedge between the Jews, who were educationally and occupationally favored by the regime, and the Muslims, who remained in a kind of traditionalist cocoon.

Not surprisingly, most urban Jews welcomed the French conquest and grew prosperous under the colonial policies that followed. Though tradition-bound rural Judeo-Berbers felt threatened by the Frenchification of their country, the urban French- and Spanish-speaking Jews identified closely, perhaps too closely, with the colonial hegemons. For them, the colonial era would offer unprecedented opportunities for socioeconomic advancement. According to Emily Gottreich, many of those employed in the colonial administration became part of the protégé system, whereby they were awarded the privileged status of extraterritoriality. Insightfully, she notes that "the jealousy their special status inspired worked to the detriment of Jewish-Muslim relations such that when French rule over Morocco came to an end in 1956, Jews were perceived by many of their neighbors (and sometimes by themselves) as being somehow less than fully Moroccan" (Gottreich 2007: 9).

Many Jewish youths left the mellahs of the old towns for the newly open and largely Westernized cities like coastal Casablanca, Rabat, and Kenitra. They adopted Western clothing, took employment with French firms, received a Western education at schools operated by the Paris-based Alliance Israelite Universelle (AIU), became literate and secular, and agitated—unsuccessfully—for French citizenship (Pennell 2000: 250).

The AIU operated a vast network of academic and vocational schools for local Jewish children and viewed modernization and Westernization as the salvation of Jewish communities. Stillman notes that they "produced cadres of Westernized Jews who possessed a distinct advantage of opportunity over the largely uneducated Muslim populace." He adds that "Jews came to have a new and unparalleled mobility and achieved a place in the economic life of the Muslim world that was far out of proportion to their numbers or their social status in the general population" (Stillman and Zucker 1993: 40). It can be argued that because the Jews tended to identify with the French and became considerably Westernized, their relations with the local Islamic population deteriorated as the twentieth century progressed.

Under Governor and resident-general Louis-Herbert Lyautey and his successors, Morocco's cities were modernized and expanded beyond the original walled confines. Lyautey's urban planners split many of the cities into two with the establishment of the European town. The dozen or so main cities became powerful magnets for commercial growth, though the "indigenous" half, which often included the Jewish ghetto, remained little changed and grotesquely overcrowded, with few modern amenities. Nevertheless, the Jewish populations of Fez, Marrakesh, Meknes, Rabat, and Casablanca grew dramatically. Morocco in general also attracted Jews from metropolitan France, who usually settled in the modern and commodious European quarters. By 1940 the country's Jewry had climbed well above 190,000. It was also in 1940 that France fell to Nazi Germany and Morocco became part of the anti-Semitic Vichy regime. Numerous anti-Semitic laws were imposed, and perhaps for the first time in the country's history, government encouraged local Muslims to harass Jewish neighborhoods and businesses. The hated Vichy regime was finally evicted by Allied forces in 1943, but the seed of modern anti-Semitism had been planted and would ultimately graft itself onto postwar pan-Arabism. Never mind that significant numbers of Moroccans did not see themselves as Arabs but as Berbers, black Africans, Jews, or French Christians.

After the war, Zionism, which had found fertile ground among Jewish intellectuals in the 1920s and '30s, took on more urgent importance with events in Palestine. Remarkably, since the early sixteenth century individual Jews of North Africa had been performing aliyah, but only in very small numbers. However, Jewish and French anxieties over the future grew after 1947, when Sultan Mohammad V asserted that Morocco must be considered part of the Arab world. And after the state of Israel was created in 1948, the urge for aliyah to the Promised Land intensified and eventually became an obsession. Anti-Semitic pogroms that year were small though destructive, and they raised fears among both the Jews and the sultan that the protection of Jewish persons and property could no longer be assured. Moreover, the sultan's aspirations to be a major player in the Arab world were compromised by his need to prevent a loss of sorely needed Jewish expertise.

France tried to stanch the growth of militant Moroccan nationalism and Islamism by deporting the sultan to Madagascar in 1953, a move that only further inflamed the masses and strengthened Istiqlal, the independence movement. Not surprisingly, Mohammad was reinstated less than two years later. Jews remained politically uninvolved in these dramatic events, and their role in the African nationalist movements throughout the Maghreb was small and rather inconsequential.

The decolonization process was already under way by then, and Morocco was given back its independence in 1956. In an effort to prevent white flight, the sultan offered equality and full citizenship to people of all faiths. Most Jews, especially those with skills that were portable, declined the invitation. Many could not countenance being a citizen in a Muslim-ruled nation. The Suez Canal crisis in the same year only exacerbated tensions between Muslims and Jews and gave further impetus to the exodus (see Stillman 1989: 160).

Coterminously, Tangier—multigenerational home to many Jews—lost its international status as a free port and was fully reabsorbed into the sultanate. For several years the Jewish Agency and Cadima, an Israeli organization, had been active in the country promoting aliyah and receiving support from such trans-Atlantic organizations as the American Jewish Committee. In the face of these promotional campaigns the exodus gained new momentum. In the late 1940s and early '50s, poor and middle-income Jews were the first to leave; among them were skilled farmers and Zionistic youths. The least skilled and educated were left behind in the teeming ghettos, barely surviving as manual laborers, clerks, and household servants (Sachar 1985: 109). And from the late 1960s, the more affluent professionals took up residence in Canada, the United States, and the Francophone world while holding on to fixed assets back home (see Pennell 2000: 277; Serels 1991: 179).

The exodus only grew after 1958 as pan-Arab activists became more vocal in response to Morocco's conciliatory gestures toward Nasser's Egypt. When Morocco joined the Arab League, Mossad (Israeli intelligence) launched a secret program of immigration, and between 1957 and 1961 they arranged for nearly 18,000 Moroccan Jews to perform aliyah. Between 1948 and 1960, Morocco's Jewish population declined from 286,000 to fewer than 162,000. By 1984, it had fallen further—to fewer than 17,000 (Diaz-Mas 2000: 183; Sachar 1985: 111).

Throughout this period, the royal family appeared to make a concerted effort to discourage emigration. Jews were given high appointments in the government, their real estate holdings were guaranteed, and after the Six-Day War in Israel, King Hassan II (Mohammed's successor in 1961) ordered the arrest of anyone engaged in anti-Semitic violence or propaganda (Pennell 2000: 334).

Through all this, Morocco, unlike nearly all nominally Arab countries, remained on friendly terms with Israel. Prime Minister Yitzhak Rabin paid a formal visit in 1976 and General Dayan a year later. Nevertheless, the exodus continued to accelerate.

In 1995 King Hassan met with both Shimon Peres and Yasser Arafat in an effort to reduce Jewish-Muslim tensions, but to little avail. As the twenty-first century unfolded, fewer than 6,000 Jews remained in the entire country—most of them too old to move on or with too many fixed assets and business connections to easily liquidate.

Egypt

Unlike Morocco, Egypt had been a province of the Ottoman Empire since the sixteenth century. Some scholars argue that for much of the period when the country was more firmly under rule from Istanbul, society was relatively open and tolerant. Jews were found in most occupations and anti-Semitic incidents were rare (Sonbol 2000: 6-7). Gradually, however, the Mamluk beys gained predominance over the operation of the government, and under Ali Bey (1760-72), the province had become almost totally self-governing. Though Ali Bey fostered commercial agriculture with some success, the government continued to be archaic and terribly inefficient. Indeed, little had changed in Egypt for centuries, and the deeply conservative Qur'anic schools pursued a curriculum totally out of touch with the modernizing Western world.

Jews did not fare well under this tyrannical ruler who, as a Mamluk child slave, apparently, was sold to the royal family by a prominent Jewish customs official (Crecelius 1981: 40-43). During his reign, Ali Bey smashed the long-established Jewish monopoly over the major customs houses, and many small businesses were ruined. He distrusted Jews and placed customs and other government offices in the hands of foreigners, mainly Coptic Christians from Syria (Winter 1987: 13; Crecelius 1981: 173). All this led to a dramatic decline in the position of the Egyptian Jewish community. Its small population chafed under this economically stultifying atmosphere and yearned for modernization of the entire state. Thus, they welcomed Napoleon's invading forces in 1798 and offered logistical assistance (Kortepeter 1991: 220). The French army easily defeated the antiquated Egyptian military and overthrew the sclerotic Mamluk oligarchy.

The French occupation did not last long enough to effect any meaningful reform. In 1801 they were expelled by the British, who saw the French in the eastern Mediterranean as a threat to their own positions in the Middle East and India. The British, with no apparent imperial designs of their own at that time, quickly restored Egypt to the Muslim central authorities in Istanbul. Nevertheless, these invasions by secular Christian nations deeply troubled Egypt's Muslim leadership and gave rise to renewed calls for independence. A young Albanian commander, Muhammad Ali, was sent to Egypt with an expeditionary force to restore law and order, and in 1807 the Ottoman authorities put him in complete control of the province.

Though a fervent Muslim, Muhammad Ali recognized that Egypt could only protect itself in the future through an aggressive program of modernization. He began with the army, building discipline, vastly enlarging its size, and equipping it with modern European-made weapons. With this national army he conquered the Nilotic Sudan, bringing to an end the Funj Kingdom of Sennar which had ruled over much of Nubia since the sixteenth century and laid the foundations for a Turco-Egyptian regime in the Sudan. But even before this he liquidated the Mamluk barons who had returned to Egypt after the French armies had retreated. Then in 1811 he gathered together the chief Mamluk leaders and had them summarily executed.

In Egypt itself, he boosted cotton cultivation by installing a modern irrigation system. Sweeping land reforms were also put into effect which broke the power of the parasitic feudal lords. In an effort to industrialize, he established a number of state-owned factories. Capital for these ambitious projects came from tax reforms that increased government revenue and from foreign borrowing. Muhammad Ali was not afraid to engage experts from Christian countries, but he also created modern secular schools modeled on those in France and Italy to train Egyptians. He believed in the need to use Western knowledge to rejuvenate Muslim institutions and to bring them into the nineteenth century. On his death in 1848 he bequeathed to Egypt the most modern and formidable army on the continent as well as the most developed economy.

Muhammad Ali had also created a dynasty of his own, and he was succeeded by his French-educated son Khedive (king) Sa'id (1854-63).

Under him, local Jews were able to secure high appointments in government. Jacob Cattawi (or Qattawi) became chief Egyptian moneylender and went on to become one of the country's leading bankers (Landau 1969: 11). Foreign investment was encouraged, and from 1858 non-Egyptians were allowed to own real estate. During his reign the government made an agreement with a French firm to construct a canal to connect the Indian Ocean with the Mediterranean via the Red Sea and Suez. As we shall see, this fateful decision would mark a turning point in Egyptian history, and for that matter in the history of the entire world.

The construction and operation of the Suez Canal had a transformative effect on Egyptian Jewry. It offered unlimited opportunities for employment as well as for investment in allied enterprises. Egypt now became extremely attractive to Jews and non-Jews throughout Europe and the Middle East.

Canal construction began during the reign of Khedive Ismail (1863-79). Like his grandfather Muhammad Ali, he welcomed foreign participation in the country's economic development. Ismail was a great admirer of the West and had a particular fondness for the French. The Ashkenazic element in the population now began to grow as Jews from France, Poland, Greece, Russia, Italy, and Germany flooded into the country. They were joined by new waves of Sephardim from the Ottoman Empire, particularly from Syria and Lebanon (Landau 1969: 3). After the canal's completion in 1869 they tended to settle in the major cities, particularly in Cairo and Alexandria. In the latter city they found small communities of relatively impoverished Arabic-Jews whose roots reached back into antiquity.

Under Ismail, Egypt underwent a Western-style transformation and the economy became strongly export oriented (Landau 1969: 7). Cotton, for years an economic mainstay, expanded in volume and fueled new textile industries. When Confederate cotton exports to Great Britain declined during the American Civil War, the Egyptians filled the vacuum. Egypt also began to expand its exports of sugar into European markets. Industrialization, which had faltered toward the end of Muhammad Ali's reign for lack of capital, was revived.

Costly state and private sector projects were undertaken on a grand scale. British and French investment poured into the country and financiers extended generous loans to the Khedive. Wealthier Jews represented overseas banks and companies and plowed their profits into the retail trade, textile industries, sugar refining, and cigarette manufacturing and distribution. The less prosperous found employment as clerks in the burgeoning local and foreign firms. By 1880, Jews could be found in practically every occupation.

Unfortunately, boom soon turned to bust and the bears beat out the bulls. By the mid-1870s the Ottoman sultanate in Constantinople as well as the Khedivate in Egypt had fallen deeply into debt. Egyptian nationals were unable to service their obligations to their Jewish and Christian creditors or to obtain refinancing. Benjamin Disraeli, the British prime minister and an ethnic Jew of reputed Moroccan ancestry, saw this as an opportunity to counterbalance the growing French presence in that volatile region. In 1875 he borrowed funds from the Rothschilds to purchase the bankrupt Khedive's own shares in the Suez Canal Company. This gave the British control over 44 percent of the company's equity and a strong voice in the canal's management. However, it also ratcheted up Anglo-French rivalry for control over the strategic canal and set into motion the ultimate British takeover.

In this Western-imposed era of free trade, Egyptian imports

had begun to exceed exports, and expenditures overtook revenues. Though Ismail followed liberal economic policies, he resisted political and administrative reform. The government itself could not honor its debts to locally based foreign creditors and to lenders overseas. By the mid-1870s Egypt as well as the entire edifice of the Ottoman Empire seemed on the verge of collapse under the weight of unsustainable debt. And such a prospect threatened the stability of the entire Middle East and North Africa.

Inevitably, the threat of sovereign bankruptcy in Egypt led to foreign financial control, just as it did ultimately in Morocco a decade or so later. In 1876 the Khedive was forced to surrender the country's fiscal institutions to the British and French, who were by far the largest creditors. Julius Blum was installed as secretary general in 1878 and was joined by other financial czars (Robinson and Gallagher 1961: 86-87; Landau 1969: 12).

The ensuing fiscal reforms coupled with external efforts to democratize the regime with a Western-style constitution provoked a national revolt against Ottoman oppression and foreign interference. In 1879 Britain pressured the Ottoman sultan in Constantinople to depose Ismail. The Khedivate as an institution virtually collapsed in 1882, after decades of European meddling. The anti-Western Egyptian army fortified by nationalist sentiments was poised to intervene into what had become a chaotic situation. Most Egyptians had already come to see Britain and France as bullying hegemons. But as France, convulsed by its own domestic crisis, hesitated to act on the unfolding situation, the British unilaterally and preemptively bombarded Alexandria and occupied the country, establishing what can only be described as a veiled colonial protectorate. Arguably, the British invasion of Egypt and the seizure of the Suez Canal was one of several key catalysts in the European scramble for, and partitioning of, the entire African continent.

Jews in Egypt overwhelmingly welcomed the British takeover

in 1882 and anticipated a strong economic revival. Jacob Landau notes that in return for their support, the British granted them legal equality with the rest of the population (Laudau 1969: 14). Though the country remained nominally a part of the Ottoman Empire until after the First World War, it was obvious to all that the British were firmly in the cockpit.

In the decades ahead the economy prospered and so did most of the country's Jews. Some of them became major powerbrokers in the country. Baron Jacques Levi Menasce (1850-1916) was perhaps one of the most prominent, having made a fortune in real estate, cotton, and sugar and then becoming a board member of the National Bank and one of Egypt's top philanthropists. A contemporary, Yusuf (or Jacob) Qattawi was a major leader in the Jewish community and served as president of the powerful Egyptian Chamber of Commerce and Speaker of the national Senate from 1927-31. He was also an ardent anti-Zionist (Goldschmidt 2000: 160). By the early 1920s, Jews had become prominent in such professions as law, medicine, accountancy, finance, and urban real estate. Not surprisingly, Jewish immigration to Egypt gained new momentum and by 1917 had brought their total numbers in the country to nearly 60,000, up from 25,000 in 1897 and a mere 4,000 in 1840 (Oppenheim 2003: 412). As we have seen, Jews flooded in from throughout the Mediterranean Basin, from Morocco to southern Europe and beyond to the Middle East. Cairo and Alexandria had again resumed their historical positions as two of the world's most cosmopolitan cities.

From the era of Khedive Ismail, Jews were playing an important role in transforming Alexandria and Cairo into bustling cosmopolises. And by the turn of the century they had become the most modern and prosperous cities in the Muslim world. Stillman notes that "both economically successful native Jews and European Jews took up residence outside the old Jewish quarters" (Stillman 1996: 67). While most Jews continued to reside in neighborhoods speaking their own languages such as Yiddish, Italian, and Arabic, the more prosperous and enterprising families left, choosing instead the French and English languages and lifestyles. This enabled them to move more easily into higher positions in government and international business and banking.

In 1922 Britain gave Egypt its nominal independence and restored the monarchy. It was a move that raised the complex issue of citizenship. With the Ottoman Empire liquidated, Egyptians were no longer Ottoman subjects. Most Jews were reluctant to opt for Egyptian citizenship because, since the days of Ismail, foreigners were exempt from a wide range of taxes and military service. Moreover, some Jews were holding out for foreign passports that might eventually lead to citizenship in France, Britain, Italy, or elsewhere. Also, Zionism was gaining ground among the intelligentsia with its emphasis on a restoration of Jewish nationality in Palestine. Consequently, when the Nationality Law was enacted in 1929, only 5,000 or so Jews became formal Egyptian citizens (Shamir 1987: 46). Most everyone else found themselves stateless and vulnerable to the whims of an Egyptian polity and society that would become progressively nationalistic and pan-Islamic.

The era of reckoning opened in the mid-1930s as the Egyptian economy faltered in the face of a global depression. Unemployment skyrocketed and Egyptians agitated for the expulsion of foreigners. Wealthy Jews were perfect targets, as they were major urban landlords and owned large department stores and labor-intensive factories in the cities (see Sonbol 2000: 65). Jews were increasingly seen as foreigners, especially those who had facility in foreign languages.

Earlier, under British rule, immigrants were offered an opportunity of special status under consular protection, but in 1936 this extraterritoriality provision was eliminated. Later in the decade, anti-Semitism reared its ugly head in various street demonstrations and in the media. Then came 1947 and the so-called Company Law, which gave Egyptian citizens a controlling share in major businesses and mandated that 75 percent of employees must be Egyptian nationals (Shamir 1987: 53-59). This marked the beginning of the Egyptianization of the foreign-dominated economy. More discriminatory regulations would soon follow.

A year later Zionist Jews found themselves in a war of liberation against Muslims and the British in Palestine, a sanguinary conflict that led to the establishment of the independent Jewish-ruled state of Israel in the Arab heartland. The creation of Israel humiliated Muslims everywhere and added fuel to religious tensions in Egypt. Riots broke out in Cairo, and in the same year some 40,000 Jews were declared ineligible for Egyptian citizenship. Many "stateless" Jews had no choice but to perform their aliyah to Israel, where as Jews their citizenship was automatic. Others incrementally departed for destinations in Europe and the Americas. Between 1949 and 1951 approximately 40 percent of a Jewish population of more than 66,000 emigrated (Opppenhein 2003: 428).

Ironically, the Suez Canal crisis of 1882 ended up attracting Jews to Egypt, while the Suez Canal crisis of 1956 had just the opposite effect. Four years earlier a military "colonels coup" toppled the corrupt King Farouk and paved the way for Gamal Abd al-Nasser, who then called for a national boycott of Jewish businesses. Subsequently, Nasser's ambitious plans for a massive Aswan Dam and irrigation project were rejected by the Americans and British. In anger he turned to the Soviet Union, which was all too happy to obtain a beachhead into the emerging African continent.

Posing as a leading pan-Arabist, Nasser became more militantly anti-West, and in July 1956 he boldly nationalized the canal, something his military predecessors had wanted to do in 1882 but, as we have discovered, were unable to accomplish because of the British. Britain and France were not only heavily invested in the canal and in the Egyptian economy; they saw it also as a vital corridor to the Indian Ocean and to the oil-rich Middle East.

That same year, Israel, in collusion with the two European powers, gave France a pretext for war by unilaterally invading the Sinai. In October, Britain and France then staged their own invasion, which quickly ended in a humiliating withdrawal in the face of American and Russian pressure. The incident was an embarrassment for Israel and a triumph for pan-Arab nationalism in Egypt. Within a year more than 2,100 Jews were expelled from the country. The exodus continued, and by 1967 fewer than 3,000 Jews remained.

In 1979 a glimmer of hope appeared when Egypt and Israel signed a peace treaty, but those hopes were dashed in 1981 with the assassination of President Anwar Sadat. By 2001 fewer than 200 Jews could be found in the entire country.

It is a daunting thought that within the next decade the last Jew may leave Egypt, ending a history of Jews and Judaism in Egypt extending back more than three thousand years.

Before closing on Egypt it is worth noting that some individuals and small groups of Jews in recent Egyptian history were ardent supporters of Egyptian nationalism (Schrand 2004: 2). One of Egypt's greatest political satirists, Sannu Ya'qub, in the 1870s was described by Khedive Ismail as Egypt's Moliere (Goldschmidt 2000: 181). His brilliant satires attacked both the indigenous and foreign elite. Though an observant Jew, he was also one of the country's earliest nationalists. It should also be said that in 1922 Jews were instrumental in founding the Communist Party, which agitated for full independence. And in the 1930s a number of Jews worked in various Egyptian nationalist movements. Still, it can be argued that since the turn of the last century, Egyptian Jewry tended to be Zionist and, excepting some Karaite descendants of Jews of antiquity, did not view themselves as indigenous Egyptians. And in turn, many Muslim Egyptians perceived them as cosmopolitans—the very antithesis of nationalists. It was that detachment that may have rendered many Jews in Egypt fatally vulnerable to attack from anti-Semites (Schrand 2004: 8).

Jews of the Anglo-Egyptian Sudan

We have already learned that Jewish communities flourished in the Upper Nile region of Africa in the days of the pharaohs and Persians, but by the eighteenth century they had almost entirely vanished. We do not hear much about Jews again until the late nineteenth century when the Egyptian khedive Ismail sent military expeditions southward in an effort to extend Egyptian trade and influence. In 1877 he appointed General Charles Gordon governor of all his Sudanese territories, and he in turn appointed Eduard Schnitzer governor of Equatoria province. A German Jew by birth, Schnitzer converted to Islam, married an Ethiopian, and assumed the name Emin Pasha. This commission was followed by a jihad led by Mohammed Ahmed ibn Abdullah, who proclaimed himself the Mahdi (messiah) and proceeded to evict the Anglo-Turco-Egyptian forces from the Sudan and declare it a theocracy.

This was arguably the West's first major confrontation with Islamic militant fundamentalism in centuries. British forces defeated the Mahdist state in 1898 at the epochal Battle of Omdurman, but not before the Mahdi had managed to lay siege to Khartoum; assassinate Gordon; evict Slatin Pasha, an Austrian-born Jew, as governor of Darfur; and occupy vast expanses west of the Nile. Emin Pasha became a celebrated figure in the Western media and was eventually evacuated from Equatoria by the world-famous explorer Henry Morton Stanley in 1889 (Lewis 1987: 41-45).

The British felt it imperative to control the headwaters of the Nile to prevent them from falling into the hands of the French. At Fashoda in 1898 in a near military confrontation the French backed down and Sudan fell under the control of the British under the guise of a joint Anglo-Egyptian condominium. The Egyptians felt cheated and dreamed of eventually absorbing the Sudan into their own country. That of course never happened.

In the same year a rail line was extended southward from Cairo, eventually reaching Khartoum, the new administrative capital on the Nile, in 1916. Exactly a decade earlier Rabbi Solomon Malka from Palestine arrived and assumed spiritual and religious leadership over what would soon become a fledgling Jewish community (Malka 1997: 27-30). As a railhead Khartoum grew rapidly and attracted representatives of leading Jewish firms from Cairo. Other Jews settled in Omdurman (Oppenheim 2003: 416). Rabbi Malka and his descendants took a leading role in the city's commercial and cultural development and became involved in a range of business ventures, including food processing, sesame oils, and tiles. In the 1920s and '30s, young Jews found employment in the civil service (Malka 1997: 51-54).

Nineteen hundred and fifty-six proved to be a turning point for the Jews of Sudan. Early that year, the British acceded to Sudanese demands for independence, and before year's end the Suez Canal crisis forced them to relinquish their preeminent position in Egypt as well. Khartoum's tiny Jewish community viewed these momentous events as a catastrophe, and within a year almost all of them had fled, some making their aliyah to Israel and others heading to Britain or Canada, which still had liberal immigration laws.

Before 1956, Jews, Christians, and Muslims had coexisted peacefully, but from then onward relations with the Islamic community deteriorated, reaching their nadir after the Six Day war in 1967. In the meantime, Sudan was plunged into a disruptive and prolonged civil war that weakened its economy and raised religious tensions between the Muslim north and the Christian south. By 1968, nearly every Jew in the country had left. Quietly and discreetly, an extremely influential though miniscule community had vanished into history.

Algeria, Tunisia, and Libya

We have grouped these states together because they were the three Maghrebian countries that were part of the Ottoman Empire and shared a somewhat similar heritage. Earlier in our narrative we noted that from at least the sixteenth century, conflicts between Turkish Muslims and Christians of Italy, Spain, and Portugal regularly fed the slave markets of Muslim Algiers and Istanbul and of Christian Lisbon, Marseilles, Livorno (Leghorn), and elsewhere (Davis 2003: 7). Christian seaports were sacked in an endless quest for slaves and plunder. Algiers and Tunis, especially, preyed upon Christian commerce and communities throughout the western Mediterranean. And until the nineteenth century, North Africa's Barbary Coast was the scene of an active slave trade in which Jews played a significant intermediary role.

Since the seventeenth century, the Emirate, or Regency, of Algiers had been operating like an independent state, even though its political and tributary ties with the Ottoman authorities in Istanbul (Constantinople) remained operative. The Turkish deys were elected from among the Janissaries of the Turkish Ojak, a body of some six thousand men of Turkish Asia Minor extraction. Gradually they became more autonomous, and in Tunis and Tripoli the militaries established semi-independent dynasties in 1705 and 1711, respectively.

By the eighteenth century a considerable portion of the wealth of the North African coastal cities rested in the hands of large Sephardic Jewish families who had emigrated generations earlier from Spain and Livorno, Italy. In Algiers they appear to have secured a virtual monopoly on trade (Kortepeter 1994: 336). The Jewish merchants of Livorno, working with their coreligionists in the Maghrebian ports, notably Tunis, constituted an extensive trading network that by the late 1700s had reached a peak in volume and value.

Yet for Algiers, much of the wealth derived from plunder. It was estimated that by the 1630s the city-state was holding approximately 25,000 Christians as slaves, including some 2,000 females who found themselves serving as concubines (Baepler 1999: 3). We have already noted that Jewish merchants sold contraband picked up by the corsairs. Indeed, since at least the sixteenth century, important Jewish trading houses were securing substantial commissions from the ransoming of captives on behalf of the dey's regime. It was an enterprise that grew in the 1770s when the Coen-Bacri family opened a branch of its Italian-based firm in Algiers. Jews, with their well-developed international mercantile networks, were ideally positioned for this activity. As Max Kortepeter notes, they had become "indispensable to the Beys of the provinces and the Deys in Algiers because of their information networks." Kortepeter adds that "the Deys, themselves members of an alien ruling class in North Africa, turned to the Jews as trusted advisers rather than to local Muslim merchants or to foreign consuls who, in any case, could barely communicate with the Deys directly in Turkish or Arabic" (Kortepeter 1991: 216).

Jews also specialized in the inspection of slaves for purchase in various Maghrebian markets. Stephen Clissold asserts that the inspection and evaluation of slaves "was a skilled business in which Jewish middlemen specialized" (Clissold 1977: 40). The slaves were then forwarded to the dey, who demanded the privilege of having first opportunity to buy his choice captives. David Voorhees observed that most of the white European and American slaves "either languished for years in slavery before being redeemed or never lived to regain their freedom" (Voorhees 1997: 10-11). A few ended up on sugar plantations in Morocco and on cotton plantations south of the Sahara in the upper Niger River valley.

From our chapter on the slave trade we learned that the Barbary corsairs raided widely, preying on ships and sweeping into coastal ports in England and as far into the North Atlantic as Iceland. In the early 1800s, the United States was especially affected and the government found itself having to pay annual tribute in the form of bullion and naval stores. Ransomed Americans returned home and composed widely read narratives of their abuse at the hands of Muslim slave masters. Curiously, this aspect of the African slave trade was given scant attention by historians of the twentieth century, and until recently it was a "lost" chapter.

The success of the Algerian dey in this extortion only encouraged his counterparts in Tunis and Tripoli. America, as a weak and essentially isolationist new nation, had to negotiate costly treaties with Algiers, Tunis, and Tripoli—treaties that the emirates often violated. Morocco, by contrast, made peace with the Americans by 1789 and ceased plundering. The corsair's harassment finally led to the creation of a United States marine corps and to the young republic's first war since independence from Great Britain. The ensuing Tripolitan War (1801-1805) involved the bombardment and blockade of Tripoli and resulted in a durable treaty (Pratt 1955: 110-11). Nevertheless, the Americans continued their tributary relationship with Algiers until 1813, when the dey declared war after not receiving timely payments. Within two years squadrons of American warships would compel the North African despot to drop all further demands, thus ending an ugly chapter in North African history (Baepler 1999: 5).

Since the Napoleonic era the French had been taking a keener interest in Algiers and its hinterland, not only for strategic reasons but as an area of trade and settlement. Mainly through

Jewish intermediaries in Algiers the dey had borrowed heavily in European financial markets, especially after the conclusion of its conflict with America. Frenchmen of both Christian and Jewish faiths joined Livornese Italians in Algiers' bustling postwar markets. It is estimated that by 1829 the coastal cities had nearly five thousand predominantly Ashkenazic Jews. There were also hundreds of remote hinterland villages containing vigorously independent-minded Judaic, Arabic, and Hispanic Berbers whose ancestors had arrived centuries earlier. For generations they had coexisted in relative peace with Muslim Berbers and Arabs, serving as artisans, itinerant petty traders, and farm laborers. Like Egypt, though to a lesser degree, the region manifested an extremely heterogeneous Jewish population.

In 1830 Charles X of France, on the verge of being deposed and anxious to divert attention from turmoil in his own country, unilaterally invaded and occupied the city of Algiers with assistance from several Algiers-based Jewish merchant families. The initial invasion was spectacularly successful but failed to preserve his position as French king. Financially, the occupation of Algiers was a bonanza for France. In 1832 the French looted the dey's treasury of an astounding 15,500 pounds of gold and 220,000 pounds of silver, more than enough to finance further military operations. The French inched along the coast, capturing a number of towns including Constantine in 1837. The new acquisitions were collectively named "Algeria."

Though an administrative presence was quickly established on the coast, the interior populations mounted a fierce resistance under the Arab-Berber warlord Abd al-Qadir (or Abdel Kader). After heavy fighting the backbone of Berber resistance was broken in 1843, though Qadir did not surrender until 1847 after French armies had pillaged the countryside and laid waste to farms and villages. France had to contend with a complex and nuanced range of resistance and collaboration manifested on numerous levels: ethnic, regional, religious, and personal.

Though resistance sputtered in isolated pockets, the conquest was largely completed by 1871 (Friedman 1988: 2-3; Laremont 2000: 17).

The French conquest opened the floodgates to foreign immigration, and by 1912 Algeria's European population exceeded 800,000, the majority being French Catholics (Mitchell 1982: 38). France provided incentives for the colonization of the temperate fertile coastlands by European winegrowers and wheat farmers. Jews settled mainly in the coastal towns. Before long, French replaced Arabic not only in government but in education and major business transactions as well.

From the onset of colonization, relations were strained between the Westernized incoming French Jews and their indigenous coreligionists, who were overwhelmingly poor and illiterate. The latter were alarmed in 1833, when assimilation-minded France acceded to pressures from the émigré Jews to place all Jews under French jurisprudence. Previously, native Jews were semi-autonomous and functioned domestically under their own religious legal system and governmentally within the Muslim shari'a. Henceforth, all Jews would fall under French secular law in civil matters. At the same time, French Ashkenazic rabbis were put in charge of organizing an indigenous rabbinate (see Friedman 1988: 9).

Culturally chauvinistic French colonists seemed to overlook the fact that since the Middle Ages there were highly educated and prosperous Hispano-Jewish communities in such interior Algerian cities as Tlemcen and Touat (or Tawat). They had drawn much of their wealth from the trans-Saharan trade in gold, ivory, salt, leather goods, and jewelry and were living in dynamic symbiosis with their Muslim counterparts.

Post-1830 Jewish émigrés were steeped in French language and culture and worked to "civilize" and thus transform their "primitive" African coreligionists. Predictably, from the 1860s the Alliance Israelite Universelle (AIU) set about establishing modern French language schools in Jewish communities throughout the country. At first indigenous Jews resisted what they saw as an extreme form of cultural chauvinism, but by 1900 most of them had become acculturated to some extent, realizing that knowledge of the French language could be an important tool for social and occupational mobility. Elizabeth Friedman summed up this process best in her observation that "while France colonized Algeria, French Jews colonized Algerian Jews" (Friedman 1988: 25). Conversely, very few Algerian Muslims were granted admission to French government schools, and thus the process of assimilation was extremely unbalanced.

The issue of citizenship was also of considerable salience to the settlers or *colons*. Adolphe Cremieux, a prominent French Jewish statesman, persuaded the National Assembly in Paris to pass the Cremieux Decree of 1870, which granted French national citizenship to Algerian Jewry. Algeria became the only North African colonial possession to enjoy this benefit. This momentous piece of legislation was supplemented in 1889 by legislation conferring automatic French citizenship on persons of European parentage born in Algeria (Abitbol 1989: 8).

Between 1889 and 1900 Algeria received a huge number of Jews from nearly every part of the Judaic world. This alarmed the Catholic European settlers, who swelled the growing number of anti-Semitic organizations. The first major pogroms, in Oran in 1897-98, did little to slow the steady stream of new arrivals who sought to take advantage of the country's impressive economic growth.

And robust it certainly was: imports soared from 55 million francs in 1840 to 260 million in 1900, while exports went from 3.6 million to nearly 250 million. Growth was especially vigorous in the wine industry, which produced a modest 228,000 hectoliters in 1872, 5.6 million in 1900, and a breathtaking 12.3 million in 1925 (Mitchell 1982: 209).

It was a prosperity that benefited commercial farmers and

merchants alike. Unfortunately, little of it trickled down to the peasants, who were overwhelmingly rural Berbers. The economic boom rolled through the 1920s as imports and exports grew to 5.7 million francs and 4.2 million francs, respectively, in 1930 (Mitchell 1982: 403). Nearly all trade was with metropolitan France, as Algeria became its major trading partner in Africa and one of its largest globally.

Per capita income among Algeria's urban Ashkenazic Jews grew faster by far than among any other ethnic group in the population. And as the economy went into recession in the late 1930s, they became the proverbial scapegoats. Anti-colonialism and anti-Semitism seemed to grow in tandem among the predominantly Muslim populace. Conversely, the white settler population in general looked upon their Islamic neighbors with increasing hostility. In France itself, many legislators lobbied for an expansion of the franchise in Algeria to include Muslims, in hopes that ultimately the colony would be fully integrated into the French nation as a province. Maurice Viollett and France's Jewish prime minister, the socialist Leon Blum, wanted to assimilate Algeria into France by eliminating restrictions on citizenship. The timing for this legislation could not have been worse, and in 1937 it was defeated.

Political Islam in Algeria had been relatively quiescent from the 1870s well into the twentieth century, but in the 1920s and '30s it was revived by a number of nationalist organizations, notably the Association of Ulama, which agitated for the renewal of Islam and the re-establishment of Arabic as the cultural base for Algerian nationalism. Anti-Semitism was given added stimulus in 1941 with the occupation of Algeria by the Nazi-supported Vichy regime (Abitbol 1989: 11-12). Prejudices lingered after the war even though the economy rebounded. By 1948 there were at least 130,000 Jews living in Algeria, and most of those of recent European origin were firmly middle and upper middle class (Deshen and Shokeid 1974: 34). Cast against this was rising unemployment among Muslim youth in the major urban areas. And along with it grew anti-colonialism, Algerian nationalism, and Islamic militancy. These forces coalesced into armed revolt in 1954 with attacks on government installations.

The long war for Algerian liberation thus began and quickly escalated into terrorist attacks on civilians as well. The military retaliated in 1957 with what came to be called the Battle of Algiers. It was a pyrrhic victory in that while the army gained militarily the National Liberation Front (FLN) grew politically and won broader support in the Muslim community. Nevertheless, throughout the liberation struggle fierce ideological battles raged within the FLN itself (Laremont 2000: 262). Secular socialists (initially a few Jewish leaders among them) clashed with Islamic socialists, with the latter ultimately prevailing.

Continued violence and destruction of European settler property provoked a counter-revolution among the colons. The Organisation de l'Armee Secrete (OAS) was a vigilante organization that nearly matched the FLN in committing atrocities. Most Jews remained politically neutral or supportive of the French forces, though a number of Jewish youth joined the OAS in hopes of "saving French Algeria" from a radical Islamic takeover (Laremont 2000: 21).

The cycle of violence became more intense and had a polarizing effect not only in Algeria but in France itself. The war was costing France dearly and may have contributed to Charles de Gaulle's election to the presidency. De Gaulle spurned the Algerian colons and set the North African possession on a rapid course toward decolonization. Full independence came abruptly in July 1962, a month after evacuation of the white population had commenced. A mass stampede followed, and by autumn only an eighth of the 800,000 Europeans remained. Most of the refugees had fled to France (Sachar 1985: 117).

From independence to 1965, Algeria's Jewish population fell precipitously from 140,000 to fewer than 4,000, leaving behind an indigenous Muslim population of more than nine million. Most of the refugees left out of a sense of insecurity. Indeed, Laskier suggests that "The fears stemmed from the continuous infiltration by Muslims into their residential quarter or the European districts" (Laskier 1991: 44). Regardless, the exodus of whites was huge and abrupt because, unlike those in Egypt, Morocco, and Tunisia, nearly all were French citizens and were immediately accepted into France.

In their rush out of the country, many Jews left behind substantial fixed assets. Most of their businesses were unrecoverable when in 1968 the xenophobic regime of Houari Boumedienne (1965-78) nationalized a broad range of private properties, including major corporations and estates owned by Jewish families. The position of whites—as well as Berbers, who comprised at least a quarter of the population—was also undermined by the government's aggressive Arabization program in the public schools and the policy of limiting access to public-sector jobs to those with an Arabic education. By 1975, the identifiably Jewish population of Algeria had been reduced to fewer than several hundred. The New York–based American Jewish Committee counted zero by the year 2001.

Like Morocco and Algeria, Tunisia and Libya were home to vibrant Jewish communities for tens of generations. The ancient Jewish island city of Jerba in Tunisia predated Christianity and Islam and was part of a chain of ancient Jewish settlements from Egypt to Mauretania. Some Jewish rabbis who studied there referred to it as the "Jerusalem of Africa." Remarkably, Jerba is still home to most of the Jews remaining in Tunisia today (Udovitch and Valensi 1984: 1-30). Similarly, numerous coastal towns in Libya had been occupied by Jews since at least the third century BCE. These communities tended to be deeply religious and operated within the context of extensive trading networks throughout the Mediterranean Basin.

In sum, Judaism was deeply rooted and its followers could be considered truly indigenous to the region. Nevertheless, here too Jews and Judaism were practically extinguished in a matter of a decade in the 1960s. Sadly, the scenario in many respects mirrors that of the other countries of North Africa. Thus, we will attempt to focus briefly on the events and historical processes that made the Jewish experience there somewhat different or unique.

For centuries, the city of Tunis served as Tunisia's chief seaport and the center of Jewish commercial life. From the late eighteenth century, Jews practically monopolized its international trade (Kortepeter 1994: 336). They were also highly influential in the royal court of the bey. Most beys were Turks, not Arabs, and thus they used the Jews as a counterbalance to the overwhelming Arab majorities. As early as 1772 Solomon Nataf was chief adviser in the bey's palace, and few decisions were made without his counsel.

The extent of Jewish influence was alluded to in 1819 when the United States Consul in Tunis wrote in a New York newspaper that Jews were entrusted with the bey's jewels, ran his customs house, oversaw tax collections, minted the coins and regulated the currency, and served in various capacities as secretaries and interpreters.

Egged on by their Jewish advisers, successive beys were anxious to develop their Ottoman province and actively sought contact with the West, particularly with France, Britain, and Italy. Ahmed Bey and an entourage of merchants journeyed to Paris in 1846 seeking out investors. One of his objectives was to wean Tunis from excessive dependence on Istanbul. This goal was shared by Tunisian Jews as well, but ironically for different reasons. They would use European consular officials in Tunis not only to expand their own businesses but to air grievances and to seek protection from religious persecution. In 1857, the bey agreed to a human rights charter that abolished the obligations of Jews to wear distinctive clothing and pay the hated poll tax (Udovitch and Valensi 1984: 14).

French, British, and Italian involvement in Tunisian internal affairs grew from the 1860s as the bey obtained foreign capital in return for monopolistic concessions. By the mid-1870s, the three powers competed against each other for lucrative contracts for the construction of railways and modern port facilities. France was especially interested in light of its investments in Egypt and its control over Algeria, which lay immediately to the west and was its most important colony in Africa.

Great Power rivalry over Tunis came to a head in 1878 at the Berlin Congress, when the British gave a green light to a future French occupation in return for French acquiescence to a British takeover of the strategic Mediterranean island of Cyprus. The moment of actual conquest came in 1881, when France launched a land invasion of Tunis on the pretext of the latter's violation of its boundary with Algeria. After a brief bombardment, the bey of Tunis, Muhammad as-Sadok, surrendered. He was persuaded to do so by his Jewish prime minister, Mustapha ben Ismael. For this, France later awarded ben Ismael the prestigious Cross of the Legion of Honor. Ottoman sovereignty was terminated and so was Tunisian self-government. Collectively, Tunis and its subject towns awakened to the reality that they were now subjects of the French Protectorate of Tunisia.

Tunisia generally prospered under French rule, but unlike Algeria, the French never intended that this protectorate would become integrally a part of the metropole. Muslims as well as Jews were brought into the colonial bureaucracies and were progressively given positions of influence. Relations among the various faith communities were relatively peaceful. During the Second World War Tunisia became the only French possession in North Africa under direct Nazi occupation and rule. Muslims and Jews (who then numbered about 90,000) mounted a fierce resistance, and with Allied assistance the Germans were expelled less than a year later in 1942.

Like most of Africa after the war, Tunisia experienced an

increase in modern nationalism, and many Jews supported the Neo Destour Party, which fell under the sway of Habib Bourguiba. A secular Jewish legislator, Pierre Mendes-France, became prime minister of France in 1954 and initiated the move towards Tunisian independence. That year, France capitulated to the Vietnamese in Indo-China and also had to face an armed revolt in Algeria.

The global pressures for decolonization seemed everywhere, and Mendes-France himself was no champion of colonialism. Nevertheless, most Jews in Tunisia were taken by surprise when independence came just two years later.

Following independence, Habib Bourguiba, who became president a year later, in 1957, acknowledged the role local Jews played in the nation's economy and pursued a conciliatory policy. Though many young Jews began aliyah to Israel, most others remained. But a confluence of local anti-Semitic riots that inevitably followed nearly every conflict between Israel and its Arab neighbors and affirmative-action government policies towards the Tunisian Arab business community had a dampening effect on Jews' vision of their own future in Africa. Gradually, it became more difficult to renew trading licenses, and preference was given to Muslims in the granting of import permits. Moreover, after independence, Bourguiba collapsed all Jewish organizations into a single Jewish Religious Council under his authority and appointed by him personally.

Jews no longer felt they had control over their destiny in a world that was becoming more self-assertively Islamic. They found it impossible to identify with Arabo-Islamic culture and felt increasingly isolated as the government began to pursue it more vigorously (Tessler and Hawkins 1980: 69). As more Jews departed, it became progressively difficult to maintain the fabric and coherence of their social, religious, and economic life. All those elements were based on a communalism and extended family construct that fell into disarray. Once a tipping point had been reached, the exodus accelerated. This loss of institutional and familial capacity contributed mightily to the decline in North African Jewry.

By 1971 approximately nine thousand Jews remained in Tunisia, and that number fell dramatically after a series of anti-Semitic incidents in 1982 (Sachar 1985: 112). As the twenty-first century opened, Tunisian Jewry had dropped to about two thousand, with nearly all of them over age sixty and huddled in small urban neighborhoods in Tunis and on the seemingly secure island enclave of Djerba. From the 1980s, Djerba would undergo a minor renaissance as a tourist destination for Jews throughout the world; and although ancient synagogues in Tunis were restored, they served mainly as museums of a golden age seemingly lost forever.

Our narrative ends with a brief examination of Libya, a Muslim country that also has a long history of Jewish involvement. The eighteenth century opened with a struggle between the Tunis bey and his superiors in Istanbul. It was a conflict that spilled over into Tripoli in 1705 and might have annihilated the local population of Muslims and Jews were it not for a plague that forced the invaders to retreat. The Karamanlis dynasty was fatally weakened by the invasion and by internal successionist disputes that followed. In 1793 Istanbul authorities dispatched an expeditionary force that overthrew the warring family and replaced it with a sadistic commander who initiated a reign of terror (Blady 2000: 318).

As we have seen, the authorities in Tunis and Tripoli had historically made handsome profits off piracy on the Mediterranean. They and their Jewish merchant consorts also participated in a lucrative trans-Saharan slave and gold trade operated by Arab caravansaries. Even before the Turks captured Tripoli in 1549 the city had been an important transit point between the oases emporia of the Fezzan and core Mediterranean markets. Fezzan continued to be Tripoli's corridor to black Africa well beyond the seventeenth century.

Already by 1810 Tripolitanian Jews had assumed important administrative and executive functions in the Ottoman government. In 1835, the Ottoman Empire established direct rule over its chaotic province and gave the local Jewish population, then numbering over 32,000, a measure of civil rights as citizens theoretically equal with Arab Muslims. Ali Ahmida notes that a number of Libyan Jews held citizenship in European countries and "defended European interests before and during colonialism" (Ahmida 2005: 62).

Italy, recently reunified as a modern nation-state, yearned for a resurrected African empire and harkened back to the days of the Roman Empire when it held sway over much of North Africa. Elaborate plans for the conquest of Tripoli were laid in 1884 but were squelched by the British, who directed their ambitions to the Horn of Africa. Undeterred, Italy updated its old plans in the early twentieth century, and the military convinced the lawmakers that its conquest would be swift and inexpensive, arguing that the Arabs would see them as liberators against their Turkish oppressors.

It turned out to be a huge miscalculation. Italy ended up deploying over 100,000 troops and nearly depleted its national treasury. Though the Libyan War was declared an Italian victory in 1912, the hinterland was not entirely "pacified" until 1932 under Mussolini. Indeed, the desert tribes had mounted a fierce guerrilla campaign that the Italians had not been militarily or fiscally prepared for (Blady 2000: 320).

Tripoli proper had fallen to the Italians in 1911 after succumbing to the first air bombardment in the history of warfare. Renamed Libya, it became part of the new Italian African Empire, which included Eritrea, a portion of Somalia, and, in the 1930s, briefly Ethiopia. When Italy took Libya and its Saharan interior, it administered the colony as two discrete dependencies: Tripoli was retained as the capital, while Benghazi became administrative headquarters for Cyrenaica. The arid and sparsely populated Fazzan was administered separately.

The status of dhimmi was abolished, and Jews and Christians were given equal status with the Arab majority. In the 1920s and late '30s the Italians modernized the economy and its infrastructure. In general, the Jewish merchants favored the fascists, who took over the administration in 1938 and increased state expenditures. Ahmida points out that "Jewish merchants...not only facilitated Italian economic and cultural interests in Tripoli city but also aided the Italian army in occupying the city" (Ahmida 2005: 65). Then in 1942 the Nazis arrived and sent Jews to local internment centers and to labor camps for work on railroad projects.

Libya was liberated by the Allied forces in 1943, and Britain and France shared in the colony's administration as the United Nations debated its future. In Libya as in other parts of North Africa, postwar Arab nationalism and anger over the creation of the Jewish state of Israel led in 1945 to a pogrom that tore at the fabric of Jewish-Muslim relations and destroyed a condition of trust and mutuality that had existed for many centuries. This tragic event was followed by another pogrom three years later that resulted in a massive Israeli government-sponsored evacuation of more than 29,000 Jews between 1949 and 1952 (Goldberg 1990: 122).

The Italian colony became independent in 1951 under Muhammad Idris, a conservative elderly monarch who, in an atmosphere of Cold War realpolitik, vowed to collaborate closely with Western powers. As part of a U.N.-brokered deal, Britain and the United States were allowed to retain their huge military installations. The Libyan army bristled under this seemingly neocolonialist arrangement and in 1969 Colonel Muammar al-Qadaffi overthrew King Idris, closed the foreign military bases, and nationalized most private properties including those belonging to Jews. In a stroke, Libyan Jewry lost its considerable fixed assets and within a few years the entire Jewish population of Libya had departed, a sizable number of them settling in Italy and North America (Goldberg 2003: 431).

References

Aberbach, Moshe, and David Aberbach. 2000. *The Roman Jewish Wars and Hebrew Cultural Nationalism.* New York: St. Martin's Press.
Abitbol, Michel, ed. 1982. *Communautés juives des marges sahariennes du Maghreb.* Jerusalem: l'Université Hebraique de Jerusalem.
_____. 1989. *The Jews of North Africa during the Second World War.* Detroit: Wayne State University Press.
Abrahams, Israel. 1955. *The Birth of a Community.* Cape Town: Hebrew Congregation.
Abun-Nasr, Jamil M. 1987. *A History of the Maghrib in the Islamic Period.* London: Cambridge University Press.
Ahlstrom, Gosta W. 1986. *Who Were the Israelites?* Winona Lake, IN: Eisenbrauns.
Ahmida, Ali Abdullatif. 2005. "State and Class Formation and Collaboration in Colonial Libya." In *Italian Colonialism.* Edited by Ruth Ben-Ghiat and Mia Fuller. London: Macmillan.
Akenson, Donald H. 1992. *God's People: Covenant and Land in South Africa, Israel, and Ulster.* Ithaca: Cornell University Press.
Alexander, Enid. 1953. *Morris Alexander: A Biography.* Cape Town: Juta.
Alhadeff, Solly, comp. 1962. *Sephardi Hebrew Congregation of Rhodesia.* Harare: National Archives.
Anon. 1972. *Israel and Uganda.* Jerusalem: Israel Ministry of Foreign Affairs.
Anon. 2004. *Great South Africans.* London: Penguin.
Apter, David E. 1961. *The Political Kingdom in Uganda.* Princeton: Princeton University Press.
Arbel, Benjamin. 1995. *Trading Nations: Jews and Venetians in the Early Modern Eastern Mediterranean.* New York: Brill.
Arkin, Marcus, ed. 1984. *South African Jewry: A Contemporary Survey.* Cape Town: Oxford University Press.
Austen, Ralph A. 1998. "The Uncomfortable Relationship: African Enslavement in the Common History of Blacks and Jews." *Tikkun* 9:2.
Baepler, Paul, ed. 1999. *White Slaves, African Masters: An Anthology of*

American Barbary Captivity Narratives. Chicago: University of Chicago Press.

Baldick, Julian. 1997. *Black Gold: Afroasiatic Roots of the Jewish, Christian and Muslim Religions*. London: I.B. Tauris.

Bar-Asher, Shalom. 1986. "The Jews of North Africa and the Land of Israel." In *The Land of Israel: Jewish Perspectives*. Edited by Lawrence A. Hoffman. Notre Dame: University of Notre Dame Press.

Barclay, John M.G. 1996. *Jews in the Mediterranean Diaspora from Alexander to Trajan, 323 BCE – 117 CE*. Edinburgh: T&T Clark.

Baron, Salo. 1975. *Economic History of the Jews*. Jerusalem: Keter Publishers.

Barron, Isadore. 2004. Oral testimony. Oudtshoorn, 6 November.

Beinart, Haim. 1992. *Moreshet Sepharad: The Sephardi Legacy* (2). Jerusalem: Magnes Press.

Benatar, David. 1988. *Three Score Years and the History of Minyan Yosef, 1926-1986*. Cape Town: UCT Printing Department.

Benbassa, Esther, and Aron Rodrigue. 2000. *Sephardi Jewry*. Berkeley: University of California Press.

Benjamin, Alan F. 2002. *Jews of the Dutch Caribbean*. London: Routledge.

Bennett, George. 1963. *Kenya: A Political History*. New York: Oxford University Press.

_____. 1965. "Politics in Kenya." In *History of East Africa, vol. 2*. Edited by Vincent Harlow and E.M. Chilver. Oxford: Clarendon.

Berger, Nathan. 1986. *Chapters from South African History* (Book Two). Johannesburg: Kayor Publishers.

Bernal, Martin. 1991. *Black Athena: Afro-Asiatic Roots of Classical Civilization* (II). New Brunswick: Rutgers University Press.

Bethell, Leslie, ed. 1987. *Colonial Brazil*. New York: Cambridge University Press.

Bettenson, Henry, ed. 1943. *Documents of the Christian Church*. London: Oxford University Press.

Birmingham, David. 1965. *The Portuguese Conquest of Angola*. Oxford: Oxford University Press.

_____. 1981. *Central Africa to 1870*. Cambridge: Cambridge University Press.

_____. 1999. *Portugal and Africa*. New York: St. Martin's Press.

Blackburn, Robin. 1997. *The Making of New World Slavery, 1492-1800*. London: Verso.

Blady, Ken. 2000. *Jewish Communities in Exotic Places*. Jerusalem: Jason Aronson.

Blakely, Allison. 1993. *Blacks in the Dutch World: The Evolution of Racial Imagery in Modern Society.* Bloomington: Indiana University Press.

Bleiberg, Edward. 2002a. *Jewish Life in Ancient Egypt: A Family Archive from the Nile Valley.* Brooklyn: Brooklyn Museum of Art.

Blom, J.C.H., ed. 2002. *The History of the Jews in the Netherlands.* Translated by A.J. Pomerans. Oxford: Littman Library.

Bloom, Herbert I. 1937. *Economic Activities of the Jews of Amsterdam in the 17th and 18th Centuries.* Williamsport: Bayard Publishers.

Blum, Charlotte, and Humphrey Fisher. 1993. "Love for Three Oranges, or, the Askiya's Dilemma: The Askiya, Al-Maghili, and Timbuktu ca. 1500." *Journal of African History* 1:34.

Bodian, Miriam. 1997. *Hebrews of the Portuguese Nation.* Bloomington: Indiana University Press.

Bovill, E.W. 1958. *The Golden Trade of the Moors.* London: Oxford University Press.

Bowser, Frederick P. 1974. *The African Slave Trade in Colonial Peru, 1524-1650.* Stanford: Stanford University Press.

Boxer, C.R. 1952. *Salvador de Sa and the Struggle for Brazil and Angola, 1602-1686.* Westport, CT: Greenwood.

_____. 1963. *Race Relations in the Portuguese Colonial Empire, 1415-1825.* Oxford: Clarendon.

Boyajian, James C. 1989. *Portuguese Bankers at the Court of Spain, 1626-1650.* New Brunswick: Rutgers University Press.

Braudel, Fernand. 1979. *The Wheels of Commerce: Civilization and Capitalism 15th to 18th Century* (2). New York: Harper & Row.

Brooks, Andree. 1997. "Jewish Voyagers to the New World Emerging from History's Mists." *New York Times*, 29 July.

Brooks, George E. 1993. *Landlords and Strangers: Ecology, Society, and Trade in Western Africa, 1000-1630.* Boulder, CO: Westview Press.

_____. 2003. *Eurafricans in Western Africa.* Oxford: James Currey.

Burstein, Stanley, ed. 2000. *Ancient African Civilizations: Kush and Axum.* Princeton, NJ: Markus Wiener Publishers.

Cantor, Norman. 1994. *The Sacred Chain: History of the Jews.* New York: Harper.

Cardoso, Gerald. 1983. *Negro Slavery in the Sugar Plantations of Veracruz and Pernambuco, 1550- 1680.* Washington, D.C.: University Press of America.

Cassell, C.E. n.d. "Bulawayo Jewry, 1894-1900." Harare: National Archives.

Cayetana, Catena Tully. 1989. "Outcasts of Jewish Descent and the

Early Development of the Sugar Industry in the New World." Ph.D. diss.

Chase, Kenneth. 2003. *Firearms: A Global History to 1700*. New York: Cambridge University Press.

Chatterjee, Margaret. 1992. *Gandhi and His Jewish Friends*. London: Macmillan.

Chazan, Naomi. 1983. "The Fallacies of Pragmatism: Israeli Foreign Policy towards South Africa." *African Affairs* 82 (April).

Chilcote, Ronald H., ed. 1972. *Protest and Resistance in Angola and Brazil*. Berkeley: University of California Press.

Chilvers, Hedley A. 1940. *The Story of De Beers*. London: Cassell.

Chissold, Stephen. 1977. *The Barbary Slaves*. London: Elik.

Chouraqui, Andre. 1998. *Histoire des Juifs en Afrique du Nord. Tome I*. Paris: Editions Du Rocher.

Coates, Timothy. 2001. *Convicts and Orphans: Forced and State-Sponsored Colonizers in the Portuguese Empire, 1550-1755*. Stanford: Stanford University Press.

Coetzee Daniel. 2000. *Immigrants to Citizens: Civil Integration and Acculturation of Jews into Oudtshoorn Society, 1874-1999*. M.A. Thesis.

Cohen, H. 1966. "Historical Facts about Rhodesian Jewry." *Rhodesian Jewish Times* (September).

Cohen, Mark R. 1980. *Jewish Self-Government in Medieval Egypt: The Origins of the Office of Head of the Jews, ca. 1065-1126*. Princeton, NJ: Princeton University Press.

Cohen, Martin A. 1971. *The Jewish Experience in Latin America* (II). New York: KTAV Publishers.

Cohen, Martin A., and Abraham Peck, eds. 1993. *Sephardim in the Americas*. Tuscaloosa, AL: American Jewish Archives.

Cohen, Robert. 1983. "Early Caribbean Jewry: A Demographic Perspective." *Jewish Social Studies* 45 (Spring): 2.

Cohen, Shayne. 1999. *The Beginnings of Jewishness*. Berkeley: University of California Press.

———. 1987. *From the Maccabees to the Mishnah*. Philadelphia: Westminster Press.

Collins, John J. 2000. *Between Athens and Jerusalem: Jewish Identity in the Hellenistic Diaspora*. Grand Rapids: Eerdmans.

Connah, Graham. 2001. *African Civilizations: An Archaeological Perspective*. 2nd ed. New York: Cambridge University Press.

Conniff, Michael, and Thomas J. Davis, eds. 2001. *Africans in the Americas*. New York: St. Martin's Press.

Constable, Olivia Remie. 1994. *Trade and Traders in Muslim Spain: The Commercial Realignment of the Iberian Peninsula, 900-1500*. Cambridge: Cambridge University Press.
Conzelman, Hans. 1981. *Gentiles, Jews, Christians: Polemics and Apologetics in the Greco-Roman Era*. Minneapolis: Fortress.
Cook, Weston F. 1994. *The Hundred Year War for Morocco: Gunpowder and the Military Revolution in the Early Modern Muslim World*. Boulder, CO: Westview Press.
Corcos, David. 1976. *Studies in the History of the Jews of Morocco*. Jerusalem: Rubin Mass.
Corinaldi, Michael. 1998. *Jewish Identity: The Case of Ethiopian Jewry*. Jerusalem: Magnes Press.
Coudenhove-Kalergi, Heinrich.1935. *Anti-Semitism throughout the Ages*. London: Hutchinson.
Crecelius, Daniel. 1981. *The Roots of Modern Egypt: A Study of the Regimes of Ali Bey al-Kabir and Muhammad Bey Abu al-Dhahab, 1760-1775*. Chicago: University of Chicago Press.
Crown, Alan D., ed. 1998. *Noblesse Oblige: Essays in Honour of David Kessler*. London: Vallentine Mitchell.
Curtin, Philip D. 1969. *The Atlantic Slave Trade: A Census*. Madison: University of Wisconsin Press.
_____. 1990. *The Rise and Fall of the Plantation Complex*. New York: Cambridge University Press.
Davenport, Rodney, and Christopher Saunders. 2000. *South Africa: A Modern History*. London: Macmillan.
David, Rosalie A. 1988. *Ancient Egypt*. Oxford: Phaidon.
Davidson, Basil, comp. 1964. *The African Past: Chronicles from Antiquity to Modern Times*. New York: Grosset & Dunlap.
_____. 1969. *The African Genius*. Boston: Little, Brown.
Davis, David Brion. 1984. *Slavery and Human Progress*. New York: Oxford University Press.
_____. 1994. "The Slave Trade and the Jews." *The New York Review of Books*, 22 December.
_____. 2001. "Slavery: White, Black, Muslim, Christian." *The New York Review of Books*, 5 July.
Davis, Robert C. 2003. *Christian Slaves, Muslim Masters: White Slavery in the Mediterranean, the Barbary Coast, and Italy, 1500-1800*. London: Palgrave.
Deshen, Shlomo. 1989. *The Mellah Society: Jewish Community Life in Sherifian Morocco*. Chicago: University of Chicago Press.
Deshen, Shlomo, and Moshe Shokeid. 1974. *The Predicament of*

Homecoming: Cultural and Social Life of North African Immigrants in Israel. Ithaca, NY: Cornell University Press.

Deshen, Shlomo, and Walter P. Zenner. 1996. *Jews Among Muslims.* New York: New York University Press.

Diaz-Mas, Paloma. 2000. *Sephardim: The Jews from Spain.* Chicago: University of Chicago Press.

Drescher, Seymour. 1993. "The Role of Jews in the Transatlantic Slave Trade." *Immigrants and Minorities* 12:2.

Dubb, Allie. 1984. "Demographic Picture." In *South African Jewry: A Contemporary Survey.* Edited by Marcus Arkin. Cape Town: Oxford University Press.

———. 1994. *The Jewish Population of South Africa.* Cape Town: Kaplan Centre.

Ebert, Christopher. 2003. "Dutch Trade with Brazil before the Dutch West India Company, 1587-1621." In *Riches from Atlantic Commerce: Dutch Transatlantic Trade and Shipping, 1585-1750.* Edited by Johannes Postma and Victor Enthoven. Leiden: Brill.

Edwards, John. 1988. "Early Caribbean Jewry: A Demographic Perspective." *Jewish Social Studies* 45 (Spring): 2.

Edwards, John. 1988. *The Jews in Christian Europe, 1400-1700.* London: Routledge.

Ehrlich, Carl S. 2003. "Judaism." In *The Illustrated Guide to World Religions.* Edited by Michael Coogan. Oxford: Oxford University Press.

Elbl, Irana. 1997. "The Volume of the Early Atlantic Slave Trade, 1450-1521." *Journal of African History* 38:2.

Eldredge, Elizabeth A., and Fred Morton, eds. 1994. *Slavery in South Africa: Captive Labor on the Dutch Frontier.* Boulder, CO: Westview Press.

Elphick, Richard, and Hermann Giliomee. 1979. *The Shaping of South African Society, 1652-1820.* London: Longman.

Eltis, David. 2000. *The Rise of African Slavery in the Americas.* New York: Cambridge University Press.

Endelman, Todd M. 2002. *The Jews of Britain, 1656-2000.* Berkeley: University of California Press.

Ennaji, Mohammad. 1998. *Serving the Master: Slavery and Society in Nineteenth Century Morocco.* New York: St. Martin's Press.

Epstein, Steven A. 1996. *Genoa and the Genoese, 958-1528.* Chapel Hill: University of North Carolina Press.

Erlich, Haggai, and Israel Gershoni, eds. 2000. *The Nile: Histories, Cultures, Myths.* Boulder, CO: Lynne Rienner.

Etherington, Norman. 2001. *The Great Treks: The Transformation of Southern Africa, 1815-1854*. London: Longman.
Faber, Eli. 1992. *A Time for Planting: The First Migration, 1654-1820*. Baltimore, MD: Johns Hopkins University Press.
———. 1998. *Jews, Slaves, and the Slave Trade*. New York: NYU Press.
Feldman, Leibl. 1989. *Oudtshoorn: Jerusalem of Africa*. Johannesburg: University of Witwatersrand Press.
Feldman, Louis H. 1993. *Jew and Gentile in the Ancient World: Attitudes and Interactions from Alexander to Justinian*. Princeton, NJ: Princeton University Press.
Finkelstein, Israel. 2001. "Biblical Iconoclaust." *Archeology* (September/October).
Finkelstein, Israel, and Neil Asher Silberman. 2000. *The Bible Unearthed: Archaeology's New Vision of Ancient Israel and the Origins of Its Sacred Texts*. New York: Free Press.
Fleischer, Delores, and Angela Caccia. 1983. *Merchant Pioneers: The House of Mosenthal*. Johannesburg: Jonathan Ball.
Forbes, Jack. 1988. *Black Africans and Native Americans*. Oxford: Blackwell.
Frankel, Glenn. 1999. *Rivonia's Children: Their Families and the Cost of Conscience in White South Africa*. New York: Farrar, Straus & Giroux.
Frankenthal, Sally, and Milton Shain. 1993. "Accommodation, Apathy and Activism: Jewish Political Behavior in South Africa." *The Jewish Quarterly* (Spring).
Frerichs, Ernest S., and Leonard H. Lesko, eds. 1997. *Exodus: The Egyptian Evidence*. Winona Lake, IN: Eisenbrauns.
Friedman, Elizabeth. 1988. *Colonialism and After: An Algerian Jewish Community*. South Hadley, MA: Bergin/Garvey.
Friedman, Saul S. 1998. *Jews and the American Slave Trade*. New Brunswick: Transaction.
Friedman, Sharon, comp. 1985. *Guide to Jewish Research Resources in the Cape Province* (II). Cape Town: Kaplan Centre.
Galloway, J.H. 1989. *The Sugar Cane Industry: Origins to 1914*. New York: Cambridge University Press.
———. 2003. "The Role of the Dutch in the Early American Sugar Industry." *De Halve Maen: Journal of the Holland Society* (Summer).
Gampel, Benjamin R., ed. 1997. *Crisis and Creativity in the Sephardic World, 1391-1648*. New York: Columbia University Press.
Gann, L.H. 1969. *A History of Southern Rhodesia: Early Days to 1934*. New York: Humanities Press.
Garfield, Robert. 1990. "Public Christians, Secret Jews: Religion and

Political Conflict on São Tomé." *Sixteenth Century Journal* 21:4.
Gastrow, Shelagh. 1987. *Who's Who in South African Politics*. Braamfontein: Ravan.
_____. 1992. *Who's Who in South African Politics*. Braamfontein: Ravan.
Gerber, Jane. 1980. *Jewish Society in Fez, 1450-1700*. Leiden: E.J. Brill.
_____. 1992. *The Jews of Spain*. New York: Free Press.
Gelfand, Michael. 1976. *A Service to the Sick: History of the Health Services for Africans in Southern Rhodesia, 1890-1953*. Salisbury: Mambo Press.
Giliomee, Herman. 2003. *The Afrikaners: Biography of a People*. Charlottesville: University of Virginia Press.
Gill, Fraser. 1956. *Cohen of South West Africa*. Windhoek: Ziv Press.
Ginio, Alisa M., ed. 1992. *Jews, Christians, and Muslims in the Mediterranean World after 1492*. London: Frank Cass.
Gitlin, Marcia. 1950. *The Vision Amazing: The Story of South African Zionism*. Johannesburg: Menorah.
Golan, Matti. 1982. *Shimon Peres: A Biography*. New York: St. Martin's Press.
Goldberg, Aleck. 1997. "Apartheid and the Jewish Board of Deputies." *Jewish Affairs* 52 (Autumn): 1.
_____. 2002. *People of a Community: South African Jewry*. Johannesburg: Aloy Foundation.
Goldberg, Harvey E. 1990. *Jewish Life in Muslim Libya: Rivals and Relatives*. Chicago: University of Chicago Press.
_____. 2003. "Libya." In *The Jews of the Middle East and North Africa in Modern Times*. Edited by Reeva Spector Simon, Michael Menachem Laskier, and Sara Reguer. New York: Columbia University Press.
Goldenberg, David M. 1999. *The Curse of Ham: Race and Slavery in Early Judaism, Christianity, and Islam*. Princeton, NJ: Princeton University Press.
Goldschmidt, Arthur. 2000. *Biographical Dictionary of Modern Egypt*. Cairo: American University in Cairo Press.
Gottreich, Emily. 2007. *The Mellah of Marrakesh: Jewish and Muslim Space in Morocco's Red City*. Bloomington: Indiana University Press.
Greenstein, Lisa, ed. 2002. *Jewish Life in the South African Country Communities* (I). Johannesburg: Hatefutsoth.
Gruen, Erich S. 2002. *Diaspora: Jews Amidst Greeks and Romans*. Cambridge: Harvard University Press.
Gubbay, Lucien. 1999. *Sunlight and Shadow: The Jewish Experience of Islam*. New York: Other Press.

Haas, Christopher. 1997. *Alexandria in Late Antiquity*. Baltimore: Johns Hopkins Press.
Harman, Nicholas. 1986. *Bwana Stokesi and His African Conquests*. London: Jonathan Cape.
Harrington, Hannah K. 2001. *Holiness: Rabbinic Judaism and the Graeco-Roman World*. London: Routledge.
Hayes, John H., and Sara R. Mandell. 1998. *The Jewish People in Classical Antiquity: From Alexander to Bar Kochba*. Louisville: Westminster/John Knox Press.
Henze, Paul. 1993. "Ethiopia and Eritrea." In *Making War and Waging Peace*. Edited by David R. Smock. Washington: U.S. Institute for Peace Press.
Herrman, Louis. 1930. *A History of the Jews in South Africa to 1895*. London: Gollancz.
Hertz, J.H. 1905. *The Jew in South Africa*. Johannesburg: CAN.
Hezser, Catherine. 2005. *Jewish Slavery in Antiquity*. New York: Oxford University Press.
Hirschberg, H.Z. (J.W.). 1963. "The Problem of the Judaized Berbers." *Journal of African History* 4:3.
_____. 1981. *A History of the Jews in North Africa* (II). Leiden: Brill.
Hiskett, Mervyn.1984. *The Development of Islam in West Africa*. London: Longman.
Hocking, Anthony. 1973. *Oppenheimer and Son*. New York: McGraw-Hill.
Hodges, Tony, and Malyn Hodges. 1988. *São Tomé and Príncipe: From Plantation Economy to Microstate*. Boulder, CO: Westview Press.
Hoffman, Tzippi, and Alan Fischer. 1988. *The Jews of South Africa: What Future?* Johannesburg: Southern.
Hoffmeier, James K. 1997. *Israel in Egypt: The Evidence for the Authenticity of the Exodus Tradition*. New York: Oxford University Press.
Hrbek, I., ed. 1993. *General History of Africa: From the Seventh to the Eleventh Century*. London: James Currey.
Hull, Richard W. 1990. *American Enterprise in South Africa*. New York: New York University Press.
Hunter, Jane. 1987. *Israeli Foreign Policy: South Africa and Central America*. Boston: South End Press.
Hunwick, John O. 1999. *Timbuktu and the Songhay Empire*. Boston: Brill.
_____. 2006. *Jews of the Saharan Oasis*. Princeton, NJ: Markus Wiener Publishers.

Iliffe, John. 1995. *Africans: A History of a Continent.* New York: Cambridge University Press.
Inikori, J.E., ed. 1982. *Forced Migration: The Impact of the Export Slave Trade on African Societies.* New York: Africana.
Innes, Duncan. 1984. *Anglo: Anglo American and the Rise of Modern South Africa.* Braamfontein: Ravan.
Isaac, Benjamin. 2004. *The Invention of Racism in Classical Antiquity.* Princeton, NJ: Princeton University Press.
Isaac, Ephraim. 1992. "Jewish Solidarity and Jews of Ethiopia." In *Organizing Rescue: National Jewish Solidarity in the Modern Period.* Edited by Selwyn Ilan Troen and Benjamin Pinkus. London: Frank Cass.
Ishemo, Sherbi L. 1995. *The Lower Zambesi Basin in Mozambique: A Study in Economy and Society, 1850-1920.* Avebury: Aldershot.
Isichei, Elizabeth. 1995. *A History of Christianity in Africa.* Grand Rapids, MI: Eerdmans.
Israel, Jonathan. 1984. "The Changing Role of the Dutch Sephardim in International Trade, 1595-1715." In *Dutch Jewish History.* Edited by Jozeph Michman. Levie: Tirtsah.
_____. 1985. *European Jewry in the Age of Mercantilism, 1550-1750.* Oxford: Clarendon.
_____. 1989. *Dutch Primacy in World Trade, 1585-1740.* Oxford: Oxford University Press.
_____. 1995. *The Dutch Republic: Its Rise, Greatness, and Fall, 1477-1806.* Oxford: Clarendon.
Jacob, Abel. 1971. "Israel's Military Aid to Africa, 1960-66." *Journal of Modern African Studies* 9 (August): 2.
Jacobs, Janet L. 2002. *Hidden Heritage: The Legacy of the Crypto-Jews.* Berkeley: University of California Press.
Jeffries, James S. 1999. *The Graeco-Roman World of the New Testament Era.* Downers Grove: Intervarsity Press.
Johnson, Paul. 1987. *A History of the Jews.* New York: Harper Perennial.
Jordan, Winthrop. 1995. "Slavery and the Jews." *The Atlantic Monthly* (September).
Joseph, Benjamin.1988. *Besieged Bedfellows: Israel and the Land of Apartheid.* New York: Greenwood Press.
Joseph, Helen. 1986. *Side By Side: A Personal Account of One South African Woman's Struggle Against Apartheid.* New York: William Morrow.
Jowell, Phyllis. 1994. *Joe Jowell of Namaqualand: The Story of a Modern-Day Pioneer.* Vlaeberg: Fernwood Press.

Kamen, Henry. 1983. *Spain, 1469-1714: A Society of Conflict.* New York: Longman.

———. 1989. "The Mediterranean and the Expulsion of Spanish Jews in 1492." *Past and Present* 119:30-55.

Kanfer, Stefan. 1993. *The Last Empire: De Beers, Diamonds, and the World.* New York: Farrar, Straus & Giroux.

Kaplan, Mendel. 1986. *Jewish Roots in the South African Economy.* Cape Town: Struik.

Kaplan, Mendel, and Marian Robertson, eds. 1991. *Founders and Followers: Johannesburg Jewry, 1887- 1915.* Johannesburg: Vlaeberg.

Kaplan, Steven. 1992. *The Beta Israel (Falasha) in Ethiopia: Earliest Times to the Twentieth Century.* New York: New York University Press.

———. 1993. "The Invention of Ethiopian Jews: Three Models." *Cahiers d'Etudes africaines* 132: xxxiii-4.

———. 2000. "Did Jewish Influence Reach Ethiopia via the Nile?" In *The Nile: Histories, Cultures, Myth.* Edited by Haggai Erlich and Israel Gershoni. Boulder, CO: Lynne Rienner Publishers.

Karis, Thomas, and Gail Gerhart, eds. 1977. *From Protest to Challenge: A Documentary History of African Politics in South Africa* (3). Stanford: Hoover Institution Press.

Karner, Frances P. 1969. *The Sephardics of Curaçao.* Assen, Netherlands: Van Gorcum.

Kedourie, Elie, ed. 1979. *The Jewish World: Revelation, Prophecy and History.* London: Thames & Hudson.

Kentridge, Morris. 1953. *The South African Jewish Board of Deputies: The Story of Fifty Years, 1903- 1953.* Johannesburg: Moss.

Kessler, David. 1982. *The Falashas: The Forgotten Jews of Ethiopia.* New York: Africana.

Ki-Zerbo, J., and D.T. Niane, eds. 1997. *General History of Africa: From the Twelfth to the Sixteenth Century* (IV). London: James Currey.

Klein, Herbert S. 1986. *African Slavery in Latin America and the Caribbean.* New York: Oxford University Press.

———. 1999. *The Atlantic Slave Trade.* New York: Cambridge University Press.

deKock, W.J., ed. 1972. *Dictionary of South African Biography.* Cape Town: Tafeberg.

Kortepeter, C. Max. 1991. *The Ottoman Turks: Nomad Kingdom to World Empire.* Istanbul: Isis Press.

———. 1994. "Jew and Turk in Algiers in 1800." In *The Jews of the Ottoman Empire.* Edited by Avigdor Levy. Princeton, NJ: Darwin Press.

Kosmin, B.A. 1980. *Majuta: A History of the Jewish Community in Zimbabwe.* Gwelo: Mambo Press.

Krikler, Dennis. n.d. "The Pioneering Jews of Rhodesia." Harare: National Archives.

Landau, Jacob M. 1969. *Jews in Nineteenth Century Egypt.* New York: New York University Press.

Landman, Isaac, and Simon Cohen, eds. 1948. *The Universal Jewish Encyclopedia.* New York: Avron.

Laremont, Ricardo R. 2000. *Islam and the Politics of Resistance in Algeria, 1783-1992.* Trenton, NJ: Africa World Press.

Laskier, Michael M. 1994. *North African Jewry in the Twentieth Century: The Jews of Morocco, Tunisia, and Algeria.* New York: New York University Press.

Law, Robin. 1991. *The Slave Coast of West Africa, 1550-1750.* Oxford: Clarendon.

Law, Robin, and Kristin Mann. 1999. "West Africa in the Atlantic Community: The Case of the Slave Coast." *William and Mary Quarterly,* 3rd series, 56:2.

Leatt, James, Theo Kneifel, and Klaus Nurnberger, eds. 1986. *Contending Ideologies in South Africa.* Cape Town: David Philip.

Leibovitz, Lief. 2005. "The Anti-Zionists." *Moment* (August).

Lerman, Anthony. 1989. *Jewish Communities of the World.* 4th ed. London: Macmillan.

Leslau, Wolf. 1951. *Falasha Anthology: The Black Jews of Ethiopia.* New York: Schocken Books.

Leveson, Marcia. 2001. *People of the Book: Images of the Jew in South African English Fiction, 1880- 1992.* Johannesburg: Witwatersrand University Press.

Levine, Donald N. 1974. *Greater Ethiopia: The Evolution of a Multiethnic Society.* Chicago: University of Chicago Press.

Levtzion, Nehemiah. 1973. *Ancient Ghana and Mali.* London: Methuen.

Lewicki, T. 1992. "The Role of the Sahara." In *General History of Africa* (III). Edited by I. Hrbek. London: James Currey.

Lewis, Bernard, ed. 1976. *Islam and the Arab World.* New York: Knopf.

Lewis, David Levering. 1987. *The Race to Fashoda.* New York: Henry Holt.

Liptz, P. 1981. "The Jewish Community in Zimbabwe." *Zimbabwe History* XII.

Livermore, H.V. 1976. *A New History of Portugal.* 2nd ed. New York: Cambridge University Press.

Lobban, Richard A. 1997. *Historical Dictionary of the Republic of Guinea-Bissau*. 3rd ed. London: Scarecrow.
Lovejoy, Paul E. 1983. *Transformations in Slavery: A History of Slavery in Africa*. New York: Cambridge University Press.
Lovejoy, Paul E., and José C. Curto, eds. 2003. *Enslaving Connections and the Changing Cultures of Africa and Brazil during the Era of Slavery*. Amherst: Humanity Books.
Lunenfeld, Marvin. 1987. *Keepers of the City: The Corregidores of Isabella I of Castile, 1474-1504*. New York: Cambridge University Press.
Macmillan, Hugh. 2005. *An African Trading Empire: The Story of Susman Brothers & Wulfsohn, 1901- 2005*. New York: I.B. Tauris.
Macmillan, Hugh, and Frank Shapiro. 2001. *Zion in Africa: The Jews of Zambia*. London: I.B. Tauris.
Makinda, Samuel. 1987. *Superpower Diplomacy in the Horn of Africa*. New York: St. Martin's Press.
Malka, Eli S. 1997. *Jacob's Children in the Land of the Mahdi: Jews of the Sudan*. Syracuse: Syracuse University Press.
Mantzaris, Evangelos. 1987. "Jewish Trade Unions in Cape Town, 1903-1907." *Jewish Social Studies* 49:3/4.
Marcus, Harold. 1994. *A History of Ethiopia*. Berkeley: University of California Press.
Marcus, Jacob R. 1970. *The Colonial American Jew, 1492-1776* (I). Detroit: Wayne State University Press.
_____. 1972. *The Jew in the Medieval World: A Source Book 315-1791*. New York: Atheneum.
Mark, Peter. 2002. *Portuguese Style and Luso-African Identity*. Bloomington: Indiana University Press.
_____. 2004. "Two Early Seventeenth Century Sephardic Communities on Senegal's Petite Cote." *History in Africa: A Journal of Method* 31.
Marlowe, John. 1971. *The Golden Age of Alexandria*. New York: Gollancz.
Martin, Phyllis. 1972. *The External Trade of the Loango Coast, 1576-1870*. New York: Oxford University Press.
McCabe, I.B., and G. Harlaftis, eds. 2005. *Diasporic Entrepreneurial Networks: Four Centuries of History*. Oberg: Oxford University Press.
McCann, James C. 1995. *People of the Plow: An Agricultural History of Ethiopia, 1800-1990*. Madison: University of Wisconsin Press.
_____. 2005. *Maize and Grace: Africa's Encounter with a New World Crop*. Cambridge: Harvard University Press.

Melammed, Rene Levine. 2004. *A Question of Identity: Iberian Conversos in Historical Perspective.* Oxford: Oxford University Press.

Mendelsohn, Richard. 1998. *The Jewish War: Anglo-Jewry and the South African War.* Pretoria: UNISA Library Conference Papers.

———. 1991. *Sammy Marks, The Uncrowned King of the Transvaal.* Athens: Ohio University Press.

Mendelsohn, Sidney. 1912. *Jewish Pioneers of South Africa.* London: Jewish Historical Society.

Meyers, Allan R. 1996. "Patronage and Protection: The Status of Jews in Precolonial Morocco." In *Jews Among Muslims.* Edited by Shlomo Deshen and Walter P. Zenner. New York: New York University Press.

Michman, Jozeph, and Levie Tirtsah, eds. 1984. *Dutch Jewish History.* Jerusalem: Tel-Aviv University Press.

Miller, Arnold. 1981. *The Jewish Community in Natal.* Cape Town: Transvaal Printers.

Miller, J.M., and John H. Hayes.1986. *A History of Ancient Israel and Judah.* Philadelphia: Westminster Press.

Miller, Joseph C. 1988. *Way of Death: Merchant Capitalism and the Angolan Slave Trade, 1730-1830.* Madison: University of Wisconsin Press.

———. 1991. "Portuguese Southern Atlantic Slave Trade." In *Slavery and the Rise of the Atlantic System.* Edited by Barbara Solow. Cambridge: Cambridge University Press.

———. 1996. "A Marginal Institution on the Margin of the Atlantic System: The Portuguese Southern Atlantic Slave Trade in the Eighteenth Century." In *Slave Trades 1500-1800: Globalization of Forced Labor.* Edited by Patrick Manning. Aldershot: Variorum.

Mitchell, B.R., comp. 1982. *International Historical Statistics: Africa and Asia.* New York: New York University Press.

Modrzejewski, Joseph M. 1995. *The Jews of Egypt from Ramses II to Emperor Hadrian.* Jerusalem: Jewish Publication Society.

Mokhtar, G., ed. 1990. *General History of Africa* (II). Berkeley: University of California Press.

Moodie, T. Dunbar. 1975. *The Rise of Afrikanerdom.* Berkeley: University of California Press.

Muller, C.F.J. 1969. *500 Years: A History of South Africa.* Pretoria: Academica.

Musiker, Naomi. 2004. "The Jews of Kenya." *Jewish Affairs* 59 (Winter): 2.

Nadav, Kashtan, ed. 2001. *Seafaring and the Jews.* London: Frank Cass.

Netanyahu, B. 1995. *The Origins of the Inquisition in Fifteenth Century Spain.* New York: Random House.
Newitt, Malyn. 1973. *Portuguese Settlements on the Zambesi.* New York: Africana.
———. 1995. *A History of Mozambique.* London: Hurst.
Newman, James L. 1995. *The Peopling of Africa.* New Haven: Yale University Press.
Nicholson, E.W. 1973. *Exodus and Sinai in History and Tradition.* Oxford: Oxford University Press.
Niditch, Susan. 1997. *Ancient Israelite Religion.* New York: Oxford University Press.
Nuland, Sherwin. 2005. *Maimonides.* New York: Schocken.
Ofcansky, Thomas P. 1996. *Uganda: A Tarnished Pearl of Africa.* Boulder, CO: Westview Press.
Ogunremi, Gabriel O. 1982. *Counting the Camels.* New York: Nok.
Oliver, Roland. 1991. *The African Experience.* New York: Harper Collins.
O'Meara, Patrick. 1975. *Rhodesia: Racial Conflict and Coexistence.* Ithaca, NY: Cornell University Press.
Oppenheimer, Jean. 2003. "Egypt and Sudan." In *The Jews of the Middle East and North Africa in Modern Times.* Edited by Reeva Spector Simon, Michael Menachem Laskier, and Sara Reguer. New York: Columbia University Press.
Ottaway, Marina. 1990. *The Political Economy of Ethiopia.* New York: Praeger.
Pallister, David, Sarah Stewart, and Ian Lepper. 1988. *South Africa, Inc: The Oppenheimer Empire.* London: Corgi.
Pankhurst, Richard. 1965. "Emperor Menelik II of Ethiopia." *Tarikh,* 1 November.
———. 1992. *A Social History of Ethiopia.* Trenton, NJ: The Red Sea Press.
———. 1998. *The Ethiopians: A History.* Oxford: Blackwell.
Parfitt, Tudor. 1992. *Journey to the Vanished City: The Search for a Lost Tribe of Israel.* New York: Random House.
———. 1999. *The Beta Israel in Ethiopia and Israel.* Edited by Tudor Parfitt and Emanuela Trevisan Semi. Surrey: Curzon.
Parfitt, Tudor, and Yulia Egorova. 2006. *Genetics, Mass Media and Identity: Case Study of the Genetic Research on the Lemba and Bene Israel.* New York: Routledge.
Park, Thomas K. 1996. *Historical Dictionary of Morocco.* Trenton, NJ: Scarecrow Press.

Paxton, George D. 2001. "Sonia Schlesin, Gandhi, and South Africa." *Jewish Affairs* 56:1.
Pennell, C.R. 2000. *Morocco since 1830: A History.* New York: New York University Press.
Penvenne, Jean Marie. 1995. *African Workers and Colonial Racism: Mozambican Strategies and Struggles in Lourenco-Marques, 1877-1962.* Portsmouth: Heinemann.
Perera, Victor. 1995. "Burning Questions: A Monumental Reinterpretation of Why the Inquisition Happened." *The New Yorker*, 6 November.
Peters, Joel. 1992. *Israel and Africa: The Problematic Friendship.* London: I.B. Tauris.
Pharr, Clyde. 1953. "The Theodosian Code." *The Jewish Quarterly Review*, n.s. (April).
Phillips, William D. 1985. *Slavery from Roman Times to the Early Transatlantic Trade.* Minneapolis: University of Minnesota Press.
Phimister, Ian. 1988. *An Economic and Social History of Zimbabwe, 1890-1948.* London: Longman.
Pollard, Justin, and Howard Reid. 2006. *The Rise and Fall of Alexandria.* New York: Penguin.
Porten, Bezalel. 1968. *Archives from Elephantine: The Life of an Ancient Jewish Military Colony.* Berkeley: University of California Press.
Postma, Johannes. 1990. *The Dutch in the Atlantic Slave Trade, 1600-1815.* New York: Cambridge University Press.
_____. 1992. "The Dispersal of African Slaves in the West by Dutch Slave Traders, 1630-1803." In *The Atlantic Slave Trade.* Edited by J.E. Inikori and Stanley Engerman. Durham: Duke University Press.
Pratt, Julius W. 1955. *A History of United States Foreign Policy.* Englewood Cliffs, NJ: Prentice-Hall.
Press, Charles. 1993. *The Light of Israel: The Story of the Paarl Jewish Community.* Paarl: Jubilee Publications.
Prichard, Denise. 2001. *Hearing Grasshoppers Jump: Story of Raymond Ackerman.* Cape Town: David Philip.
Pullan, Brian S. 1983. *The Jews of Europe and the Inquisition of Venice, 1550-1670.* New York: Barnes & Noble.
Quirin, James. 1992. *The Evolution of the Ethiopian Jews: A History of the Beta Israel to 1920.* Philadelphia: University of Pennsylvania Press.
Rawley, James A. 1981. *The Transatlantic Slave Trade.* New York: W.W. Norton.
Reiser, Stewart. 1989. *The Israeli Arms Industry: Foreign Policy, Arms*

Transfers and Military Doctrine of a Small State. New York: Holmes & Meier.
Robinson, Ronald, and John Gallagher. 1961. *Africa and the Victorians.* New York: St. Martin's Press.
Rodrigues, José H. 1965. *Brazil and Africa.* Translated by Richard Mazzara. Berkeley: University of California Press.
Rohl, David M. 1995. *Pharaohs and Kings: A Biblical Quest.* New York: Crown.
Rosen, Chaim, and Steven Kaplan. 1994. "Ethiopian Jews in Israel." In *American Jewish Yearbook.* New York American Jewish Committee.
Rosenthal, Eric, comp. 1966. *Southern African Dictionary of National Biography.* London: Voix.
Ross, James R. 2000. *Fragile Branches: Travels through the Jewish Diaspora.* New York: Riverhead Books.
Rotberg, Robert I. 1965. *A Political History of Tropical Africa.* New York: Harcourt, Brace.
____. 1965. *The Rise of Nationalism in Central Africa, 1873-1964.* Boston: Harvard University Press.
____. 1988. *The Founder: Cecil Rhodes and the Pursuit of Power.* New York: Oxford University Press.
Roux, Edward. 1964. *Time Longer than Rope: The Black Man's Struggle for Freedom in South Africa.* Madison: University of Wisconsin Press.
Rubens, Alfred. 1973. *A History of Jewish Costume.* London: Weidenfeld & Nicolson.
Rubin, Martin. 1977. *Sarah Gertrude Millin: A South African Life.* Johannesburg: AD Donker.
Runia, David. 2002. "Christian Reception of Philo the Jew in Egypt." In *Shem in the Tents of Japhet.* Edited by James L. Kugel. Leiden: Brill.
Ryder, Alan. 1969. *Benin and the Europeans, 1485-1897.* New York: Humanities Press.
Sachar, Howard M. 1985. *Diaspora: An Inquiry into the Contemporary Jewish World.* New York: Harper & Row.
____. 1994. *Farewell España: The World of the Sephardim Remembered.* New York: Alfred A. Knopf.
Salamon, Hagar. 1999. *The Hyena People: Ethiopian Jews in Christian Ethiopia.* Berkeley: University of California Press.
Sanders, Edith. 1969. "The Hamitic Hypothesis." *Journal of African History* 10:4.
Saron, Gustave. 2001. *The Jews of South Africa to 1953.* Johannesburg: Scarecrow.

Saron, Gustave, and Louis Hotz, eds. 1955. *The Jews in South Africa.* Cape Town: Oxford University Press.

Saunders, A.C.D. 1982. *A Social History of Black Slaves and Freedmen in Portugal, 1441-1555.* New York: Cambridge University Press.

Schafer, Peter. 1997. *Judeophobia: Attitudes toward the Jews in the Ancient World.* Cambridge: Harvard University Press.

Scheindlin, Raymond P. 1998. *History of the Jewish People: From Legendary Times to Modern Statehood.* New York: Oxford University Press.

Schorsch, Jonathan. 2004. *Jews and Blacks in the Early Modern World.* New York: Cambridge University Press.

Schrand, Irmgard. 2004. *Jews in Egypt: Communists and Citizens.* Munster: Lit Verlag.

Schrire. 2000. "Mostly Smous?" *Jewish Affairs* 55:1.

Schroeter, Daniel J. 1988. *Merchants of Essaouira: Urban Society and Imperialism in Southwestern Morocco, 1844-1886.* New York: Cambridge University Press.

_____. 1992. "Slave Markets and Slavery in Moroccan Urban Society." In *The Human Commodity: Perspectives on the Trans-Saharan Slave Trade."* Edited by Elizabeth Savage. London: Frank Cass.

_____. 1993. "The Jewish Quarter and the Moroccan City." In *New Horizons in Sephardic Studies.* Edited by Yedida K. Stillman and George K. Zucker. Albany: State University of New York Press.

_____. 2002. *The Sultan's Jew: Morocco and the Sephardi World.* Stanford: Stanford University Press.

Schwartz, Stuart B. 1985. *Sugar Plantations in the Formation of Brazilian Society.* New York: Cambridge University Press.

Seltzer, Robert M. 1980. *Jewish People Jewish Thought: The Jewish Experience in History.* New York: Macmillan.

Semi, Emanuela T. 1998. "Faitlovitch, Margulies and the Alliance Israelite." In *Noblesse Oblige: Essays in Honour of David Kessler.* Edited by Alan D. Crown. London: Vallentine Mitchell.

Serels, M. Mitchell. 1991. *A History of the Jews of Tangier in the Nineteenth and Twentieth Centuries.* New York: Sepher-Hermon.

Shain, Milton. 1983. *Jewry and Cape Society: The Origins and Activities of the Jewish Board of Deputies for the Cape Colony.* Cape Town: Historical Publication Society.

_____. 1994. *The Roots of Antisemitism in South Africa.* Charlottesville: University Press of Virginia.

_____. 1998. *Antisemitism.* London: Bower Dean.

_____. 2002. "South African Jewry: Emigrating? At Risk? Or

Restructuring the Jewish Future?" In *Continuity, Commitment, and Survival: Jewish Communities in the Diaspora.* Edited by Sol Encel. Westport, CT: Praeger.

Shain, Milton, and Richard Mendelsohn, eds. 2000. *Memories, Realities and Dreams: Aspects of the South African Jewish Experience.* Cape Town: Jonathan Ball.

Shamir, Shimon, ed. 1987. *The Jews of Egypt: A Mediterranean Society in Modern Times.* Boulder, CO: Westview Press.

Shaw, Stanford J. 1991. *The Jews of the Ottoman Empire and the Turkish Republic.* New York: New York University Press.

Shelemay, Kay Kaufman. 1990. *Music, Ritual, and Falasha History.* East Lansing: Michigan State University Press.

Shimoni, Gideon. 1980. *Jews and Zionism: The South African Experience (1910-1967).* Cape Town: Oxford University Press.

———. 1983. "South African Jewry." In *The Jews of South Africa.* Tel Aviv: National Goldmann Museum of the Jewish Diaspora.

———. 2003. *Community and Conscience: The Jews in Apartheid South Africa.* Lebanon, NH: Brandeis University Press.

Sichel, Frieda H. 1966. *From Refugee to Citizen.* Cape Town: Balkema.

Simon, Reeva Spector, Michael Menachem Laskier, and Sara Reguer, eds. 2003. *The Jews of the Middle East and North Africa in Modern Times.* New York: Columbia University Press.

Slingerland, H. Dixon. 1997. *Claudian Policymaking and the Early Imperial Repression of Judaism at Rome.* Atlanta: Scholars Press.

Sly, Dorothy I. 1996. *Philo's Alexandria.* New York: Routledge.

Smallwood, E.M. 1976. *The Jews under Roman Rule.* Leyden: Ranana.

Snow, Philip. 1988. *The Star Raft: China's Encounter with Africa.* Ithaca, NY: Cornell University Press.

Sonbol, Amira El-Azhary. 2000. *The New Mamluks: Egyptian Society and Modern Feudalism.* Syracuse, NY: Syracuse University Press.

Spector, Stephen. 2005. *Operation Solomon: The Daring Rescue of the Ethiopian Jews.* New York: Oxford University Press.

Stein, Miriam. 1997. "The Past Is All About Us: Jewish Women and Apartheid." *Jewish Affairs* 52 (Autumn): 1.

Stein, Robert Louis. 1979. *The French Slave Trade in the Eighteenth Century: An Old Regime Business.* Madison: University of Wisconsin Press.

Stern, Maureen, comp. 1972. *South African Jewish Biography, 1900-1966.* Cape Town: University of Cape Town Libraries.

Stillman, Norman A. 1996. "Middle Eastern and North African Jewries Confront Modernity." In *Sephardi and Middle Eastern*

Jewries. Bloomington: Indiana University Press.
Stultz, Newell. 1974. *Afrikaner Politics in South Africa, 1934-1948.* Los Angeles: University of California Press.
Summerfield, Daniel P. 2003. *From Falashas to Ethiopian Jews: The External Influences for Change, 1860-1960.* New York: Routledge.
Suttner, Immanuel, ed. 1997. *Cutting Through the Mountain: Interviews with South African Jewish Activists.* New York: Viking.
Swainson, Nicola. 1980. *The Development of Corporate Capitalism in Kenya, 1918-1977.* London: Heineman.
Swetschinski, Daniel. 2000. *Reluctant Cosmopolitans: The Portuguese Jews of Seventeenth Century Amsterdam.* London: Littman.
_____. 2002. "The Middle Ages to the Golden Age, 1516-1621." In *The History of the Jews in the Netherlands.* Edited by J.C.H. Blom. Translated by A.J. Pomerans. Oxford: Littman Library.
Tambs, Lewis A. 1996. "Expulsion of the Jewish Community from the Spains." In *Religion in the Age of Exploration: The Case of Spain.* Edited by Benjamin LeBeau and Menachem Mor. Towon: Creighton University Press.
Tavares, Maria. 1997. "Expulsion or Integration?" In *Crisis and Creativity in the Sephardic World, 1391-1648.* Edited by Benjamin Gampel. New York: Columbia University Press.
Tcherikover, V. 1963. "The Decline of the Jewish Diaspora in Egypt in the Roman Period." *Journal of Jewish Studies* 14.
Tessler, Mark, and Linda Hawkins. 1980. "Political Culture of Jews in Tunisia and Morocco." *International Journal of Middle East Studies* II.
Thomas, Hugh. 1997. *The Slave Trade: The Story of the Atlantic Slave Trade, 1440-1870.* New York: Simon & Schuster.
Thompson, L., and J. Ferguson. 1969. *Africa in Classical Antiquity.* Ibadan, Nigeria: Ibadan University Press.
Thornton, John. 1992. *Africa and Africans in the Making of the Atlantic World, 1400-1680.* New York: Cambridge University Press.
Toaff, Ariel, and Simon Schwarzfuchs, eds. 1989. *The Mediterranean and the Jews.* Jerusalem: Bar-Ilan Press.
Tomeh, George J. 1973. *Israel and South Africa.* New York: New World Press.
Trimingham, J. Spencer. 1970. *A History of Islam in West Africa.* New York: Oxford University Press.
Troen, Selwyn I., and Benjamin Pinkus, eds. 1992. *Organizing Rescue: National Jewish Solidarity in the Modern Period.* London: Frank Cass.
Trzebinski, Errol. 1985. *The Kenya Pioneers.* London: Heinemann.
Tyrrell-Glynn, W., comp. 1977. *Guide to the South African Manuscript*

Collections in the South African Library. Cape Town: South African Library.

Udovitch, Abraham, and Lucette Valensi. 1984. *The Last Arab Jews: The Communities of Jerba, Tunisia.* New York: Harwood.

Van den Boogaart, Ernst. 1992. "The Trade between Western Africa and the Atlantic World, 1600- 1690." *Journal of African History* 4:33.

Van Onselen, Charles. 1982. *Studies in the Social and Economic History of the Witwatersrand, 1886-1914* (I). Johannesburg: Ravan.

Vansina, Jan. 1966. *Kingdoms of the Savanna.* Madison: University of Wisconsin Press.

Veen, Ernest W., and Mohammed Achaari. 2005. *Morocco: 5000 Years of Culture.* Amsterdam: KTT.

Verlinden, Charles. 1995. "Italian Influences in Iberian Colonization." In *The European Opportunity.* Edited by Fernandez-Arnesto Felipe. London: Ashgate.

Vogt, John L. 1973. "The Early São Tomé-Príncipe Slave Trade with Mina: 1500-1540." *International Journal of African Historical Studies* 6:3.

Voorhees, David. 1997. "Captured: The Turkish Slavery of Leisler's Susannah." *Seaport Magazine* (Summer).

Wagaw, Teshome. 1993. *For Our Soul: Ethiopian Jews in Israel.* Detroit, MI: Wayne State University Press.

Walker, Eric. 1957. *A History of Southern Africa.* London: Longman.

Walshe, Peter. 1971. *The Rise of African Nationalism: The African National Congress, 1912-1952.* Berkeley: University of California Press.

Watzman, Haim. 2001. "Biblical Iconoclaust." *Archeology* (September/October).

Weinstein, James. 1997. "Exodus and Archeological Reality." In *Exodus: The Egyptian Evidence.* Edited by Ernest S. Frerichs and Leonard Lesko. Winona Lake: Eisenbrauns.

Weisbord, Robert G. 1968. *African Zion: The Attempt to Establish a Jewish Colony in the East African Protectorate, 1903-1905.* Philadelphia: The Jewish Publication Society of America.

Westheimer, Ruth, and Steven Kaplan. 1992. *Surviving Salvation: The Ethiopian Jewish Family in Transition.* New York: New York University Press.

Wheatcroft, Geoffrey. 1985. *The Randlords.* London: Cass.

Wilks, Ivor. 1993. *Forests of Gold: Essays on the Akan and the Kingdom of Asante.* Athens: Ohio University Press.

Willis, John R. 1971. "The Spread of Islam." In *Horizon History of Africa*. Edited by Alvin Josephy. New York: American Heritage.

Wills, A.J. 1964. *The History of Central Africa*. New York: Oxford University Press.

Winter, Michael. 1987. "Egyptian Jewry during the Ottoman Period." In *The Jews of Egypt*. Edited by Shimon Shamin. Boulder, CO: Westview Press.

Wiznitzer, Arnold. 1960. *Jews in Colonial Brazil*. New York: Columbia University Press.

Yogev, Gedalia. 1978. *Diamonds and Coral: Anglo-Dutch Jews and Eighteenth-Century Trade*. New York: Holmes & Meier.

Index

Aaron, Benison 130
Abayudaya 183-184
Abbasid 43, 45, 48
Abdel Kader 238
Abraham 3-5, 8-9, 11-12, 58, 82, 110, 116, 119, 182-183, 254, 270
Abraham of Bija 119
Abravanel, Samuel 85
Abu Zikri Kohen 47
Abyssinia 185
Ackerman, Gus 138, 156
Ackerman, Ray 156
Adowa, Battle of 202
Adulis 188-191
Afonso IV, King 81, 92, 95, 117
African National Congress (ANC) 150-151, 154, 158-161, 163-165, 271
Afrikaner 122, 126, 129-132, 137, 139, 141-144, 149, 152, 154-155, 174, 177, 269
Agaw 187-191, 193
Ahmed Bey 244
Akhenaten 6
Aksum 185, 188-193
Alawis 212
Albany Settlement 120
Albu, George and Leopold 127
Alexander, Morris 134, 251
Alexander the Great 14, 16, 19
Alexandria 17-18, 22-24, 26-27, 29-34, 36, 68, 190, 226, 228-229, 258, 263, 266, 269
Alexandria, Great Library at 30
Alfasi, Isaac 48
Algarve 81
Algeciras 218
Algeria 20, 22, 28, 30, 33-34, 45, 59, 66, 71, 210, 217, 235, 238-243, 245-246, 262
Algiers 52, 66, 68, 217, 235-238, 242, 261
Algiers, Battle of 242
Ali Killis 47
Aliens Act (1906) 139, 141
Aliyah 154, 166, 201, 203-206, 221-223, 231, 234, 246
Allied Forces 221, 249
Almohads 52-55
Almoravids 52-53
Alvaro II, King 100
Amenemhat III, Pharaoh 4
American Association for Ethiopian Jews 203
American Civil War 227
American Jewish Committee 222, 243, 267
Amerindians 97, 99
Amharic 186, 192, 194
Amin, Idi 184
Amsterdam 102-106, 109-115, 213, 253, 270-271
Andalusia 52, 60-61, 71-72
Anglo-American Corporation 136-137
Anglo-Boer War 130-131, 133
Anglo-French rivalry 227
Angola 78, 84, 90, 95-96, 98, 100, 103-104, 107-108, 111, 162, 169, 171, 252-254
Antwerp 98, 102-103, 112
Apartheid xiv, 145, 153-164, 166, 258, 260, 269
Arab League 223
Arabs 39-40, 42, 44, 171, 191, 221, 238, 244, 248
Aragon 56-59, 69, 81, 84, 86-88
Arenstein, Rowley Israel 151
Arguin 82-83
Ark of the Covenant 192
Asentistas 100, 113
Ashkenazi 204
Ashkenazic 123, 136, 176, 226, 238-239, 241
Asia Minor 47, 66, 235
Asiento 96, 103, 111-112, 114-116
Association of Ulama 241
Aswan 15, 33, 231
Atlas Mountains 21, 30, 53, 57, 213

Babylon xvi, 10-11, 15
Babylonian 10-11, 15-16, 35
Babylonian diaspora 11

Babylonian Talmud 35
Baghdad 43-46
Bahia 97-98
Balfour Pledge 143
Bani Hilal 49-50, 54
Bar Kokhba 30
Barbary Coast 235, 255
Barcelona 56-57
Barnato, Barney 125-127
Barreto, Luis Gomex 102-103
Basner, Hyam 150
Baumann, Gustave 122
Bayruk family 212
Beira 171-172
Beit, Alfred 125, 127
Belmont, Diego Nunes 105
Belmonte, Manuel de 111
Benghazi 248
Berbers 20-22, 30, 34, 40, 43-44, 46, 49, 52, 83, 221, 238, 241, 243, 259
Bergtheil, Jonas 121
Berlin Congress (1878) 245
Bernstein, Lionel 151
Beta Israel 186-187, 195-196, 198-201, 203-204, 261, 265-266
Bey, Ali 224, 255
Bight of Benin 90
Bight of Biafra 92
Block, Abraham 182-183
Bloemfontein 122, 128
Blum, Julius 228
Blum, Leon 241
Boers 121-122, 128-129, 133, 141
Boumedienne, Houari 243
Bourguiba, Habib 246
Brazil 78-79, 96-100, 101-104, 106-108, 110-114, 125, 252-254, 256, 263, 267, 272
Breyner & Wirth 172
British South Africa Company 172, 174-175
Bruce, James 199
Bulawayo 143, 174-176, 181, 253
Byzantine xv, 34-36, 39-40, 66
Byzantium 33, 66, 191

Caesar 22-23
Cairo 46-47, 55, 59, 67-68, 174, 226, 229, 231, 234, 258

Caligula 22, 24, 26
Cambyses 13
Camels 21, 30, 265
Canaan 3-5, 8, 11-12, 20, 35
Canada 223, 234
Canaries 82, 84-86
Cão, Diogo 84
Cape Bojador 82-83
Cape Colony 116, 120-123, 128, 132, 268
Cape of Good Hope 119
Cape Town xx, 120, 122-125, 128, 134-135, 137, 143, 145-146, 164, 174, 251-252, 256-257, 261-264, 266-270
Cape Verde Islands 82, 84, 90
Cardoso, Isaac 215
Carthage 20-21, 28, 40
Casablanca 220-221
Castile 69, 84, 86-88, 90, 263
Catalan 56
Catalonia 81
Catholics 87-88, 122, 239
Cattawi, Jacob 226
Caxito, Battle of 95
Central African Federation 177-178
Central African Zionist Organization 181
Central Selling Organisation 137
Ceuta 58, 68, 82
Chamberlain, Joseph 181
Charles X 238
Chaskalson, Arthur 161, 165
Chosen people xii, 3, 8, 193
Claudius 26-27
Clegg, Johnny 158
Cleopatra 24
Coen-Bacri family 236
Cohen, Benjamin and Leon 171
Cohen, Lionel 127, 137
Cohen, Sam xx, 170
Coheno, Samuel 113
Colombus, Christopher 85
Colons 240, 242
Company Law (1947) 231
Concalves, Antao 83
Constantine, Emperor 32
Constantinople 33-34, 66, 81, 227-228, 235
Conversos xii, xvii, xx, 60, 70-72, 75,

INDEX 275

78-81, 83, 85, 87-89, 91, 93, 95-99, 101-103, 105, 107, 109, 111-116, 263
Copperbelt 169, 178
Coptic Christian Church 185
Correa, Manuel Alvares 114
Corsairs 236-237
Council of Elvira (306) 32
Cremieux, Adolphe 240
Cremieux Decree (1870) 240
Cresques, Abraham 58
Crypto-Jews 70, 79, 87, 103, 106, 108, 110, 210, 260
Curaçao 112-114, 261
Curse of Ham 193, 258
Cushitic 185, 188, 190
Cyprus 29, 245
Cyrenaica 20, 29, 34, 40, 50, 249
Cyrus 10, 13

Darfur 67, 233
Darius, king 13
Dayan, General 223
De Beers 125-126, 136-137, 156, 254, 261
De Beers Consolidated Mines 125
Defiance Campaign 159
De Gaulle, General Charles 242
Degredados 93, 100, 110
De Klerk, President 163
Delamere, Lord 182
De Lomega, Joseph 119
Dengal, Sarsa 196
De Pass, David 121
De Pass, Elias and Aaron 121
De Souza, Thomas 97
Deuteronomy, Book of 3
Dhimmi 41, 219, 249
Djerba. *See* Jerba
Diamonds 77, 124-126, 131, 156, 261, 272
Disraeli, Benjamin 227
DNA xii, 20, 50, 65, 173, 189
Dom Afonso I, King 81, 92, 95, 117
Dudimose, Pharaoh 7
Dulcert, Angelino 58
Durban Marxist Club 148
Dutch 72, 77, 79, 102-116, 119-120, 122, 128, 176, 252, 256-257, 260, 264, 266

Dutch Batavian Republic 120
Dutch East India Company 116, 119
Dutch Reformed Church 120, 128
Dutch Republic 105, 115, 120, 260
Dutch West India Company 107-108, 110, 115, 256

Edict of Expulsion 88
Egypt 4-8, 10-20, 22-25, 27-29, 34-36, 39-47, 49-52, 55, 63, 65-68, 80, 119, 144, 174, 184, 190-191, 196, 200, 210, 217, 223-234, 238, 243, 245, 253-255, 258-259, 262, 264-265, 267-270, 272
Egyptian Chamber of Commerce 229
Egyptians xv, 5-7, 9-11, 13-16, 18, 24-26, 29, 225, 227-228, 230, 233-234
Elephantine 14-16, 187-188, 266
Eliot, Sir Charles 181-182
Elizabeth I, Queen of England 212
Elmina castle 84
Emin Pasha 233
Engenho 96, 98
England xxi, 73, 115-116, 125, 136, 139, 212, 237
Equatoria Province 233
Eritrea 188, 196, 203, 248, 259
Essaouira 212, 214, 268
Evil eye xiii
Ezana, King 190

Fagan, Henry 159
Fagan Commission Report 159
Faitlovitch, Jacques 200
Falas Muras 206
Falasha 186, 195-197, 200, 261-262, 269
Fashoda 234, 262
Fatimids 45-51
Fazendas 91
Fazendeiros 91
Ferdinand, King 63, 88
Fernandes, Diego Dias 98
Fez 44, 47-49, 55, 57, 61-62, 71, 213, 216, 219, 221, 258
Fez, Treaty of 219
First, Ruth 161
First World War 123, 143, 147, 229
Flaccus 24
Florence 58, 59, 151

Fortes, Meyer 146
Fourth Anglo-Dutch War 116
Frame, Phillip 138
France 40, 58, 110, 115, 212, 215, 217-218, 221-222, 225-226, 228, 230, 232, 238-246, 249
Franco, Abraham and Jacob 115-116
Frankel, Dr. Siegfried 120
Freedom Charter 160
French 77, 110, 113-114, 200, 214, 217-221, 224-228, 230, 234, 237-243, 245, 269
Friedman, Nathan 130

Gama, Gaspar 119
Gama, Vasco da 119
Gandhi, Mohandas 146
Garamantes 20-21
Ge'ez 185-186, 190
Genoa 45, 50, 58-59, 256
Genoese 79, 81, 84-86, 256
Germany 106, 123, 131, 136, 140, 142, 218, 221, 226
Ghana xiv, 44, 48, 52, 65, 84, 151, 262
Ghetto 24, 52, 62, 210-211, 221
Gluckman, Emanuel 149
Gluckman, Max 146
Gold 14-15, 22, 28, 30, 43-45, 47-48, 53-54, 56, 59, 63, 73-74, 77, 81-84, 88, 90-91, 93-94, 104, 108-109, 115, 124, 126, 128-131, 174, 190, 212-213, 238-239, 247, 252, 271
Goldberg, Bennie 177
Gold Coast 84, 90-91, 94, 108
Gomes, Fernao 84
Gondar 198-199
Gordimer, Nadine 157
Gordon, Donald 156-157
Gordon, General Charles 233
Gordon, Max xxi, 150
Goree 110
Gradis, Abraham 110
Granada 49, 53, 55, 63, 71-72
Graumann, Harry 133
Great Trek 121, 141, 152
Great Zimbabwe 173
Greeks xv-xvi, 14, 16, 18, 20, 23-27, 29, 176, 185, 258
Greite, Augustus 174
Gulf of Guinea 90-91, 96

Hafsid 57, 59
Haile Selassie, Emperor 202-203
Halakhah xiii, xvi
Ha-Levi, Samuel 49
Halevy, Joseph 200
Hamburg 106, 112, 125
Harber, Anton 157
Hassan II, King 223
Hatherly Distillery 130
Hebrews xii, 5, 8-9, 13, 15, 204, 253
Henriques, Duarte Dias 100
Herzl, Theodor 143, 181
Holland 104-106, 110, 257
Hollander, Felix Charles 133
Holocaust 137, 176
Horn of Africa 188-189, 248, 263
Hyksos 5, 7

Iberian Peninsula 40, 54-55, 60, 63, 69-70, 73, 81, 86, 89, 102-103, 105, 112, 254
Iberians 72, 81
Iceland 237
Ifriqiya 21, 49-50, 54, 59, 61
Iltizams 67
India 13, 47, 49, 98, 106-108, 110-111, 115-116, 119, 146-147, 182, 190, 225, 256
Indian Ocean 46, 81, 116, 119, 171, 173, 181, 188-189, 197, 226, 232
Indonesian Archipelago 116
Indo-China 246
Isaacs, Nathaniel 121
Isabella, Queen 63, 88
Ismail, Sultan 213
Israelites xii, 6-9, 11-12, 192, 251
Istanbul 66, 210, 224-225, 235, 244, 247, 261
Italian African Empire 248
Italians 77, 81, 202, 238, 248-249

Jacobson, Dan 157
Jameson Raid 131
Janissaries 66, 235
Jerba 28, 243, 271
Jerusalem xii-xiii, 7, 9-10, 15, 18, 26-28, 30, 34, 43, 51, 192, 243, 251-252, 254-255, 257, 264, 270
Jewish Socialist Society 148
Jihad 39, 53, 233
Joal 109

Joao III, King 102
Johannesburg xx, 124, 126-129, 131, 133, 135, 137, 140, 145, 150, 156-157, 161, 175, 252, 257-259, 261-262, 267, 271
Johannesburg Stock Exchange 127
Joseph, Helen 149, 151, 260
Josiah, King 12
Judah xvi, 9-13, 80, 82, 202, 264
Judea 18, 22, 30
Judeo-Berbers 220
Judeophilia 144
Judeophobia xiv, 31, 60, 62, 268
Justinian, Emperor 34

Kadalie, Clements 149
Kairwan 40, 44-45, 48, 50, 52
Kallenbach, Hermann 147
Karaite 232
Karamanlis dynasty 247
Kasrils, Ronnie 161
Kebra Nagast 191-194
Kenitra 220
Kentridge, Morris 134, 261
Kerzner, Sol 157
Khaldun, Ibn 84
Khartoum 233-234
Khedivate 227-228
Kimberley xx, 124-127, 129, 136
Kirsch, Sam 138
Kisch, Daniel 174
Kongo, kingdom of 89, 91, 95
Kruger, Paul 129
Kush 14, 185, 253

Ladino 80, 176
L'Alliance Israelite Universelle (AIU) 200
AIU 200, 220, 239
Lancados 93, 109
Land Apportionment Act (1931) 179
Las Casas, Bartolomé de 99
Latvians 135, 139
Law of Return 204
Lebanon 5, 226, 269
Lemba 173, 189, 265
Leon, Tony 164
Levant 5, 20, 80-81, 102, 119
Levantine 81
Levy, Leon 149
Libya 20, 36, 59, 71, 235, 243, 247-251, 258
Libyan War 248
Limpieza de sangre 87
Lippert, Edward 175
Lippert Concession 175
Lisbon 81, 83-85, 92-95, 97, 99, 100, 102-103, 105-106, 112, 235
Lithuanians 135, 139
Litvaks 124, 129
Livorno 235-236
Loango 94-95, 108, 111, 263
Lobengula, King 175
London 113, 116, 121, 124, 136-137, 145, 179, 182, 199, 251-256, 258-268, 270-271
London Society for the Promotion of Christianity among the Jews 199
Lopes, Andrew 114
Lopes, Duarte 108
Low Countries 102, 213
Luanda 100, 108, 111-112
Lubavitch Hasidic 164
Luthuli, Albert 151
Lyautey, Governor Louis 219, 221

Maccabi Games 146, 152
Madagascar 222
Madeira 82, 84, 90, 97-100
Maghili, al- 62-64
Maghreb 40, 43-46, 49, 52-54, 56-57, 63, 66, 68, 71, 222, 251
Mahdi, Sultan al- 212
Maimonides, Moses 55
Maisels, Isie 161
Malan, D.F. 141, 152
Malka, Rabbi Solomon 234
Malocello, Lanzarotto 81
Mamluks 43, 50-52, 269
Mandela, Nelson 160, 163, 165
Mansur, Ahmad al- 73, 211
Manuel, King 89, 92-93
Mappa mundi 58
Maqnin, Meir Cohan ben 216
Marinids 55
Marks, Sammy 127, 129-132, 138, 264
Marrakesh 47, 52-54, 57, 216, 218, 221, 258
Marranos 88-89, 102, 106-107
Marseilles 235
Matabeleland 174-175

Mauritania 83
Mauritanian coast 82
Mawlay Abd al-Hafidh 219
Mbemba Nzinga, King 92
Mecca 43, 59, 67
Medes 10
Mediterranean 4, 10, 17, 19-22, 34, 36, 40-41, 45-47, 50-54, 56, 60, 66, 68, 72, 74, 80-81, 90, 102-103, 119, 144, 176, 189, 209, 217-218, 225-226, 229, 235, 243, 245, 247, 251-252, 255, 258, 260, 269-270
Mediterranean Basin 34, 47, 80, 189, 229, 243
Meknes 216, 221
Mellah 62, 211, 214, 255, 258
Menasce, Baron Jacques Levi 229
Mendes-France, Pierre 246
Menelik I, King 187, 192-193
Menelik II, King of Shoa 202, 265
Mengistu 204-205
Mesopotamia 3, 5-6, 11, 13, 29
Mesticos 91
Mestre Filipe 109
Mexico 114
Middle East xii-xiii, xvi, 4, 6-7, 10, 17, 19, 22, 27, 34-35, 39, 41-42, 48-51, 152-154, 165, 196, 225-226, 228-229, 232, 258, 265, 269-270
Middle Kingdom xvi, 4-5
Middle Passage 97
Millin, Sarah Gertrude 267
Mkhize, Florence 151
Moffat, Reverend John 175
Mogador 214
Mohammad V, Sultan 221
Mohammed Ahmed ibn Abdullah 233
Montefiore, Sir Moses 218
Morgan, J.P. 136
Morocco, Sultanate of 70, 211
Moroccan Royal Army 72, 213
Mosenthal brothers 122-123, 126
Moses, Prophet 7-8, 12, 173
Mossad 205, 223
Mozambique 127, 130, 162, 170, 172-174, 180, 260, 265
Mozambique Company 172, 174
Mugabe, Robert 162
Muhammad Ali 225-227
Muhammad as-Sadok 245

Muhammad, King Idris 249
Muhammad, Prophet 39, 44
Muhammad III, Sidi 214
Muslims xi, xx, 36-37, 40-45, 47-49, 51, 53, 55-61, 63-65, 67-71, 73, 77, 80-81, 83, 86, 88, 192, 197-198, 210, 212, 219, 221-222, 231, 234-235, 240-241, 243, 245-248, 256, 258, 264
Mussolini, Benito 202
Mustapha ben Ismael 245

Nairobi Zionist Association 182
Napoleon 224
Nasser, Gamal Abd al- 184, 223, 231
Nataf, Solomon 244
Natal xx, 121, 132-133, 139, 145-147, 151, 264
Nathanson, Smoel 130
National Liberation Front (FLN) 242
National Party 142, 144, 152, 159, 161
Nationality Law (1929) 230
Naude, Reverend Beyers 155
Nazis 140, 142, 249
Ndongo, kingdom of 95
Nellmapius, Alois 131
Neo Destour Party 246
Netherlands 102, 104-105, 109, 111, 212, 253, 261, 270
New Christians xii, 60, 70, 78-80, 82, 86-89, 93-94, 96-97, 101-105, 109-110, 112, 116
New Holland 106, 110
New Testament 86, 183, 260
Ngoyi, Lilian 151
Nicholas V, Pope 93
Nigeria xiv, 51, 64-65, 108, 270
Nile Delta 4-7, 10
Nile River valley 4, 16, 187
Nilotic Sudan 225
Nis, Filipe de 96
Norden, Benjamin 120
Noronha, Fernao de 97
North America xiv, 112-113, 250
Northern Rhodesia 146, 169, 176-179
Nubians 13-14, 51
Numidia 20, 30
Nunez, Joao 119
Nuremberg Laws 140

INDEX 279

Nyasaland 177, 179

Obote, President 184
Ochs, Albert 171
Old Christians 32, 70, 87, 94, 96, 101
Old Kingdom 5
Olmert, Ehud 165
Omdurman 233-234
Omdurman, Battle of (1898) 233
Operation Entebbe 185
Operation Joshua 205
Operation Solomon 205, 269
Oporto 97, 105
Oppenheimer, Ernest 136-137, 144
Oppenheimer, Harry 156
Oran 58, 213, 240
Orange Free State 121, 126, 128, 135, 141
Ossewa Brandwag 142
Ottoman Empire 66, 68, 70-71, 87-88, 197, 210, 224, 226, 228-230, 235, 248, 261, 269
Oudtshoorn 123, 252, 254, 257

Palache, Moses 213
Palache, Samuel 213
Pale of Settlement 123
Palestine xii-xiii, 3-5, 8-9, 12-13, 17-20, 24-25, 29-30, 43, 47-48, 66, 80, 143, 146, 152, 161, 182, 187, 191, 194, 201, 221, 230-231, 234
Pan-Arabism 221
Papal bulls 83
Pentateuch 11-12, 19
People of the Book 42, 214, 262
Peregrino, Jacob 109
Peres, Shimon 223, 258
Perez, Manuel Bautista 114
Pernambuco 97-98, 105, 110, 253
Persia 14, 41
Persians 13, 15-16, 191, 233
Phillips, Lionel 127
Philo 26-27, 30-31, 267, 269
Phoenicians 20
Pinto, Isaac 215
Pioneer Column 174
Pogroms xiv, 26, 65, 69, 182, 211, 222, 240
Polak, Henry 147
Pollak, Otto 127
Pombeiros 79

Portugal 63, 68-71, 73, 79, 81-82, 84, 86, 88-92, 94-100, 102-106, 109-110, 115, 171, 235, 252, 262, 268
Portuguese Crown 84, 89, 94, 100, 109
Portuguese Royal Guinea Company 114
Pozo, Jean Barroso del 112
Prince Henry 82-83
Príncipe Island 93
Promised Land xii, 3, 8, 152, 182, 201, 205-206, 221
Ptolemaic 17-18, 22, 24-25, 190
Ptolemy I Soter 17

Qadaffi, Colonel Muammar al- 249
Qadir, Abd al- 238
Qattawi, Jacob 226, 229
Quota Act (1930) 140, 142
Qur'an 86

Rabat 220-221
Rabin, Yitzhak 223
Ramesses II, Pharaoh 7
Ramesside era 7
Ramires, Lopo 104
Rand 124, 126, 130, 137, 172
Randlords 128, 130, 132-133, 271
Recife 106, 108, 111, 113
Red Sea 185, 188-190, 196-197, 200, 226, 265
Reynal, Pedro Gomez 103
Rhodes, Cecil 125-126, 172, 174, 267
Rivonia 161, 257
Robben Island 161
Rudolph, Samuel 121
Romans xv-xvi, 22, 24-26, 28, 30, 32, 258
Romanus Pontifex 83
Rose, Max 123
Rothschild, Baron Edmond de 200
Rothschild, N.M. 125
Royal African Company 115
Rubin, Leslie 134
Rufisque 109

Saadian dynasty 211-212
Sachs, Albie 161, 165
Sachs, Solly 149
Sadat, Anwar 232
Sahara 20-22, 30, 35-36, 44, 52, 57-

58, 60, 62, 73, 237, 262
Sahel 64
Sa'id, Khedive 226
Salisbury 175-177, 258
Salt 61-62, 90, 212, 239
Sandton City 157
Sannu Ya'qub 232
Sao Salvador 106
São Tomé 82, 84, 89-97, 99-102, 257, 259
Schauder, Adolph 133
Schetz, Erasmo 98
Schlesin, Sonja 147
Schlesinger, I.W. 137
Schnitzer, Eduard 233
Schoonenbergh, François van 112
Schreiner, Olive 157
Second Temple 28
Second World War 137, 151-152, 155, 182, 202, 245, 251
Segal, Leon 138
Senegambia 109
Sennar, kingdom of 225
Sephardic xiii, 55, 60-61, 63, 68, 71-72, 85-86, 89, 91, 103-107, 110-112, 114, 176, 200, 204, 235, 257, 263, 268, 270
Sephared 50
Septuagint 19, 27, 30-31
Sepulveda, Gonzalo Nunes 100
Seville 60, 85, 94, 100
Shaka 121
Shari'a 67, 239
Sharpeville Massacre 154, 160
Sheba, Queen 192-193
Sherifian dynasty 211
Shtetls 124
Sijilmasa 43-45, 47, 56-58
Simon, Barney 158
Simons, Jack 146
Simons, Rachel Ray Alexander 151
Sinai, Mount 8
Sion, Amda 186, 195
Sisulu, Walter 160
Six-Day War xiv, 153, 223
Slatin Pasha 233
Slave Coast 84, 108, 262
Slovo, Joe 160, 165
Smith, Ian 162, 180
Smous 122, 268
Smuts, Jan Christian 143

Solomon, Harry 127, 133
Solomon, Saul 120
Solomonic dynasty xii, 194
Somen, Issy 183
Songhay 64-65, 73-74, 212, 259
Sonnenberg, Max 138
South Africa xiii, xxi, 79, 83, 117, 119-127, 129, 131-147, 149-151, 153-157, 159-167, 169-170, 172-175, 177, 189, 211, 251, 254-262, 264-265, 267-270
South African Communist Party (SACP) 148-151, 158, 160
South African Jewish Board of Deputies 145, 154, 261
South African Republic 121, 126, 128, 131, 174
South African War 130, 133, 135
South African Zionist Federation 143, 166
South African Zionist Federation in Israel 166
South Atlantic 77, 83-84, 86, 120
Southern Rhodesia 143, 169, 175-179, 257-258
Soveral, Francisco de 100
Soviet Union 231
Soweto Rebellion 154, 161
Spain 34, 36, 40-41, 44, 49-50, 52-56, 63, 68-73, 79, 81, 86-87, 91, 96-97, 99, 102-106, 109-111, 114-115, 197, 212, 217-218, 235-236, 253-254, 256, 258, 260, 264, 270
Spanish Netherlands 102
Spanish-Dutch Treaty 111
Stalin 150
Stanley, Henry Morton 233
Stern, Irma 158
Sudanic 43-44, 48, 51, 54, 58, 63-65, 212
Suez Canal 144, 200, 217, 222, 226-228, 231, 234
Suez Canal Company 227
Suez Canal crisis 222, 231, 234
Sugar 72-73, 77-81, 84-86, 89-91, 96-107, 112-114, 116, 121, 172, 212-213, 227, 229, 237, 253, 257, 268
Sulayman, Mulay 215
Suppression of Communism Act (1950) 160
Suriname 114-115

INDEX

Susman Brothers & Wulfson 178
Susneyos III, King 197
Suzman, Helen 159-160
Swahili 171, 173

Table Bay 120
Tacitus 25
Taghaza 212
Talmud 15, 35, 186, 204
Talmudic scholar 82
Tangier 68, 71, 215-219, 222, 268
Tawat 30, 56, 58, 239
Tewodros, Emperor 199
Theodosius 32
Three Kings, Battle of 73-74
Timbuktu 58, 64-65, 73, 253, 259
Tlemcen 57, 62-63, 65, 71, 239
Tomeans 90-92, 94-95, 99
Tondibi, Battle of 73, 211
Torah 19, 49, 73, 186, 203-204
Tordesillas 84-85
Touat 239
Transvaal 121-122, 126, 128-132, 134-135, 139, 141, 145, 147, 149, 152, 161, 174, 264
Tripoli 40, 54, 58, 66, 235, 237, 247-249
Tripolitan War (1801-05) 237
Tripolitania 20, 50, 59
Trotsky, Leon 150
Tuat 30, 56, 58, 60, 62-65
Tunis 49, 57, 59, 61, 68, 84, 235-237, 244-245, 247
Tunisian 34, 40, 244-247
Turco-Egyptians 197, 225, 233
Turks 65-66, 68, 71, 197, 244, 247, 261
Turok, Ben 161
Tutu, Bishop Desmond 155
Twelve Year Truce (1609-21) 104

Uganda xiv, 181-185, 251, 265
Uganda Scheme 182
Uitlanders 128-129, 132
United Jewish Appeal 205
United Provinces 102
United States xix, 128, 136, 177, 215, 223, 237, 244, 249, 266
Upper Guinea coast 82, 84-85, 91, 94, 109
Upper Niger 212, 237

Utrecht, Treaty of 115

Valencia 56, 94
Venetians 79, 251
Venice 52, 58-59, 266
Verwoerd, H.F. 141
Vichy regime 221, 241
Viollett, Maurice 241
Volksraad 122, 128

Washington, President George 215
Weinbren, Bennie 149
Weizmann, Dr. Chaim 143
Welensky, Sir Roy 177
Witwatersrand xx, 124, 126, 130, 146, 257, 262, 271

Yazid, Sultan 215
Yehudim 10
Yekunno-Amlak 194
Yemen 173, 188-189, 193
Yiddish 124, 135, 139, 146, 170, 176, 230
Yohannes, Emperor 198
Yom Kippur War 153, 183
Yutar, Percy 161

Zacuto, Abraham 82
Zagwe dynasty 193
Zambesi 172, 260, 264
Zambia 163, 173, 176, 179, 181, 263
Zara Yakob 196
Zayyanid 57
Zimbabwe, Republic of 154, 173, 175, 181, 189
Zionism 143-144, 148, 152-154, 165, 221, 230, 258, 269
Zionists 143, 170, 182
Zulu 121, 158

About the Author

Richard Hull is a Professor of African history at New York University. He holds a Ph.D. in African history and two M.A. degrees from Columbia University. He is the winner of three awards for Teaching Excellence at N.Y.U. and a United Nations Distinguished Service Award and is a Fulbright-Hays Fellow. He has written and presented two 30-episode series on "African Civilizations" for CBS Television and served for several years as a curriculum consultant on Africa for the New York State Department of Education. In 2006 he was given the "Distinguished Africanist" Award by the New York African Studies Association. At New York University he served on the Faculty Council and Senate for many years and as Director of Undergraduate Studies in the History Department. He was a founder of the university's Institute for African-American Affairs. At NYU he teaches a wide variety of lecture courses and seminars, including Jews and Judaism in African History, Religions of Africa, Genocide in Africa, African Slavery and the Atlantic Slave Trade, Ancient Africa, Contemporary Africa, and History of South Africa. Over the past four decades, he has conducted research in eight African countries.

Professor Hull is the author of numerous works on Africa, including *African Cities and Towns before the European Conquest* (W.W. Norton), *American Enterprise in South Africa* (NYU Press), *Munyakare: African Civilization before the Batuuree* (John Wiley), *Modern Africa: Change and Continuity* (Prentice-Hall), and *Southern Africa: Civilizations in Turmoil* (NYU Press). He is also a co-author of numerous editions of W.W. Norton's two-volume *World Civilizations: Their History and Culture*.

www.ingramcontent.com/pod-product-compliance
Lightning Source LLC
Chambersburg PA
CBHW030230170426
43201CB00006B/171